More Praise for *Everyone at the Table*

"*Everyone at the Table* places teacher leaders squarely where they need to be—at the table in shaping policies and making decisions that impact classroom practice and student learning."

—Katherine Bassett, director,
National Network of State Teachers of the Year

"Meaningful change in our schools will only take hold when educators are included in the design and implementation of policies that affect their classrooms and careers. By highlighting the importance of giving teachers a seat at the policy table, *Everyone at the Table* moves the profession in a positive direction."

—Syndey Morris, cofounder, co-CEO,
Educators4Excellence

"Mobilizing educators to come together in an effort to redesign schooling, rethink the profession, and professionalize their craft can play a vital role in educational improvement. In *Everyone at the Table: Engaging Teachers in Evaluation Reform*, the authors offer useful guidance for engaging teachers in conversations about teacher evaluation. They sketch a road map for policymaking that promises to draw upon the wisdom and address the concerns of educators and educational policy leaders alike. This is an endeavor that we can all support."

—Frederick M. Hess, PhD, director,
Education Policy Studies, American Enterprise Institute

"This book makes clear why it's critical to engage teachers in designing and implementing teacher support and evaluation systems. And it's chock-full of concrete ideas, tools, and examples for making those conversations authentic and meaningful."

—Lynn Olson, advisor to the director of
College-Ready Education, Bill & Melinda Gates Foundation

D1401437

everyone
at the table

ABOUT THE SPONSORS

About AIR

Established in 1946, with headquarters in Washington, DC, the American Institutes for Research (AIR) is a nonpartisan, nonprofit organization that conducts behavioral and social science research and delivers technical assistance both domestically and internationally in education, health, and workforce productivity. AIR's Education program includes work in all fifty states and internationally and involves more than five hundred staff working to improve the conditions of teaching and learning from early childhood through college and careers, with a special focus on the most underserved and vulnerable populations. For more information, visit www.air.org.

About Public Agenda

Public Agenda partners with citizens and leaders to help them better navigate complex and divisive issues. Through nonpartisan stakeholder opinion research and public engagement, Public Agenda provides the insights, tools, and support that people need to build common ground and arrive at solutions that work for them. Public Agenda works in K–12 education, higher education, the federal budget, health care, and other critical issues. A national, nonprofit, nonpartisan organization, Public Agenda was founded in 1975 by the social scientist and public opinion expert Dan Yankelovich and former secretary of state Cyrus Vance, and is based in New York City. For more information, visit www.publicagenda.org.

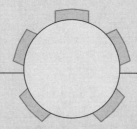

everyone at the table

Engaging Teachers in Evaluation Reform

Ellen Behrstock-Sherratt • Allison Rizzolo
with Sabrina Laine and Will Friedman

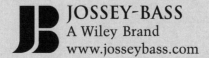

JOSSEY-BASS
A Wiley Brand
www.josseybass.com

Copyright © 2013 by John Wiley & Sons, Inc. All rights reserved.

Published by Jossey-Bass
A Wiley Brand

One Montgomery Street, Suite 1200, San Francisco, CA 94104-4594—www.josseybass.com

Jossey-Bass books and products are available through most bookstores. To contact Jossey-Bass directly call our Customer Care Department within the U.S. at 800-956-7739, outside the U.S. at 317-572-3986, or fax 317-572-4002.

Wiley publishes in a variety of print and electronic formats and by print-on-demand. Some material included with standard print versions of this book may not be included in e-books or in print-on-demand. If this book refers to media such as a CD or DVD that is not included in the version you purchased, you may download this material at http://booksupport.wiley.com. For more information about Wiley products, visit www.wiley.com.

Library of Congress Cataloging-in-Publication Data
Behrstock-Sherratt, Ellen.
    Everyone at the table : engaging teachers in evaluation reform / Ellen Behrstock-Sherratt,
  Allison Rizzolo with Sabrina Laine and Will Friedman.
       pages cm
    Includes bibliographical references and index.
    ISBN 978-1-118-52634-7 (pbk.); ISBN 978-1-118-54013-8 (ebk.);
    ISBN 978-1-118-54015-2 (ebk.); ISBN 978-1-118-54022-0 (ebk.)
       1. Teachers—Rating of—United States.   2. Teaching—United States—Evaluation.   I. Title.
  LB2838.B47   2013
  371.14'4—dc23

                                                                                    2013006257

Printed in the United States of America
FIRST EDITION
PB Printing   10 9 8 7 6 5 4 3 2 1

CONTENTS

Superintendent Amelia Baker wakes up excited and nervous. Today she will share the new teacher evaluation system with the five hundred–plus teachers in Merryville School District. Superintendent Baker worked for two years on the system, in coordination with other district leaders and several content experts. They planned carefully, developed research-tested tools, and deliberated endlessly among themselves on the definition of effective teaching and the appropriate weights of different evaluation measures. Today, it's finally time to present to teachers the new, carefully constructed approach to teacher evaluation. The union—indeed, all relevant parties—have come around to seeing the benefits of a more rigorous teacher evaluation system. So what could go wrong?

Sitting down for her morning coffee, Baker scans the day's news: "Dunrock School District Returns to the Drawing Board on Teacher Evaluation System." But how could this be? Baker wonders. She had discussed their evaluation reforms with the superintendent of nearby Dunrock, and they had found so many similarities in their approaches. Not to mention that Dunrock's superintendent was well known for her thoughtfulness and positive reputation.

Standing at the podium, ready for the big presentation, Baker scans the faces of her teachers and notes the many crossed arms in the audience. She suddenly wonders if she and her committee had missed a step. She opens her mouth but doesn't get past "Good morning" before an arm shoots up and a teacher asks, "I understand that the district has developed a new way to do evaluations—why is this the first time many of us are hearing about it or being asked to give input?"

Baker's heart sinks as she realizes that, even today, her fifteen-minute presentation leaves no space for "input." Her heart sinks further, and she mutters under her breath, "It is going to be a long fifteen minutes and a long week, month, and school year."

◉

Superintendent Baker's predicament is unfortunately not unique. Even the most well-intentioned education leaders often fail to consider the input of those most deeply affected by teacher evaluation: teachers themselves. It is rarely a case of malicious intent; rather, education leaders don't have the time to engage teachers, don't know how, or are fearful of handing over power. They see engagement—or collaborative decision making, distributive leadership, or other variations on that theme—as difficult or unpredictable, and they worry that engaging teachers will just lead to venting and resentment, making the problem worse, not better.

We believe, however, that engaging the stakeholders who are most directly affected by change can be a transformative experience, not a threatening one. Teacher engagement, when done right, has the potential to bring vital, firsthand knowledge and ideas to problem solving; facilitate smoother implementation; help education leaders circumvent potential roadblocks or unintended consequences resulting from new policies; create legitimacy through shared ownership; and lead to policies that stick.

Authentically engaging teachers is not an easy process—it requires a good amount of planning, foresight, and, yes, time. Nonetheless, ensuring that teachers are engaged up front will often help prevent adversity that can delay or derail reform and force education policymakers back to the drawing board once again. *Everyone at the Table: Engaging Teachers in Evaluation Reform* is intended to make the seemingly overwhelming task of engaging teachers in evaluation more straightforward and more effective. The book provides a rationale for increased teacher leadership in reform, as well as actionable strategies *to get everyone around the table* and partaking in meaningful, research-driven conversations that will result in reforms that can be implemented successfully and sustained over time.

Teacher evaluation reform is already well under way, with thirty-six states and Washington, DC having adopted new laws concerning evaluation systems. As these reforms take place at a faster and faster pace, with time often too scarce to carefully develop policies (let alone *collaboratively* develop them), the absence of teacher voice in education reform has become more acute, and we've seen the repercussions. The anger of frustrated teachers boiled over into the 2012 Chicago Public Schools teacher strike. Principals from Long Island in New York sued that state's education department over their dissatisfaction with the teacher evaluation system. We've also seen the absence of teacher voice spark the formation of the numerous teacher voice organizations that we profile in this book.

These organizations understand, as we and many frustrated teachers and principals do, that successful reform is impossible without the active support of those who will be most affected. It is best practice for any good leader or manager, in any sector, to take the time to consult with those on the ground doing the work, before deciding how to evaluate or improve their jobs. And it is likewise best practice for any teacher to embrace this opportunity.

In September 2012, an adviser for teacher quality to the secretary of education led a presentation and panel discussion at a convening of state-level education leaders for the National Comprehensive Center for Teacher Quality. The event aimed to help state leaders visualize how the teaching profession would ideally be transformed into one that met the needs of all students. Participants concluded that in order to transform the teaching profession, teachers and leaders at all levels of the system would need to develop a common vision through ongoing collaboration. Creating structures to facilitate consistent dialogue at the school, district, and state level would aid this collaboration. State education leaders further articulated the need for states to encourage teacher-initiated solutions and to develop formal avenues for teacher leadership as key elements to transforming the teaching profession to one that meets the needs of every student. This book answers that call.

Everyone at the Table presents an array of well-tested engagement and discussion approaches that can help generate deep thinking about the design and implementation of a comprehensive approach to teacher evaluation—one that will align with state and federal policy requirements and, more important, work in a given local context.

This book equips readers with a variety of resources: the research base behind teacher effectiveness and quality; the key policy questions reflected in the national debate around measuring teacher effectiveness; practical, hands-on recommendations for taking action to promote dialogue and collaborative problem solving on policy design; and ready-made, flexible, and well-tested materials for teacher-led dialogue on teacher evaluation.

The strategies introduced in this book are intended to genuinely include teachers in conversations that affect the future of their profession as well as their own careers. They are designed to include all teachers—not just the outspoken "usual suspects" who are already active in policy debates—and to go beyond what many typically think of as "dialogue," challenging local leaders to create a new vision for inclusive decision making.

The approach and materials in *Everyone at the Table* also depoliticize the issue of measuring teacher effectiveness and provide teachers with a framework to transcend an either-or pattern of thinking, talk about the real values and trade-offs inherent in any evaluation strategy, generate new insights on complex problems, and start moving toward workable solutions for their own contexts.

The book is divided into three parts, each of which contains a number of chapters. Part One focuses on the need for teacher engagement and the context of evaluation reform; Part Two focuses on the entry points for and principles of teacher engagement; and Part Three focuses on the process, or "how-to," of engaging teachers in the dialogue. This last part also broadens the discussion to talk about the need to engage principals and the community in teacher evaluation (and teacher quality more broadly), as well as the need to apply the concepts in this book to other education policies.

Part One: Understanding the Teacher Evaluation Conversation and Why It Matters

Chapter One, "Why Now? The Importance of Cultivating Teacher Leadership and Teacher Voice in the Age of Accountability," provides an overview of engagement in evaluation reform, including its wider goals of strengthening the teacher workforce.

Chapter Two, "The Teacher Effectiveness Question: How Can Effectiveness Be Measured?" focuses on the contemporary controversies, emerging research on best practice, and trends in assessing teacher effectiveness, and provides a brief contextual history of this important but complex issue.

Part Two: What We Know About Effectively Engaging Teachers

Chapter Three, "The Who, When, and How of Evaluation: Engaging Teachers on Issues That Matter," provides a crash course in Teacher Evaluation 101, detailing the technical aspects involved in designing a new teacher evaluation system and the key decision points for teacher engagement. This chapter also includes a section about teacher involvement in the evaluation process, as peer observers and in other capacities.

Chapter Four, "The Elements of Authentic Engagement," highlights research, theory, and innovative practices from the field of public engagement, detailing the core principles of authentic engagement and exploring why engaging teachers on hot-button topics like evaluation is so critical.

Part Three: The Engagement Process

Chapter Five, "Planning: Steps for Engaging Teachers," lays out strategies for engaging teachers, sample plans for teacher engagement to help organizers envision a timeline, and activities to help organizers envision how they will engage teachers in their school or district.

Chapter Six, "Strategies for Ensuring Authentic Engagement in Evaluation Reform," includes the most essential strategies for teacher engagement—recruiting teachers to the conversation and then conducting facilitated discussions that get to the heart of the issues of greatest importance.

Chapter Seven, "Optional Activities for Teacher Engagement in Evaluation Reform," details a number of optional activities for promoting teacher conversations, including resources for further reading and sharing, and an interviewing exercise.

Chapter Eight, "Other Stakeholders: Engaging Principals, Parents, and Community Members," presents strategies for engaging these other stakeholders in teacher and principal evaluation reform.

Chapter Nine, "Conclusion: Teacher Voice in Evaluation and Beyond," discusses how to move the conversation beyond teacher evaluation to address a range of other pressing policy issues related to teacher quality, including compensation, induction and mentoring, recruitment and hiring, working conditions, and professional learning opportunities. To truly advance the teaching profession, it argues, evaluation reform is only the beginning.

The approach taken in this book is based on the Everyone at the Table: Engaging Teachers in Evaluation Reform project, developed by Public Agenda and the American Institutes for Research (AIR), with funding from the Bill & Melinda Gates Foundation. The Everyone at the Table website (www.everyoneatthetable. org) includes several multimedia resources that you may wish to access, such as

- A two-minute video that captures the importance of broader, more genuine involvement of teachers in evaluation reform and demonstrates the enthusiasm of education leaders around the country for this involvement (http://www.everyoneatthetable.org/leadersVideo.php).

- An eight-minute discussion-starter video that gives teachers the chance to think and talk about the pros and cons of different kinds of evaluation systems (http://www.everyoneatthetable.org/gtt_video.php).
- A PowerPoint presentation and a number of Word documents that can be modified and used for teacher discussion activities.

In some cases, the recommendations in this book guide you to these online resources. Recognizing that readers will approach this book from many different school and district contexts, the supporting materials have been designed to be customizable and flexible. All downloadable materials are formatted as Word documents and can be easily modified to suit the particular local context of your school and community.

WHO SHOULD READ THIS BOOK?

This book is intended for a variety of audiences, including school district leaders, union leaders, teacher leaders, school principals, school board members, and other community members.

Teacher leaders (particularly those who aim to be on-the-ground leaders of discussions about policy) are a key audience for this book, and they can promote and lead all the undertakings recommended here. The approach is always most effective, however, if those charged with overseeing teacher evaluation (for example, district and school administrators) are supportive of the way teachers' voices are included in the process.

School district leaders can read this book to understand how to better include teachers in local policymaking related to teacher quality. School district leaders set the tone for how teacher voice will be considered when important decisions are made, and their support is key to generating fruitful conversations with teachers, many of whom are often reluctant to speak up for fear of getting into trouble or wasting their time. District leaders are in an ideal position to identify teacher leaders, or teachers with leadership potential, to discuss the strategies in this book.

Union leaders may consult this book for an innovative approach to engaging teachers at scale and soliciting more representative and in-depth teacher input than may normally be achieved through a survey or a single union meeting. In unionized districts, the structured and solutions-oriented approach that is recommended in this book can build collaboration among teachers across a district and between union leaders and district administration.

School principals may wish to become familiar with the approaches recommended in this book to encourage teacher engagement and become a conduit between classroom teachers and district decision makers. Many teachers express a desire to serve in leadership positions outside the classroom, and principals can use the contents of this book to facilitate teachers continually expanding their horizons on educational policy, building leadership skills, and collaborating with colleagues in new and interesting experiences.

School board members can use this book to identify strategies for conveying to other leaders in the district and community the importance of meaningfully bringing teachers into the conversation on new policies as they develop. They can also identify ways to improve their own dialogue and decision-making processes, as well as the quality of dialogue with their constituent community members.

Parents and community members who are concerned about teacher effectiveness can read this book to gain insight on the topic of teacher evaluation and to find ways of convening structured dialogues to incorporate the noneducators' perspective on this important issue.

This book is intended for anyone concerned with developing strong and sustainable teacher evaluation systems that are created with and for teachers to inform their practice and improve student learning. In addition to the groups we've listed here, state education agency staff who are charged with supporting districts in improving teacher effectiveness, as well as the many national organizations that are committed to elevating teaching and learning in our schools, will find this book valuable.

ACKNOWLEDGMENTS

This book would not have been possible without the contributions of many dedicated individuals. First, we thank our three research assistants from American Institutes for Research (AIR): Lauren Bivona, Jenni Fetters, and Catherine Jacques. For her valuable contributions to the seminal research that underlies this book, we thank Public Agenda senior fellow Jean Johnson, who also contributed helpful reviews of the manuscript and key suggestions.

Others who reviewed and contributed to the Everyone at the Table: Engaging Teachers in Evaluation Reform project include Jonathan Rochkind; Amber Ott; Jeremy Hess; Gretchen Weber, NBCT; Molly Lasagna; Jill Shively; Sheri Frost Leo; Jane Coggshall, PhD; Sara Wraight, JD; Lisa Lachlan-Haché, EdD; Ellen Cushing; Catherine Barbour; Lynn Peloquin; and Cass Daubenspeck. For their extensive contributions to the field of public engagement, which undergirds the approach described in this book, we thank Public Agenda founder Dan Yankelovich along with Alison Kadlec and the rest of the Public Agenda public engagement team.

We give particular thanks to the Bill & Melinda Gates Foundation for supporting the Everyone at the Table project and to the many inspiring individuals who provided feedback at the Gates Teacher Voice convenings, in particular John King, Sydney Morris, Evan Stone, Rhick Bose, Dina Rock, Wendy Uptain, Jeanne Bliss, Alesha Daughtrey, and Lindsay Sobel. We thank the American Federation of Teachers, each district, and the many teachers and principals who participated in focus groups to field-test this approach, including Hazelwood, Missouri;

Nataki Talibah Schoolhouse in Detroit; Cranston, Rhode Island; Prince George's County, Maryland; and New Orleans, Louisiana, among others. We also thank Representative Sharon Tomiko Santos (WA) for sharing valuable insights on the Everyone at the Table concept.

This book would not have been possible without the support of the individuals and organizations that are highlighted in the text as examples of effective teacher voice initiatives: Teach Plus, Educators4Excellence, VIVA Teachers, New Millennium Teachers, Hope Street Group, Advance Illinois, and Teachers United.

Finally, our sincere gratitude goes out to all of the teachers and school and district leaders who are working each day to reshape the teaching profession into one that is more collaborative and more engaged, and one in which teacher leaders can succeed in realizing a shared vision for advancing teaching as a profession.

Ellen Behrstock-Sherratt, PhD, is a senior policy analyst on educator quality at the American Institutes for Research. Behrstock-Sherratt supports education policy stakeholders through the national Center on Great Teachers and Leaders, has authored or coauthored numerous articles, briefs, and reports on teacher and principal quality, and is coauthor of the book *Improving Teacher Quality: A Guide for Education Leaders* (Jossey-Bass, 2011). She led the Everyone at the Table: Engaging Teachers in Evaluation Reform initiative to increase teachers' engagement in the process of designing the policies that affect them, and she has supported both national teachers' associations and state policymakers in Illinois, Ohio, Washington, Maine, and Massachusetts on improving teacher and principal effectiveness. She is a frequent presenter on such topics as teacher incentives, equitable teacher distribution, Generation Y teachers, and human capital management in education. Behrstock-Sherratt earned her doctorate in education from the University of Oxford.

Allison Rizzolo is the communications director at Public Agenda. She develops and leads the organization's communications strategy. Rizzolo writes frequently on such issues as K–12 education reform, teacher engagement, public engagement, and improving our country's democratic processes. Rizzolo also contributes to various programs for Public Agenda. In addition to her deep involvement in Everyone at the Table, she produced Public Agenda's 2012 Citizens' Solutions Guides, nonpartisan discussion guides that improve collaborative problem solving by using the Choicework framework to help citizens better grasp their practical choices. Rizzolo is a coauthor of "Energy: A Citizens' Solutions Guide" and "Health Care: A Citizens' Solutions Guide," and the author of "Immigration: A Citizens' Solutions Guide." Rizzolo is a former middle school and high school teacher. She is a graduate of Tufts University, where she studied international relations and anthropology.

Sabrina W. M. Laine, PhD, is vice president, Education Program at the American Institutes for Research. She is a principal investigator on multiple technical assistance initiatives focused on educator quality that are funded by the U.S. Department of Education, such as the national Center on Great Teachers and Leaders. Laine has spearheaded efforts to contribute to policy research and resource development related to every aspect of managing and supporting educator talent, including recruitment, compensation, evaluation, distribution, and professional development. She leads a team of more than twenty-five researchers and policy analysts who are focused on the challenges faced by educators in urban, rural, and low-performing schools. Laine has worked for the last several years to ensure that policies and programs are in place that enable all children to have access to highly effective teachers and leaders. She is the primary author of the book *Improving Teacher Quality: A Guide for Education Leaders* (Jossey-Bass, 2011) and is a frequent presenter in states and districts across the country on topics ranging from ensuring teacher effectiveness to equitable teacher distribution. Laine earned her doctorate in educational leadership and policy studies from Indiana University.

Will Friedman, PhD, is the president of Public Agenda. After founding the organization's public engagement department in 1997, Friedman has overseen Public Agenda's steady and expanding stream of work aimed at helping communities and states build capacity to tackle tough issues in more inclusive, deliberative, and collaborative ways. In 2007, he established Public Agenda's Center for Advances in Public Engagement (CAPE), which conducts action research and evaluation to assess the impacts of public engagement and improve its practice.

Friedman is the author or coauthor of numerous publications, including "Reframing Framing," "Transforming Public Life: A Decade of Public Engagement in Bridgeport, CT," "Deliberative Democracy and the Problem of Scope," "Deliberative Democracy and the Problem of Power," and "From Employee Engagement to Civic Engagement: Exploring Connections Between Workplace and Community Democracy." He is also the coeditor, with Public Agenda chairman and cofounder Daniel Yankelovich, of the book *Toward Wiser Public Judgment* (Vanderbilt University Press, 2011).

Friedman holds a doctorate in political science with specializations in political psychology and American politics.

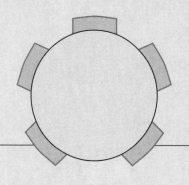

PART
ONE

Understanding the Teacher Evaluation Conversation and Why It Matters

CHAPTER
ONE

Why Now?

The Importance of Cultivating Teacher Leadership and Teacher Voice in the Age of Accountability

Big Study Links Good Teachers to Lasting Gain

—*New York Times,* January 6, 2012

Good Teachers Lead to Test Success

—*Wall Street Journal,* January 8, 2013

Teacher quality is making headlines and has risen to the top of the national education policy agenda in recent years. In many ways, effective teachers have come to be seen as a panacea for all that ails society—from crime and prejudice to inequality—a pathway to a healthy democracy and a means of strengthening our national economy. In spite of facing one of the deepest economic recessions in history, policy leaders continue to invest in new approaches to attract and retain effective teachers to staff our ninety-nine thousand public schools. The public, political, and financial commitment to securing effective teachers is unprecedented, and it creates a critical window of opportunity to develop a truly world-class teaching profession for all students.

This unparalleled focus on enhancing teacher effectiveness has tremendous potential to improve both student learning and the working lives of teachers. Although pockets of innovation around teacher career ladders, professional learning communities, job-embedded professional development, coteaching and peer observations, and induction and mentoring programs for new teachers have sprouted across the country, those working to promote high-quality teaching have emphasized improving teacher evaluation over all else (National Council on Teacher Quality, 2011). With the twin goals of strengthening accountability and creating a culture of continual instructional improvement, redesigning teacher evaluation systems to be more comprehensive, fair, and reliable appeals to policymakers and education leaders across the political spectrum. Evaluation redesign has become a key element of achieving the goal of securing excellent teachers for all students.

At the same time that policymakers and education leaders are making a massive push for teacher evaluation reform, many teachers themselves are actively seeking to have a greater voice both in education policy and in the direction of their own profession. For example, a number of highly engaged teacher groups (many of which are highlighted in this book) are widening teacher leadership in schools, districts, and beyond, expanding the scope for teachers to shape policy. There is also a growing acceptance, indeed enthusiasm, among policymakers and education leaders for a heightened teacher role in leading a stronger profession.

It is within this context that we make the case that teachers need to be at the table and engaged in the conversation when it comes to teacher evaluation reform. Sound and authentic teacher engagement informs the design of teacher evaluation by drawing on the knowledge of those closest to the problem. In doing so, it minimizes unintended consequences and communication gaffes that can impede and even derail implementation. It legitimizes the new policy and fosters a sense of shared responsibility for its success that makes it more durable and sustainable. It also opens up channels of communication and builds trust in ways that foster teacher engagement and leadership, and builds capacity to resolve other issues that educators need to address, from school safety to technology-enhanced pedagogy.

THE CURRENT CLIMATE

With thirty-six states and Washington, DC recently passing new laws concerning teacher evaluation, the transformation of teacher evaluation systems is already well under way and is moving at a fast pace in some parts of the country. In some cases, the time frame for designing and implementing new evaluation systems was so aggressive that engaging a wide variety of stakeholders in the reform effort was purely an afterthought, if it happened at all.

Nonetheless, many of the country's fourteen thousand school districts and three thousand charter schools have yet to embark on the teacher evaluation reform journey. This book is written with these schools and districts in mind—those in the earliest stages of reform as well as those in the process of reconsidering their system—where fast action is needed for teachers' voices to meaningfully rise above the many competing perspectives that are sweeping through schools around the United States.

Research finds that most teachers want a strong evaluation system—but they want a say about what that system should look like. Nearly two-thirds of teachers, for example, would prefer a principal who frequently observes them and provides detailed feedback to one who comes in once a year and gives just cursory, general comments (Public Agenda, 2010), but building an evaluation system that meets the needs of all parties is complex. It is only through the inclusion of many voices that the complexities inherent in teacher evaluation can be unearthed and addressed.

At present, however, teacher voice is woefully lacking. In her book on engaging stakeholders in education decision making, *You Can't Do It Alone,* Public Agenda senior fellow Jean Johnson states, "Most teachers believe they have been left out of conversations on improving schools and enhancing learning, even though they have vital, firsthand knowledge to offer" (2012, p. 17). Citing research from several studies, Johnson finds that

- 70 percent of teachers believe that they are left out of the loop in the district decision-making process.
- 80 percent feel that they are rarely consulted about what happens in their schools.
- 70 percent believe that district leaders only talk to them to win their support.
- Only 23 percent believe that district leaders speak to them to gain a stronger sense of teachers' concerns.

Half of the teachers surveyed felt that they were not even heard by their union and that decisions were made by a small group of highly engaged, typically veteran union members (Duffett, Farkas, Rotherham, & Silva, 2008; Farkas, Foley, & Duffett, 2001; Farkas, Johnson, & Duffett, 2003).

District leaders are often surprised at the backlash that ensues from their well-meaning reforms when teachers are left out of the equation. Teachers are loath to execute a policy that they had no say in—and that has no clear benefit for them—and principals find themselves putting out fires not just with students but also with their staff. Methods that seemed practical prove to be unfeasible, and challenges set policymakers back a few steps, if not back to the beginning.

In the worst cases, forward progress is entirely stymied or derailed, and teachers, unions, and education departments find themselves in a seemingly interminable cycle of dispute and gridlock. Yet these stumbling blocks are often predictable and preventable.

Although there are hurdles to authentically engaging teachers—it is time-consuming and requires careful attention and at least modest resources—there are instances where not taking the time and care to institute a process of authentic engagement will ultimately set policy back substantially by producing outcomes that are less effective and legitimate. In the case of evaluation policy, schools and districts have sometimes ended up with evaluation plans that were unrealistic and impossible to implement, as well as poorly received by teachers, who resented being denied a voice when plans were being developed.

It is our strong belief, informed by research and our practical experience with the design and implementation of educator evaluation systems and with engagement processes, that these evaluation reforms are more likely to succeed if teachers play a meaningful role at each stage of the reform process. Perhaps few would argue that point, but often the logistics and know-how around creating opportunities for teachers—whose time, like that of school and district leaders, is always at a premium—to do so poses the problem.

Arguments against teacher engagement and apprehensions about it are understandable, and most of us have seen instances where opening up decision making to other stakeholders has wrought conflict and confrontation rather than collaborative problem solving. Our point, however, is that these instances were often poorly planned and facilitated. There are plenty of useless and even harmful ways of designing engagement, as well as instances of pseudo-engagement that was never authentic in the first place; this book is about how to do engagement well.

THE STRENGTHS OF ENGAGING TEACHERS IN TEACHER EVALUATION

Education leaders have begun to acknowledge and embrace the need for teachers to weigh in on education policy reform. In February 2012, the U.S. Department of Education launched a project called RESPECT: Recognizing Educational Success, Professional Excellence and Collaborative Teaching. The project exemplifies a change in tide when it comes to heightening teachers' role in shaping their own profession. RESPECT's goal is to rebuild the profession, increase educators' voices in policymaking, and make teaching the most important and respected occupation in the United States. "Our goal is to work with educators in rebuilding their profession—and to elevate the teacher voice in shaping federal, state and local education policy," said Secretary of Education Arne Duncan during the launch of the project.

Teacher voice in education policy will only strengthen that policy. Teachers can, and should, weigh in on how evaluation results will be used—what happens to teachers who get bad evaluations, and how will those who shine be recognized and rewarded? Teachers can also help shape the implementation approach, including the use of pilot programs and their design. They can inform decisions about program monitoring and midcourse modifications that are needed to address system flaws. Teachers are also in the best position to design an evaluation system that contributes to continuous improvement, supporting all teachers as they work to improve their practice. Finally, teachers can shape the evaluations themselves, serving as peer evaluators, self-evaluators, and partners with their evaluators, as well as in other capacities. Teachers ought to be leading the development of these policies through on-the-ground conversations and interactions among peers and through larger-scale involvement in the policymaking process that empowers teachers individually and advances the perception of teaching as a profession.

According to *The MetLife Survey of the American Teacher,* teacher morale has dropped to a twenty-year low; the number of teachers who are very satisfied with their jobs fell from 59 percent in 2009 to 44 percent only two years later in 2011 (Markow & Pieters, 2012). Given the contentious nature of various approaches to evaluation reform, some current reform efforts have the unfortunate potential to further lower morale before they raise it.

The need for teacher input into changes that will raise morale in the profession is best expressed by the 2012 Teacher of the Year—seventh-grade California English teacher Rebecca Mieliwocki. In her speech at the White House, Mieliwocki said, "I want to spend my time restoring dignity and admiration to teachers. . . . I'm simply not going to let teachers get kicked around" (Heitin, 2012). With each passing reform that excludes teachers, however, more dignity is lost that needs to be restored, and it will take more than a speech by the Teacher of the Year to do so. We believe that it will take the widespread application of the types of professional and collaborative conversations that are recommended in this book.

Teacher engagement in evaluation will influence the eventual success of evaluation systems in three key ways; namely, it will promote (1) sound design, (2) effective implementation, and (3) sustainability.

Sound Design

Meaningful teacher involvement in evaluation will enable teachers to provide input as to which elements of the system will likely improve their practice, resulting in evaluation systems that are truly helpful. Accurately identifying what satisfactory and exemplary performances look like and determining the evaluation processes that will minimize disruptions and time wasting in the teacher's day, for example, are important elements of an accountability system that simultaneously affect how well teachers can serve their students.

Teachers are in the best position to envision how the details of a new system will play out on the ground, and to offer precautions. Well-intentioned policies (for example, compensation for growth tied to student test scores) can create perverse incentives, which in turn lead teachers to prioritize personal gain over the needs of students by working in competition rather than in collaboration with colleagues, or to cheat on a test, as exemplified by recent scandals in Atlanta and Washington, DC (Mathews, 2012; Sarrio, 2011). These serious, unforeseen complications might be avoided by incorporating teachers' insights into design conversations. In short, including the knowledge and wisdom of those most closely involved with and affected by the evaluation system will lead to better policies in practice.

Effective Implementation

Policies developed locally with significant teacher input are also likely to be better supported by teachers when the time comes for broad-based implementation. Teachers can make or break the implementation of a school policy, and they are much more likely to be supportive of the change if they have been properly engaged. With teacher participation, implementation is likely to go more smoothly, and there will be fewer confrontational meetings, fewer headaches, greater clarity around the purpose of the new initiative, and, in many cases, more enthusiasm for the changes and the increased professionalism that they bring.

Sustainability

As we've noted, teacher engagement is likely to lead to policy that teachers view as legitimate and to teacher support of and participation in implementation; thus, through engagement, teachers develop a stake in the new policies. Teacher engagement promotes sustainable policies that stand the test of time, and there is little point passing a new policy if mounting resistance ends up causing its eventual demise. Unfortunately, many high-profile teacher evaluation initiatives have experienced setbacks that threaten their sustainability. In trying to implement its Race to the Top teacher evaluation reforms, for example, New York State faced legal battles in the courtroom, district resistance to signing on to the policy, and an open letter of concern signed by fifteen hundred school principals (one-third of all principals in the state), causing both the chief education officer and the governor to question whether the new system would work (McNeil, 2012). Elena Silva, a leading policy analyst from the Carnegie Foundation for the Advancement of Teaching, described how failure to acknowledge teachers and their concerns hindered Race to the Top evaluation reforms across the country: "The movement around teacher evaluation reform was pushed fairly boldly and quickly around the accountability issue and that was a mistake. It left teachers behind and didn't attend to the vulnerabilities and insecurities teachers feel" (Paulson, 2012, p. 6). Properly engaging teachers reduces the likelihood of the skepticism and resistance that too often lead to short-lived reforms.

Involving teachers in the conduct of the evaluation—as evaluators of their own performance or that of others—can also lead to increased teacher investment in the policy and can create opportunities for meaningful feedback from grade-level or subject-area peers, provide professional learning and growth opportunities, and, in the right circumstances, result in more accurate and fair ratings of teachers' instructional effectiveness.

Considering that so many teachers are experiencing "reform fatigue," redesigning evaluation systems can easily be shrugged off as just another initiative "that too shall pass." The strategies detailed in Chapters Five through Eight of this book, however, offer education leaders, teachers, and other stakeholders a new approach for tackling a controversial reform initiative such as teacher evaluation. The key to the approach laid out in these chapters is to avoid top-down decision making and instead to create conditions in which teachers themselves are active participants in the process and are using their wisdom, experience, and creativity to strengthen their profession.

As described in the vignette that follows, Educators4Excellence has championed teacher engagement in New York City and Los Angeles to ensure that teachers are included in policy decisions that affect them and their students. Throughout this book, examples of similar organizations that bring together excellent teachers and are actively promoting teacher voice in education policy will be shared to illustrate the many ways teacher voice can shape policy and to highlight how this has led to successful outcomes for the teacher leaders involved.

Educators4Excellence

Bringing Out the Expertise

"If we can trust teachers with the education of our future and of our next generation, we should be able to trust teachers with conversations around where their profession is going." When Evan Stone made this statement, he was not just expressing an opinion; he was describing the teacher engagement initiative that he and fellow mover and shaker NYC teacher Sydney Morris began several years earlier. After noting the paucity of opportunities for teachers to discuss their profession with colleagues from different schools and different parts of the city, Stone and Morris cofounded Educators4Excellence (E4E), an organization that strives to ensure that teachers' voices are included in decisions that impact teachers and students. The organization started in 2010 as a small group of teachers working to improve policy. Just two years later, E4E engages more than six thousand educators nationally, all of whom are united around a common set of beliefs and norms.

Central to the organization's mission is the affirmation that expertise lives in the classroom. E4E prides itself on being an organization run by teachers for teachers. All staff members have teaching experience, and more than half of the members of the board of directors are current classroom teachers. The true stars of the organization, however, are the teacher members of E4E who engage in opportunities to learn about policy, network with like-minded colleagues and important policymakers, and take action around policy changes that will improve outcomes for students and elevate the teaching profession. E4E teachers have already made their impact on policy in multiple ways, including through the E4E policy team program.

The E4E policy team engages in an intensive and authentic policymaking process. E4E assembles groups of fifteen to twenty teacher volunteers who commit to spending three to four months researching a specific, relevant, and pressing reform issue, such as teacher compensation, teacher evaluation, or principal evaluation. Beginning with an extensive review of the existing literature and research, E4E challenges teachers to view the issue from multiple perspectives and to look at examples and models from a range of other districts and states. Through surveys and other feedback mechanisms, the policy team hears from hundreds of fellow educators and brings their voices back to the table. After extensive research, polling, and careful thought, the policy group publishes a white paper articulating the changes they want to see.

E4E does not ask teachers to leave their teacher hats at the door. Rather, E4E encourages teachers to draw on their firsthand classroom experiences as they deliberate on solutions-oriented policy questions. As Morris noted, "oftentimes in the education conversation, it's easiest to focus on what's wrong with the current system rather than thinking about building that system in a more ideal way." Rather than viewing teaching and policymaking as distinct, the policy group members use questions about how a policy would work in their classroom to guide their policymaking process:

Would this work in my school?

Would this help me improve as a practitioner?

Would this benefit my students?

In just a short time, E4E teachers have impacted state and local policy by raising awareness and influencing final outcomes. In 2011, the New York City E4E team released *Beyond Satisfactory: A New Teacher Evaluation System for New York,* a proposal for an evaluation system based on multiple measures of performance. Policy team members presented this paper to the district, to the union, and to the governor—and their voices were heard. The final teacher evaluation appeals process in New York State, for example, closely reflects the recommendations from the E4E policy team. More recently, the release of *Breaking the Stalemate: LA Teachers Take on Teacher Evaluation* stirred conversation in Los Angeles. Newspapers, including the *Los Angeles Times,* have profiled the paper, and Superintendent John Deasy, after hearing a presentation of the paper, praised the model presented by E4E teachers for its thoughtfulness. Ultimate outcomes remain unclear, but the accomplishments of E4E and its members demonstrate how teacher-created policy can be smart policy.

Reflecting on their accomplishments to date, Stone attributed E4E's success to its treatment of educators as experts. Yet the cofounders noted that too often districts and policymakers fail to tap the expertise of educators. Stone and Morris admit that going to schools, holding lunch meetings, sending out surveys, and engaging teachers in the policymaking process from the very beginning, in an authentic and meaningful way, require time—something that both teachers and policymakers often lack. However, taking time to authentically engage teachers is a worthwhile investment. According to Morris, efforts to engage teachers will "result in a better policy [that is] created with the input of those who will be responsible for implementing it." In the words of Stone and Morris, "Expertise lives in the classroom; we just need to help bring it out."

Source: Interview with Sydney Morris and Evan Stone, June 15, 2012.

TEACHER LEADERSHIP AND TEACHER ENGAGEMENT

Along with expanding the role of teacher voice in education policy, groups like Educators4Excellence tackle the related mission of expanding the role of teachers as leaders in their profession. Although to date most teacher leadership opportunities reside in schools, districts, and teachers' associations, in some cases, teacher leaders are members of policy-oriented groups (including Educators4Excellence and many other organizations described in subsequent chapters), and they publish influential reports and policy briefs that they present to their school boards, mayors, governors, and, in some cases, the president of the United States. Teacher leaders from the Center for Teaching Quality, for example, published a book titled *Teaching 2030* (Berry, 2011), which outlines their vision for a future profession that capitalizes on instructional technology and other twenty-first-century advances. Similarly, the twenty-one teacher leaders who made up the National Education Association's Commission on Effective Teachers and Teaching called for a greater role for effective teachers in teacher selection, evaluation, and dismissal; a teacher-led system of teacher preparation, licensure, and certification; and more opportunities for teachers to grow in the areas of instructional leadership, educational management, and school and district leadership (Commission on Effective Teachers and Teaching, 2011).

This is not a movement relegated to organizations. Teachers are also making independent efforts to expand teacher leadership. In some cases, teacher leaders have created campaigns—such as Chicago teacher Adam Heenan's "Use Your Teacher Voice" YouTube video campaign—that showcase short, homemade videos from teachers nationwide about their views on teacher policy and the profession. Other teacher leaders blog in online policy forums, as guest bloggers on education policy maven Rick Hess's Straight Up blog, for example, or on *Teaching Ahead,* a joint project of *Education Week Teacher* and the Center for Teaching Quality, where National Board Certified teachers (NBCTs) and other teacher leaders regularly contribute posts. Indeed, in many cases teacher leaders write about the need for more teacher leaders (as illustrated in the box "Teachers Blog on Teacher Leadership"). In other cases, teacher leaders do not necessarily write about their viewpoints but instead serve on boards of nonprofit and governmental organizations outside the schoolhouse.

TEACHERS BLOG ON TEACHER LEADERSHIP

Recent reflections by NBCTs on *Teaching Ahead,* the joint project of *Education Week Teacher* and the Center for Teaching Quality, include the following insights:

> As professionals, we need to be sitting down with management to thoughtfully develop and execute evaluation systems. We need to get serious about teacher evaluation and its purpose; and when I say "we," I mean teachers in the classroom, as well as administrators. Teachers

must share responsibility for the professional practice of every teacher in their school. Teachers ceded our role as quality guardians in our profession when we allowed the role of evaluation to be placed solely in administrators' hands.

—Maddie Fennell (Omaha, 2007 Nebraska Teacher of the Year)

It is time for us to realize as teachers we are the ones who must speak out about education, and we should use the most powerful tool currently available to do so: *social media*. Until we do, other people who know little about schools will do the speaking for us . . . incorrectly.

—Lillie Marshall (Boston, prominent blogger)

I appreciate how the Teacher Leader Model Standards identify different domains in which teachers can lead and not specify how they should lead. Just as students have strengths and areas to build upon, so do teachers. There are many ways to lead—some more visible than others, but all vital to our profession.

—Jane Fung (Los Angeles, National Board Certified Teacher)

Teachers are called on all the time to give feedback on new standards, policy, and curricula. Sometimes the people who wrote the originals are just looking for a rubber stamp; other times they genuinely want our insights to inform their revisions. But either way, there's a big difference between helping to build something and just giving it a thumbs-up or thumbs-down once it's built.

—Justin Minkel (Springdale, Arkansas, 2007 Arkansas Teacher of the Year)

The perception from teachers is that sharing ideas is going to create a problem; that speaking about changes means you are causing trouble. Where does this negative assumption come from? The expectation of negativity is a roadblock to progress.

—Cheryl Suliteanu (Oceanside, CA, National Board Certified Teacher)

Source: These comments first appeared on EdWeek.org, July 20–25, 2012. Reprinted with permission from the authors.

At the same time that current and former teachers are building up their efforts to increase teacher voice in education policy, parallel attention is being paid to the role of teacher voice and teacher leadership among education leaders and policymakers. The growing interest in teacher leadership is reflected in recent developments from the schoolhouse to the statehouse. For example:

- Boston's new Teacher Leader Certificate program, created by the city's Teacher Leadership Resource Center, provides courses for experienced teachers on shared leadership, supporting instruction, using data, and professional expertise. All the courses are designed and facilitated by practicing Boston Public

School teachers, and this provides instructors and course participants alike with a meaningful leadership opportunity.

- Kansas, Ohio, Delaware, Alabama, and Kentucky have formed a consortium on teacher leadership, known as the KODAK group, to develop a curriculum for higher education institutions to prepare teachers for leadership. The KODAK group has been supported by the Council for Chief State School Officers, which works with the leaders of departments of education in all fifty states to share ideas and innovations around teacher quality. The curriculum includes courses on such topics as leading change and facilitating productive collaboration.
- Kansas, Louisiana, Georgia, and Illinois have developed teacher leader certifications or endorsements to recognize teacher expertise in subject-matter knowledge, pedagogy, or child development, and to encourage additional training and responsibilities for teachers who wish to remain in the classroom.
- Virginia Commonwealth University's Center for Teacher Leadership, University of West Georgia's Teacher Leadership Endorsement Program, and Montclair State University's master of education in teacher leadership have begun to redesign their teacher preparation programs to equip their graduates with the skills to be leaders, reflecting an emerging recognition of the formal role teacher leaders play in a twenty-first-century education system.

Indeed, more than sixty colleges now offer master's programs in teacher leadership (Rebora, 2012). We must leverage this unprecedented movement toward stronger teacher leadership and teacher voice in the education policy debate to foster the practice of meaningful, productive teacher engagement on issues like evaluation reform. Engagement initiatives can have the greatest impact when they are led by teachers with strong leadership qualities who are dialed into the policy world and understand its workings.

At the same time that the movement toward stronger teacher leadership nourishes the kind of teacher engagement described in this book, the practice of teacher engagement itself fosters teacher leadership. Teacher engagement on *any* policy, and particularly on teacher evaluation, will create stronger leaders of teachers.

The strategies set forth in Chapters Five through Seven promote teacher leadership in evaluation reform in two ways: first, they develop specific leadership skills, such as organizing colleagues, mastering the content of the policies considered, and listening and public speaking skills for teachers who lead this initiative as moderators; second, they provide a forum for other teachers to expand their knowledge of education policy, empowering them to better judge the merits of that policy and craft and articulate a common vision of what meaningful evaluations can look like.

Why is fostering teacher leadership so critical? For the national effort to reinvigorate the teaching profession through improved teacher evaluation to succeed, teachers must be engaged as leaders within and beyond their classroom walls. Teacher leadership, in this and many other ways, is the key to unlocking the potential of the profession.

Unlocking the potential of teachers as leaders has many other benefits as well. As the role of school principals evolves to focus more on instructional leadership than on managerial duties (Darling-Hammond, LaPointe, Meyerson, & Orr, 2007; Davis, Kearney, Sanders, Thomas, & Leon, 2011), teacher leaders are perfectly suited to take on some of the principals' managerial tasks, which would free up the principals' time to focus on instructional leadership while simultaneously expanding teachers' skill sets, exposing teachers to opportunities outside of the classroom, and building a principal pipeline.

There is also growing evidence that providing opportunities for leadership is an important part of any effort to recruit and retain excellent teachers for all students. Smart, dynamic, motivated teachers fear stagnating in their growth. In 2011, researchers at Scholastic asked teachers what factors were important to teacher retention, and a "greater decision-making role for teachers in regards to school policies and practices" was cited as "absolutely essential" or "very important" by over 75 percent of teachers. Similarly, providing "opportunities for additional responsibility and advancement while staying in the classroom" was seen as "absolutely essential" or "very important" by nearly 60 percent of those surveyed (Scholastic & Bill & Melinda Gates Foundation, 2012, p. 59). So great is the desire to both remain in the classroom and assume additional leadership responsibilities that over 60 percent of teachers would be interested in working at a school that was run and managed by teachers themselves (for example, at a charter school) (Public Agenda, 2010). Expanding teacher leadership opportunities is one way to allow these talented professionals to fulfill their desire to continually expand their horizons while still spending the bulk of their time teaching students.

Of course, not all teachers are interested in being leaders, but for those who are, teaching must be able to provide the kind of authentic leadership roles, avenues for ongoing professional growth, and opportunities to collaborate that can be found in other professions that are competing for the same teacher talent. This means that full-time teachers need dedicated time away from their students to reflect on their practice and their profession and to participate in enhancing both.

Teacher leadership in teacher evaluation, and teacher leadership more generally, are mutually reinforcing, and districts with a strong history of developing teachers as leaders will have an easier time translating their teachers' leadership skills to this particular arena to craft stronger teacher evaluation systems. Regardless of a district's starting place, however, using teacher evaluation as a means of improving teachers' skills and knowledge and of expanding teacher voice will create the conditions that will enable future school policy dialogue to benefit from teachers' leadership.

Teachers United provides an illustration of a targeted initiative to extend teachers' voices beyond the red brick walls.

Teachers United

Showing Up and Working for Change

Ask anyone where to find a teacher, and you're likely to get the response, "in a school" or "in a classroom." But teachers with Teachers United can be found in a variety of places: in the boardroom of a nonprofit organization, in a union executive committee meeting, on the steps of the state capitol, or out in the community. The Seattle-based organization encourages teachers to contribute their voices not only in schools but also in broader arenas where policies and practices impact students and education.

Teachers United began as a discussion between cofounders Chris Eide and Kirby Green one evening. "We were frustrated by our school system's inability to effectively help a lot of kids who needed support. So we started thinking about ways we could actually get involved in some of the things we were talking about. . . . The more we read about 'last in, first out' practices, the more we thought it wasn't necessarily the best thing for students," Eide explained. "So we went down to Olympia, our state capital, to testify against this practice." After the *Seattle Times* and other local news sources covered the teachers' testimony in 2010, other teachers approached Eide and Green to ask how they could become involved. Teachers United, an organization dedicated to empowering teachers to advocate for the policies they believe in, was born.

Since then, Teachers United staff and members have sent hundreds of emails to legislators, given testimony to education committees in the state capital, and assumed leadership positions within teachers' unions and other organizations. "The voice of teachers is not really represented on boards of nonprofits and other organizations that claim to be education advocates," Eide explained. Often, the voice of teachers—who are in some cases ultimately charged with implementing policies—is missing. "So we're bringing that voice to the table so these organizations can make better, more balanced decisions that will have a much greater chance of success on the ground." It's important that Teachers United encourages its members to seek leadership positions within the teachers' union. According to Eide, unions are vital to the success and well-being of teachers in Washington, but the messaging and dialoguing at times can be stagnant and should be reframed to promote more informed conversation around the critical issues in education.

Source: Interview with Chris Eide, August 8, 2012.

TYING IT TOGETHER

Given the heated national discourse that permeates teacher quality reforms, there is an urgent need to rethink how new education policies and programs are designed, communicated, and implemented to ensure long-term, positive change in the delivery of education.

The strategies outlined in Chapters Five through Seven intend to empower teachers as leaders around the teacher evaluation table. Although it may be possible to communicate with and engage teachers effectively using other approaches, the road can be rocky, and it is lined with cliffs. The safer route, outlined in this book, involves meaningfully engaging *all* interested teachers in a sustained and genuine way.

Highly engaged teachers and the persistent, authentic inclusion of their voices will create strong evaluation systems comprising more meaningful tools, measures, and processes. These stronger systems will, in turn, provide greater avenues for high-quality instructional feedback and support, collaboration, and other culture changes associated with improved classroom instruction. Changing teachers' practices in this way will result in student learning, engagement, and achievement. This theory of action is illustrated in Figure 1.1.

The theory of action illustrates that the many outcomes of teacher engagement benefit principals, teachers, and students alike. Principals will benefit from a more content and collaborative staff. Teachers will see dysfunction and top-down directives replaced by new school policies that "just make sense"; they will receive

Figure 1.1. The Outcomes of Teacher Engagement

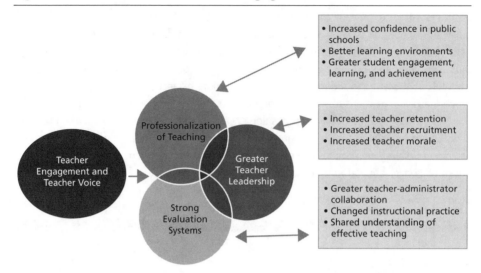

- Increased confidence in public schools
- Better learning environments
- Greater student engagement, learning, and achievement

- Increased teacher retention
- Increased teacher recruitment
- Increased teacher morale

- Greater teacher-administrator collaboration
- Changed instructional practice
- Shared understanding of effective teaching

Teacher Engagement and Teacher Voice

Professionalization of Teaching

Greater Teacher Leadership

Strong Evaluation Systems

targeted guidance for improving student behavior and increasing student learning and engagement; and they will be recognized for their achievements in realizing these successes. Lastly, students, and society at large, will be the ultimate beneficiaries of more efficient, effective educational policymaking that results in greater feedback and ongoing learning for teachers.

It is the premise of this book that elevating teacher engagement and teacher voice (particularly through the process outlined in Chapters Five through Seven) will result in these positive outcomes. But in practice, the ideal approach to widespread engagement in teacher evaluation can take many forms. What does this ideal look like in your school, district, or state? Is it a handful of teachers joining administrators on a school or district committee? Is it teachers running the local evaluation system as peer evaluators? Is it detailed teacher survey data that administrators or the teachers' association compiles into a fancy report? Is it teachers taking an activist stand or even running for political office? Or is it something different? In the best-case scenario, how would teachers' voices be incorporated when tough decisions are made around assessing teacher effectiveness or other policies?

There is no single answer, but these questions should be kept in mind while you are reading the chapters that follow, and your reactions and responses should be weaved into your expanding ideas to help make this vision a reality on the ground in the school(s) you serve.

TWO

The Teacher Effectiveness Question

How Can Effectiveness Be Measured?

According to the *Oxford English Dictionary,* the word *widget* was derived from the word *gadget,* which *Merriam-Webster Dictionary* claims was coined in 1886, when the firm that created the Statue of Liberty (Gaget, Gauthier & Cie) began selling miniature versions of the statue, bearing the cofounder's name, to tourists. Little did Mr. Gaget know that his name, associated then with the statue representing the U.S. ideal of liberty and equality of opportunity, would one day be associated with the means to achieve that ideal—education and effective teachers—through the publication of another New York City phenomenon, the New Teacher Project's report titled *The Widget Effect.*

Published in 2009, *The Widget Effect* shed light on the dire state of teacher evaluation, drawing attention to the fact that, at present, fewer than 1 percent of teachers are rated "Unsatisfactory," even when large portions of their students are failing. Surveying fifteen thousand teachers and thirteen hundred administrators across twelve districts in Illinois, Ohio, Colorado, and Arkansas, the report found that our nation's current approach to measuring teacher effectiveness is so broken and lacking in rigor that three-quarters of teachers do not receive any useful feedback from these empty checklist exercises (Weisberg, Sexton, Mulhern, & Keeling, 2009).

The report argued that treating teachers like interchangeable widgets does nothing to benefit teachers or students. Fixing the system so that it meaningfully recognizes and differentiates teachers' unique strengths sends a message to teachers that what they do in the classroom matters and that time and resources will be devoted to assessing how well they implement key instructional practices so that feedback can be provided to help them improve in the areas where they do not already excel. By failing to separate the wheat from the chaff, the current approaches to assessing performance have allowed—and even encouraged—many students (and particularly those from disadvantaged backgrounds) to be taught by ineffective teachers who stymie their chances for a successful career and a successful life. Following the publication of the report in 2009, thirty-six states, along with Washington, DC and countless school districts, have passed reforms with the goal of more meaningfully assessing teacher effectiveness.

There is a pair of old adages: "That which gets measured, matters" and "That which gets assessed, gets addressed." When it comes to teacher effectiveness, paying more attention to performance may lead to improved results if teachers have access to, and can apply, performance data to instructional improvements. Equally important, however, is that it may also change how policymakers and the public see teachers.

Although there is widespread recognition of the important role education plays in our society, and for teachers on an individual level, the teaching profession as a whole does not always command the same respect. The 2011 annual Phi Delta Kappa/Gallup Poll of the Public's Attitudes Toward the Public Schools, for example, found that although 71 percent of the public have trust and confidence in the men and women teaching in our public schools and 74 percent would encourage the brightest person they know to become a teacher, only 29 percent thought they heard more good stories than bad stories in the media about teachers (Bushaw & Lopez, 2011). It is hoped that through the measurement and demonstration of the student learning taking place, however, teaching will come to be seen as more rigorous and as something that people care about enough to carefully assess what is taking place in classrooms and whether it is helping students grow.

THE CHALLENGE OF MEASURING TEACHER EFFECTIVENESS

Leading up to the publication of *The Widget Effect* (and the numerous legislative changes that followed) was No Child Left Behind, the 2001 reauthorization of the Elementary and Secondary Education Act. This required, among other things, that school districts report on the percentage of classes that were taught by highly qualified teachers (HQTs), defined as those with at least a bachelor's degree, full state certification, and proven content knowledge of each subject they teach. The U.S. Department of Education required not only that all teachers become HQTs but also that states take action based on these data. Specifically, states were required to ensure that districts were equitably distributing their HQTs so that students from low-income and minority backgrounds would not be systematically taught by teachers assigned outside their content-area major or without full certification.

When HQT data were first released at the national level in 2005, states reported that 87 percent of classes were taught by HQTs. Over the following six years, the number inched up to 97 percent, as illustrated in Figure 2.1. Although still shy of the 100 percent target, the most notable accomplishment resulting from the HQT mandate is that the number of teachers on waivers and renewable emergency certification has declined significantly; when emergency certified teachers do appear on the rolls, they now tend to be aligned with federally approved alternative route provisions.

Nonetheless, it quickly became clear that HQT status was an insufficient measure of the quality of teaching that students experience and, hence, might mask inequities in access to effective instruction. The HQT criteria set the bar too low to meaningfully assess whether teachers were high quality or not. The other available and quantifiable aspect of teacher quality was teacher experience, but experience levels were also found to be only marginally useful for measuring a teacher's actual effectiveness. Studies by the National Center for the Analysis of Longitudinal Data in Education Research found that teachers tend to rapidly become more effective during their first five years in the classroom, but that

Figure 2.1. Percentage of Highly Qualified Teachers over Time

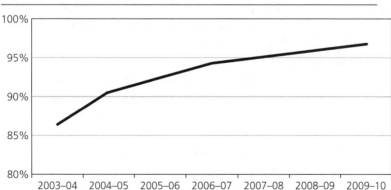

their effectiveness at raising student test scores then plateaus (Rice, 2010). Thus the need to identify better data to inform decisions about teacher advancement, placement, and compensation became another rallying cry for reforming how teacher effectiveness is assessed.

Recognizing that the HQT standards were a necessary but insufficient measure of teacher quality, the U.S. Department of Education, national policy organizations, and states and districts across the country began transitioning the public lexicon from highly qualified teachers (HQTs) to *highly effective teachers* (HETs). In so doing, they began creating assessments of teacher effectiveness based on outcomes, or performance measures, rather than on inputs tied to the number of years in the classroom or the number of advanced degrees. Although credentials still matter from a hiring perspective, career decisions are increasingly based on what teachers are able to accomplish in the classroom and the extent to which this can be demonstrated by the academic growth of their students. Of course, questions related to how performance would be reliably measured for our nation's 3.2 million public school teachers was, and continues to be, the subject of much debate. Spurred by *The Widget Effect* report, however, redesigning teacher evaluation systems came to be seen as the starting place for rethinking what constitutes an effective teacher.

In the rush to respond to this new reform agenda, referred to by some as the "teacher evaluation binge" (Mead, Rotherham, & Brown, 2012), many states introduced policies without thoroughly considering the complexities that the changes would bring. New approaches to measuring teacher effectiveness were mandated with very short timelines for implementation and before the tools needed to implement them were or could be made available. Tests that teachers trusted as an indicator of their effectiveness, for example, were unavailable, as were protocols for ensuring that classroom observers were sufficiently trained to rate teachers' practice consistently. Insufficient time was allotted to pilot new approaches and generate an evidence base in regard to what types of measures work best, and, most unfortunate of all, policies were passed without input from those most intimately impacted by the change: teachers.

The nationwide revamping of methods for measuring teacher performance was born of the desire to use data to enable the identification of more and less effective teachers so that education leaders could better guarantee that students (and particularly high-need students) would not be shortchanged by the education system. However, a more cynical dimension took hold as the inadequacies of the new evaluation systems surfaced and the prolonged national economic recession simultaneously necessitated public spending cuts in education. To cut spending, a number of states, most notably Wisconsin, curbed teachers' collective bargaining rights. The anti-union sentiment that accompanied this period of economic downturn also fueled an existing rhetoric of "firing the bad teachers," and to some, firing teachers for the purposes of cost-cutting came to be seen as the dominant goal of these reforms.

DIMENSIONS OF TEACHER EFFECTIVENESS

As policymakers and the public turned their focus to better differentiating among teachers, challenges associated with the paucity of existing valid and reliable measures of effectiveness, as well as with determining how to weigh the importance of student outcomes data as part of a larger assessment model, quickly surfaced.

Because measures of effectiveness were highly underutilized in the past—teachers were often only evaluated once every three years, and few useful tools and models existed to inform this emerging reform agenda—the reality of reforming how teachers are assessed surfaced many more questions initially than it offered solutions (Bill & Melinda Gates Foundation, 2010; Brandt, Mathers, Oliva, Brown-Sims, & Hess, 2007; Weisberg et al., 2009).

One of the first challenges to measuring teacher effectiveness has to do with the multiple dimensions associated with *defining* teacher effectiveness. Defining effectiveness provides a common language around the practices, knowledge, and dispositions, and a starting point for rethinking the overall design of a teacher evaluation system. Multiple organizations filled this void by introducing standards that define what effective teaching should comprise. The National Comprehensive Center for Teacher Quality, for example, provided the following definition of an effective teacher:

1. Effective teachers have high expectations for all students and help students learn, as measured by value-added or other test-based growth measures, or by alternative measures.
2. Effective teachers contribute to positive academic, attitudinal, and social outcomes for students, such as regular attendance, self-efficacy, and cooperative behavior.
3. Effective teachers use diverse resources to plan and structure engaging learning opportunities; monitor student progress formatively, adapting instruction as needed; and evaluate learning using multiple sources of evidence.
4. Effective teachers contribute to the development of classrooms and schools that value diversity and civic-mindedness.

5. Effective teachers collaborate with other teachers, administrators, parents, and education professionals to ensure student success, particularly the success of students with special needs and those at high risk for failure. (Goe, Bell, & Little, 2008, p. 8)

Similarly, the Interstate Teacher Assessment and Support Consortium at the Council of Chief State School Officers offered ten model core teaching standards, and the National Board for Professional Teaching Standards offered five core propositions and related standards for defining effective teaching. In addition, many districts have opted to develop their own frameworks or rubrics to define the elements of effective teaching and what constitutes exemplary, proficient, or ineffective teaching, often using one or more national models as a starting place before defining locally what constitutes an effective teacher.

For many schools and districts, Charlotte Danielson's Framework for Teaching (1996) provided a detailed definition of effective teaching. The framework articulates, in very practical terms, four levels of teaching performance—Unsatisfactory, Basic, Proficient, and Distinguished—across twenty-two components (and seventy-six smaller elements) of effective teaching, organized into four domains: (1) planning and preparation; (2) classroom environment; (3) instruction; and (4) professional responsibilities, as illustrated in Figure 2.2.

This framework offered "face validity" for teachers—that is, it "just made sense"—but it was also supported by research which suggested that teachers' ratings on this framework were correlated with student test score growth, lending additional credibility to its use (Sartain, Stoelinga, & Brown, 2011). Most important, it clearly articulated what constituted effective teaching for each element of the framework. Specifically, Danielson's Framework for Teaching (1996) defines performance levels as follows:

Unsatisfactory. The teacher does not yet appear to understand the concepts underlying the component. Working on the fundamental practices associated with the elements will enable the teacher to grow and develop in this area.

Basic. The teacher appears to understand the concepts underlying the component and attempts to implement its elements. But implementation is sporadic, intermittent, or otherwise not entirely successful. Additional reading, discussion, visiting classrooms of other teachers, and experience (particularly supported by a mentor) will enable the teacher to become proficient in this area. For supervision or evaluation, this level is minimally competent;

Figure 2.2. Danielson's Framework for Teaching

Domain 1: Planning and Preparation	Domain 3: Instruction
1a. Demonstrating Knowledge of Content and Pedagogy	3a. Communicating Clearly and Accurately
1b. Demonstrating Knowledge of Students	3b. Using Questioning and Discussion Techniques
1c. Setting Instructional Outcomes	3c. Engaging Students in Learning
1d. Demonstrating Knowledge of Resources	3d. Providing Feedback to Students
1e. Designing Coherent Instruction	3e. Demonstrating Flexibility and Responsiveness
1f. Assessing Student Learning	
Domain 2: Classroom Environment	**Domain 4: Professional Responsibilities**
2a. Creating an Environment of Respect and Rapport	4a. Reflecting on Teaching
2b. Establishing a Culture for Learning	4b. Maintaining Accurate Records
2c. Managing Classroom Procedures	4c. Communicating with Families
2d. Managing Student Behavior	4d. Contributing to the School and District
2e. Organizing Physical Space	4e. Growing and Developing Professionally
	4f. Showing Professionalism

Source: Adapted from Danielson, 1996, p. 61.

improvement is likely with experience, and little or no actual harm is done to students.

Proficient. The teacher clearly understands the concepts underlying the component and implements them well. Most experienced, capable teachers will regard themselves and be regarded by others as performing at this level.

Distinguished. Teachers at this level are master teachers and make a contribution to the field, both in and outside their school. Their classrooms operate at a qualitatively different level, consisting of a community of learners, with students highly motivated and engaged and assuming considerable responsibility for their own learning.

Despite the availability of standards and model frameworks to determine what should be measured, successful communication about teacher effectiveness is often hampered by the terminology associated with the different dimensions of high-quality teaching. To aid communication around defining and measuring teacher effectiveness, a much-cited resource is Jane Coggshall's *Communication Framework for Measuring Teacher Quality and Effectiveness* (2007), which specifies seven key dimensions of teacher quality and is commonly used in conversations about teacher evaluation design.

The definitions of these key dimensions, and the range of measurement instruments associated with them, are illustrated in Table 2.1. Understanding the nuances in terminology is an important first step for productive communication about the measurement of teacher effectiveness. The purpose of considering these seven dimensions is not so much to determine which has priority or which is best, but rather to make sure that everyone in the conversation is using a common vocabulary so as to avoid confusion and miscommunication.

Discussing and defining good teaching using rubrics and tools like Danielson's Framework for Teaching or Coggshall's *Communication Framework for Measuring Teacher Quality and Effectiveness* can be a highly rewarding opportunity for teachers to reflect and grow as they talk through examples of classroom practices and tackle the question that is so fundamental to their everyday work: how to teach well. Teachers we have spoken to have reported that some of the richest conversations of their careers have been about what good teaching looks like, and these conversations have taken place in the process of creating new approaches to measuring teacher effectiveness.

CONTEMPORARY APPROACHES TO MEASURING TEACHER EFFECTIVENESS

Reaching consensus about terminology and the definition of effective teaching is the first step for any district or state concerned with improving teacher effectiveness. The next step is to decide what measures and instruments will be used to assess teacher effectiveness. At this stage, disagreements often emerge, and positioning for or against a particular measure or approach begins to drive teachers and other stakeholders to take opposing positions. The tools and activities presented in Chapters Five through Eight are designed specifically to assist with this challenging task.

Table 2.1. Seven Dimensions of Teacher Quality

Dimension of Teacher Quality	Definition	Measurement Instruments and Indicators
Teacher effectiveness	In the research on teacher quality and in many policy communities, the word *effective* connotes some direct impact—or effect—on outcomes. In the case of teachers, this term is usually defined as the teacher's contribution to student academic achievement test scores, though it is possible to measure other valued student outcomes, such as high school graduation rates; student motivation; academic efficacy beliefs; or other social, behavioral, or intellectual outcomes. Thus, *highly effective* teachers can be defined as those teachers who show evidence of producing high student outcomes (however defined or measured).	• Student achievement (including value-added methods, growth models) • Dropout rates • Documented student work • Student affect, engagement, persistence
Teacher qualifications	*Qualified* teachers hold credentials certifying that they have successfully completed a state-approved (often nationally accredited) teacher preparation program, have demonstrated their good character (usually through a criminal background check), and hold a bachelor's degree. Moreover, states almost always require an examination of content and pedagogy for state certification. Qualifications can also include certification by professional groups, such as the National Board for Professional Teaching Standards, as well as experience, advanced degrees, and certification endorsements; however, such credentials are not necessary for teachers to be considered minimally qualified. *Highly qualified* teachers, as defined in the No Child Left Behind Act, are those who are fully certified by the state, hold a bachelor's degree, and demonstrate that they have content-area expertise in the subject that they are actually teaching.	• Degrees • Coursework or transcript review • Certification or licensure requirements • Preparation program status (such as alternative, traditional, accreditation status, prestige level) • Test cut scores for certification

(continued on next page)

Table 2.1. Seven Dimensions of Teacher Quality (*continued from previous page*)

Dimension of Teacher Quality	Definition	Measurement Instruments and Indicators
Teacher expertise	*Expert teachers* have a deep and broad working knowledge of both the content of the subject matter they are teaching and how to teach that content. Expert teachers also have knowledge of how students learn in general, as well as of a range of effective pedagogies to help all students learn. Expert teachers are also culturally competent for the context in which they teach.	• Exams (including multiple-choice tests or constructed response tests of content or pedagogical knowledge, or content knowledge for teaching) • Teaching portfolios • Classroom observation • Assessments related to professional development
Teacher capacity	Teachers with *capacity* for success demonstrate an ability to leverage their professional context into better teaching. For example, they have been well prepared, are committed to continued learning, are reflective, are organized, demonstrate verbal ability, and are able to analyze their teaching and articulate and refine their teaching philosophies.	• Teacher interviews • Qualification review • Teaching cases or classroom vignettes • Classroom observation • Intelligence testing, tests of verbal ability • Teaching philosophy statements
Teacher character	*Teachers of character* have certain traits and dispositions that are observed to be related to quality teaching: sensitivity, warmth, enthusiasm, passion, creativity, persistence, caring, commitment, self-efficacy, and genuineness.	• Teacher interviews • Personal and professional references • Student surveys and interviews • Parent surveys and interviews • Classroom observations • Teaching philosophy statements • Background checks or fingerprinting

| Teacher performance | *High-performing* teachers are those whose actions are observed to meet or exceed high standards of teaching practice. High-performing teachers demonstrate the knowledge and skills to provide high-quality instruction to all their students. These teachers will likely produce high student learning outcomes but may be unable to provide valid, reliable, or sufficient evidence of student learning outcomes. | • Teaching portfolios
• Principal, peer, or specialist evaluation with structured observation protocols
• Performance Assessment for California Teachers (PACT), Teaching Advancement Program (TAP), Connecticut Beginning Educator Support and Training (CT BEST), Danielson Framework, and other state and local evaluation systems
• Praxis III
• Teacher work samples
• Video evaluation
• Student surveys and interviews
• Parent surveys and interviews
• Teaching cases analysis
• Teacher logs
• Surveys of Enacted Curriculum |
| Teacher success | The term *successful teachers* could mean teachers who are "highly effective" in producing student success (however defined) or "high performing" (or both), so they likely will produce student growth and success. | • Combined measures of effectiveness and performance |

Source: Adapted from Coggshall, 2007, pp. 7–8.

Research provides some, albeit limited, guidance on how to measure effective teaching. Of greatest importance is the general consensus among the policy and research communities that a strong evaluation system includes multiple performance ratings and multiple measures of teacher effectiveness. Researchers support rating systems that categorize teachers not on two levels of effectiveness—Satisfactory and Unsatisfactory—but on four or five levels instead (Weisberg et al., 2009). Using a "nonbinary" rating scale provides a much more meaningful portrait of teachers' performance. Not only can principals and district leaders see a greater spread of performance levels when looking at the aggregate picture, but teachers themselves can obtain a more detailed assessment of their areas of strength and weakness. By receiving a 1–4 or 1–5 rating overall and in five, ten, twenty, or thirty different areas of performance, teachers—few of whom believe they excel at everything—can see where their 1s, 2s, 3s, 4s, and 5s are, and can focus their efforts accordingly. Considering that almost every teacher receives *some* 1s and 2s and almost every teacher receives *some* 4s and 5s, the message is conveyed that at every level, a teacher will have strengths and weaknesses and that the system is intended to identify specific areas for growth and to help teachers improve in those areas over time.

Researchers (Goe et al., 2008; Bill & Melinda Gates Foundation, 2013) also recommend using multiple teacher effectiveness measures, including but not limited to

Classroom observations. Used by evaluators to make consistent judgments of teachers' instructional practice, classroom observations are the most common measure of teacher effectiveness; they vary widely in how they are conducted and what they assess. High-quality classroom observation instruments are standards based and contain well-specified rubrics that delineate consistent assessment criteria for each standard of practice. To be accurate, evaluators should be trained to ensure consistency in scoring.

Student growth on standardized tests. Student growth on standardized tests refers to the test score *change* from one point in time to another point in time. The related concept of value-added measures refers to student growth measures that include a pre-test score and a post-test score *as well as* a number of other variables (for example, poverty, special needs, and so on) that are outside a teacher's control yet tend to affect students' academic growth. (See a more detailed discussion of student test scores later in this chapter.)

Other student growth data. Other student growth data include information about the change in students' performance on some other measure, such as a teacher- or district-developed test, over two or more points in time. It may also include growth in terms of behavior, musical performances, or portfolios of student work.

Instructional artifacts. Instructional artifacts are used by evaluators to rate lesson plans, teacher assignments, teacher-created assessments, scoring rubrics, or student work on particular criteria (such as rigor, authenticity, intellectual demand, alignment to standards, clarity, and comprehensiveness). Evaluators typically use an evaluation tool or rubric to make judgments about the quality of student artifacts.

Teacher portfolios. Portfolios are a collection of materials that exhibit evidence of exemplary teaching practice, school activities, and student progress. They are usually compiled by the teacher, and they may include teacher-created lesson or unit plans, descriptions of the classroom context, assignments, student work samples, videos of classroom instruction, notes from parents, and teachers' analyses of their students' learning in relation to their instruction. Similar to portfolios, evidence binders often require specific criteria for inclusion and require a final, teacher-led presentation of the work to an evaluation team.

Teacher self-assessments. Self-assessments consist of surveys, instructional logs, or interviews in which teachers report on their work in the classroom, the extent to which they are meeting standards, and, in some cases, the impact of their practice. Self-assessments may include checklists, rating scales, and rubrics, and they may require teachers to indicate the frequency of particular practices.

Student surveys. Student surveys are questionnaires that typically ask students to rate teachers on an extent scale (for example, from 1 to 5, where 1 = very effective and 5 = not at all effective) regarding various aspects of teachers' practice (for example, course content or usefulness of feedback), and to rate how much they believe they learned or the extent to which they were engaged.

Parent surveys. Parent surveys are questionnaires that typically ask parents to rate teachers on an extent scale (for example, from 1 to 5, where 1 = very effective and 5 = not at all effective) regarding various aspects of teachers' practice (for example, course content, usefulness of feedback, quality of homework, or quality of communication), and to rate the extent to which they are satisfied with teachers' instruction.

The instruments and tools that are developed to put the measures into practice must be created or selected wisely, and any of the aforementioned measures will be inappropriate if certain conditions are not met. Observations, for example, will be a poor measure if the observers do not follow appropriate protocols for conducting fair, accurate observations and providing effective feedback. Likewise, student growth on tests will be a poor measure if the tests are poor indicators of what students should be learning, or if students do not take the tests seriously. Researchers refer to these considerations as issues of *validity* and *reliability* (see box), and any sound teacher evaluation system must use only those measures that are deemed valid and reliable.

VALIDITY AND RELIABILITY

Validity refers to the ability of an instrument to measure the attribute that it intends to measure.

Reliability refers to the ability of an instrument to measure teacher performance consistently across different raters and different contexts.

The important caveat is that researchers do not provide recommendations regarding *which* measures to use. The Measures of Effective Teaching Project, the largest study to date on this topic, focuses on three measures: student gains on state tests, classroom observations, and student surveys (Bill & Melinda Gates Foundation, 2013). But choosing appropriate measures is something that must be decided locally, based on local values, with everyone's voice—that of teachers, their principals, students and their parents, and others—at the table. That is, it is a community's values regarding the importance of student test scores, of student or parent perceptions of teachers, and of principals' or peers' professional judgment that determine which measures of teacher effectiveness ought to be considered.

Individuals at the table may not immediately know which measures of teacher effectiveness are the most appropriate, but two useful starting places are (1) to revisit the priorities and purposes of measuring teacher effectiveness, noting that different measures are more appropriate for different purposes; and (2) to consider existing state and district policies that govern how teacher performance will be measured in your own setting and elsewhere.

Table 2.2 illustrates how various measures of teacher effectiveness align to different purposes. Clarifying your purposes for measuring teacher effectiveness is good practice under any circumstances, but it can also aid decision making about the most appropriate measures to use.

Table 2.2. Alignment of Evaluation Measures with Purposes

Purpose of Evaluation of Teacher Effectiveness	Value-Added Measures	Classroom Observation	Analysis of Artifacts	Portfolios	Teacher Self-Reports	Student Ratings	Other Reports
Find out whether grade-level or instructional teams are meeting specific achievement goals.	X						
Determine whether a teacher's students are meeting achievement growth expectations.	X		X				
Gather information in order to provide new teachers with guidance related to identified strengths and shortcomings.		X	X	X			X
Examine the effectiveness of teachers in lower elementary grades for which no test scores from previous years are available to predict student achievement (required for value-added models).		X	X	X			X
Examine the effectiveness of teachers in nonacademic subjects (for example, art, music, and physical education).		X		X		X	X
Determine whether a new teacher is meeting performance expectations in the classroom.		X	X	X		X	X
Determine the types of assistance and support a struggling teacher may need.		X	X		X	X	

(continued on next page)

Table 2.2. Alignment of Evaluation Measures with Purposes (continued from previous page)

Purpose of Evaluation of Teacher Effectiveness	Value-Added Measures	Classroom Observation	Analysis of Artifacts	Portfolios	Teacher Self-Reports	Student Ratings	Other Reports
Gather information to determine what professional development opportunities are needed for individual teachers, instructional teams, grade-level teams, and so on.	X	X			X		X
Gather evidence for making contract renewal and tenure decisions.	X	X					X
Determine whether a teacher's performance qualifies him or her for additional compensation or incentive pay (rewards).	X	X					
Gather information on a teacher's ability to work collaboratively with colleagues to evaluate needs of at-risk or struggling students and to determine appropriate instruction for them.				X	X		X
Establish whether a teacher is effectively communicating with parents and guardians.				X			X
Determine how students and parents perceive a teacher's instructional efforts.						X	
Determine who would qualify to become a mentor, coach, or teacher leader.	X	X	X	X			X

Note: X indicates measures approved for the specified purpose.
Source: Little, Bell, and Goe, 2009, p. 16.

Researchers emphasize that it is not enough to use just one form of measurement (for example, *either* observations *or* student test scores *or* classroom artifacts). According to Goe (2010), multiple measures

- *Strengthen teacher evaluation* by providing a more complete picture of the teacher's contribution to student learning, including collaboration among teachers; multiple measures also result in greater confidence in evaluation results.
- *Contribute to teachers' professional growth* by creating learning opportunities during the evaluation process that provide teachers with insights about their instruction.
- *Set the stage for improved teaching and learning* by offering more complete information about student learning, including students' areas of strength and weakness. This is particularly important for teachers of nontested subjects and grades and for English language learners and students with disabilities.

Multiple measures yield more information about a teacher than any single measure can, and more information helps administrators, instructional coaches, and teachers understand and address teachers' strengths and needs more fully. Looking at aspects of student achievement alone, for example, provides very little insight into which elements of a teacher's practice may have contributed to those results. Moreover, few student achievement tests accurately measure all the domains of learning that teachers seek to enhance in their students. At the same time, omitting measures of student learning outcomes when assessing teacher effectiveness risks allowing mediocre practice to go unaddressed.

Although using multiple measures can be more expensive due to the time commitment that is necessary to train observers, conduct multiple observations, and assess multiple pieces of data on teacher performance, it is important that judgments about a teacher's effectiveness are not based on inadequate evidence. Indeed, within a given measure, multiple sources of evidence are often recommended. For example, classroom observations should include multiple observers on multiple occasions in order to fully capture teachers' effectiveness from many angles. Likewise, stronger systems will include multiple measures of student learning (for example, growth on standardized tests, teacher-developed tests, performances, or a combination of these) as opposed to just one, and will balance the need for multiple measures with the need to avoid overtesting of students.

Organizations that promote teacher leaders, such as Hope Street Group (see box), have already begun reading the research, exploring systems around the country, and using what they have learned to get this balance right.

Hope Street Group

Moving from Hope to Action

"It never occurred to me that I should be involved in policy or reform; those words were not even part of my vernacular."

Dina Rock has been a lifelong educator. For the past twenty-four years, she has worked as a classroom teacher in a variety of contexts, ranging from an inner-city public school in Los Angeles, California, to a private school in Beachwood, Ohio. Although Rock frequently talked with colleagues about policies that could be improved and reforms that could be better implemented, discussions did not extend beyond the teachers' lounge.

In 2009, Rock found her voice. A colleague directed her to Hope Street Group, a non-profit and nonpartisan public policy organization that provides forums—both online and in person—for teachers and other professionals to engage in conversations about education reform. Rock participated in an online discussion thread about what makes a teacher effective and, as she described, experienced an "amazing awakening." "I knew there were teachers around me who felt the same way or thought the same things," explained Rock, "but I had no clue that these thoughts extended [nationally] beyond my teachers' lounge or my friends who are teachers."

After Rock became more involved in online discussions, Hope Street identified her as a team leader. As one of five leaders, Rock led a group of educators in discussing measures associated with teacher effectiveness. Four work groups produced eight recommendations for teacher evaluation systems, which Rock presented at the National Press Club and to policymakers in 2009. Reflecting on the event, Rock noted that many participants had stated, "It's so good to hear from a teacher." She had always assumed that teachers were involved in education policymaking decisions, but at that event she realized that this was not always the case. Rock decided that she needed to do more to engage teachers.

Engaging teachers has been challenging, however. In general, teachers are unaware of opportunities to engage in reform conversations and lack sufficient time to participate. To overcome these challenges, organizations like Hope Street have engaged teachers at a level at which they can commit. Hope Street works toward building an opportunity economy through collaborative problem solving in reforming education, health care, and jobs. The organization draws on "crowdsourced" solutions created with new voices, world-class talent, and modern tools, including state-of-the-art online discussion forums. Hope Street has provided private, collaborative work spaces to partner stakeholder groups, including the New York State Regents Task Force on Teacher and Principal Effectiveness, Florida Race to the Top implementation committees, and the Teacher and Leader Evaluation Multi-State Network.

Rock explains, "It is such a ripe time for teachers to become involved and engaged." Teacher effectiveness is a prominent issue, and administrators and policymakers are listening to teachers more than ever before. Hope Street teacher fellows have met with Secretary of Education Arne Duncan and other members of the administration to talk about their work in teacher evaluation reform, and Duncan has since referenced their work in speeches and articles. More recently, more than one hundred key stakeholders—including Superintendent John Deasy of Los Angeles, former chancellor of schools Joel Klein, and Senator Michael Bennett—gathered at the 2012 Hope Street Colloquium. As a keynote presenter, Rock helped unveil the new Teacher Evaluation Playbook—Hope Street's new Web tool that provides suggestions for teacher engagement in policy and effective educator reform. (The Teacher Evaluation Playbook is available online at http://playbook.hopestreetgroup.org/.)

Source: Interview with Dina Rock, May 2, 2012.

Two evaluation systems that are often referenced as models of a nuanced and comprehensive approach to assessing teacher performance are Hillsborough County, Florida, and the Teaching Advancement Program (TAP).

Hillsborough County, Florida—Measuring Effectiveness with Tests

In close collaboration with its union, the Tampa, Florida, district of Hillsborough County Public Schools developed a new system for assessing teacher effectiveness that includes multiple measures, including both teacher performance (as judged by their principal and accounting for 40 percent of a teacher's rating) and student learning (as measured by district assessments and accounting for 60 percent of a teacher's rating). Hillsborough County was in a unique financial position, with funding from the Bill & Melinda Gates Foundation and other sources, to build a stronger evaluation system for their own teachers so that lessons could be learned nationally for other districts' consideration.

In order to avoid punishing teachers of challenging or low-performing students, Hillsborough County adopted pre- and post-tests in each grade and subject so that students' *growth* could be ascertained. This approach meant that teachers of gifted or high-performing students were, if anything, at a disadvantage because their students' pre-test scores were so high.

The challenge that emerged early on was that pre- and post-tests did not exist for many grades and subjects, so Hillsborough County took on the mammoth task of designing such tests for every class. In total, the district designed more than six hundred tests.

On their first pass, the tests were not perfect, and concerns arose about variations in the level of rigor that made it difficult to compare teacher effectiveness across the district. However, these concerns were addressed over several years as the tests were strengthened. Key to improving the district tests was the involvement of teachers from the full diversity of subject areas, as well as content supervisors and the use of validity testing.

For the grades and subjects where it is relevant, the Florida Comprehensive Assessment Test (FCAT) is also used, as are various national norm-referenced tests.

TAP—Measuring Effectiveness Differently for Different Teachers

One of the most popular teacher effectiveness programs—TAP: The System for Teacher and Student Advancement—provides an example of weighting different measures of effectiveness for different purposes. TAP, which was created in 1999 (and referred to at the time as the Teacher Advancement Program), involves an innovative career ladder for teachers that includes

- *Career teachers.* These are regular classroom teachers.
- *Master teachers.* Along with teaching students for about two hours per day, master teachers work with the principal to analyze student data and create a schoolwide academic achievement plan; lead professional learning communities; coach; provide demonstration lessons; identify research-based instructional strategies to share with career teachers; evaluate other teachers; and interact with parents.
- *Mentor teachers.* These teachers support career teachers through leadership teams that involve analyzing student data and creating a schoolwide academic achievement plan; lead cluster meetings; provide extensive feedback and follow-up on career teachers' instructional practices; collaboratively plan for instruction; and engage in self- and team-directed professional development.

To reflect that a teacher's responsibility differs depending on his or her placement on this career ladder, different weights are assigned to different areas of performance. Although every teacher is rated on a 1–5 scale on four key areas—designing and planning instruction, the learning environment, instruction, and responsibilities—certain categories count more for some teachers than for others, as depicted in Figure 2.3.

Figure 2.3. Weighting Evaluation Criteria

Domain Weights	Career	Mentor	Master
Designing and Planning Instruction	15%	15%	15%
Learning Environment	5%	5%	5%
Instruction	75%	60%	40%
Responsibilities	5%	20%	40%

Source: Daley and Kim, 2010.

In addition to teachers' scores on this skills, knowledge, and responsibilities rubric, TAP teachers' evaluations include schoolwide (or, where possible, classroom-level) student achievement gains in mathematics and language arts.

TAP is used to assess the performance of more than seventy-five hundred teachers in districts across thirteen states and Washington, DC.

◉

As we have just discussed, Hillsborough County created over six hundred different student assessments to measure student learning growth from year to year in each subject area, and TAP created a career ladder program that includes peer evaluations. Other salient components of evaluation systems are found in school districts around the country, including the following:

Frequent observations. In Harrison County, Colorado (Colorado Springs), teacher evaluations include eight unannounced walkthroughs per year (and sixteen for new teachers) to ensure that teachers receive regular feedback and that their principals have a truer understanding of what is happening in the classrooms on a day-to-day basis.

Student surveys. Pittsburgh Public Schools include student surveys, not only for the purposes of giving teachers feedback, but also as a measure that gets factored into teachers' evaluations.

Competitive salaries. Washington, DC's IMPACT program stands out as an example of linking salary to high evaluation ratings. Whereas before, a "highly effective" teacher could earn $87,500 after twenty-one years in the district, these teachers can earn more than $130,000 under the new system, and it can take less than ten years to begin doing so (Doyle & Han, 2012).

It is also worth considering how other local organizations assess the effectiveness of their staff. Approaches to performance assessment outside of education might be of particular interest to parents and community members as they discuss the best way to measure teacher effectiveness. (See Chapter Eight for detailed strategies for promoting parent and community engagement.) Public Impact—an education policy think tank based in Charlotte, North Carolina—conducted a review of the literature on *noneducational* organizations' approaches to measuring employee effectiveness in the private, government, and nonprofit sectors and found that 60 percent of the more than five hundred HR managers in large and midsize companies conduct employee evaluations annually, and many leaders advocate for twice-yearly evaluations. Likewise, 60 percent of Fortune 100 companies use five levels of performance ratings in their evaluation systems, and an additional 20 percent use more than five rating levels (Kowal & Hassel, 2010; Thomas & Bretz, 1994).

Within or outside the field of education, no measure is perfect. Using multiple, high-quality measures of teacher performance—and then collaboratively deciding on a system for weighting those different measures—is therefore seen as a stronger approach than simply choosing the "best" measure (be it test scores, observations, surveys, or other measures). A report by Sheri Frost Leo and Lisa Lachlan-Haché (2012) at the American Institutes for Research profiles three leading approaches to weighting effectiveness measures: (1) a numerical approach, whereby scores from multiple measures are averaged to obtain a final rating number; (2) a profile approach, whereby a graphic maps out how various combinations of multiple measures translate to a final rating; and (3) a holistic approach, whereby evaluators "eyeball" each measure and use their judgment to determine a final rating. In practice, Leo and Lachlan-Haché argue, most summative rating systems adopt a hybrid of these three approaches.

In summary, the research base on measuring teacher effectiveness is still growing, and there is no evidence to suggest that one approach to measuring effectiveness is the most promising. As a result, states and districts have adopted a variety of approaches, and in doing so they have stirred tremendous controversy and debate in the field. Part of the controversy stems from the fact that there are aspects of effective teaching that are not readily measurable, such as instilling a love of learning or developing skills like empathy, tenacity, or creative problem solving in students. At the same time, a whole host of other considerations related to child poverty, parental neglect, gang and peer influence, illness, and mobility cannot be ignored. A balance must be struck between capturing objective measures and capturing the full range of the teacher's work, and this requires much thoughtful consideration. A significant amount of time—ideally using the materials provided in Chapters Five through Eight—must be spent discussing what can and should be measured and how best to measure it.

ROADBLOCKS TO MEASURING EFFECTIVENESS— IMPLEMENTATION AND THE NEED FOR TEACHER ENGAGEMENT

Much of the controversy around measuring teacher effectiveness stems from the potential consequences associated with these measures. Teacher concern over the use of student test scores or subjective observations would probably be more muted if performance-based evaluation data were primarily used for formative evaluations with the sole goal of improving teacher learning. Once high-stakes decisions—those tied to teachers' salaries, tenure, and promotion—are involved, however, the fairness of the data that inform those decisions becomes the object of much more scrutiny. These controversies should not become a reason to shy away from the conversation; instead, they make it even more important to ensure that teachers are engaged and heard, through their associations or otherwise, throughout the process of deciding how teacher effectiveness measures will be used. The key topics of debate, and the arguments in favor and against, are presented in this section.

Tying Teachers' Salaries to Their Effectiveness Ratings

The popularity of alternative teacher pay schemes has waxed and waned in the education policy realm for several decades—in the 1950s, 1980s, and today—for reasons that are easy enough to grasp. Compensation is an effective strategy for recruiting and retaining top talent, but for most districts it is an unaffordable one. Pay-for-performance schemes allow employers to spend what little they have to incentivize great teachers to accept offers and then stay in their schools, while at the same time not wasting money on those doing a mediocre job or worse—those whom the district would rather not have on their staff at all. On the flip side, pay for performance is seen by many teachers as offensive because it suggests that teachers do not already put in 100 percent of their effort for their students, but would do so for more money. Sensitive about their already comparatively low pay, teachers do not want to see their congenial school culture replaced by infighting over shares in what is feared will be—if not immediately, then down the road—a limited pot of money, nor do they want to see colleagues succumb to "teaching to the test" (or to the classroom observer) in order to afford supporting their families.

If teacher effectiveness measures were tied to informal incentives alone—recognition at a staff meeting, a high-five in the hallway, a spotlight in a school or district newsletter, pizza parties, gift cards, or school or district paraphernalia—then the choice of measures and their weights would not seem nearly as critical. However, tying teachers' salaries to these measures (as is done in most other professions) is highly divisive, particularly along generational lines. When teachers were asked how effective various policies would be at improving teacher effectiveness, for example, 49 percent of Generation Y teachers (that is, those born between 1977 and 1995) thought that pay for performance would be somewhat or very effective, compared with only 29 percent of older teachers, as illustrated in Figure 2.4.

Whether this difference in opinion is due to Gen Y teachers' greater openness or naïveté, their forward-looking attitude, or the potential for them to increase

Figure 2.4. Percentage of Teachers Indicating the Effectiveness of Paying Teachers Based on Performance

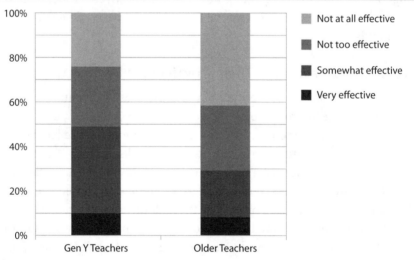

Source: Public Agenda, 2010.

their salaries at a faster pace is unclear. Nonetheless, the controversy can cause unproductive intergenerational tension that can only be resolved through open, constructive dialogue (as is modeled in this book); engaging teachers of all backgrounds, including all age and experience levels, is therefore crucial.

The importance of teacher engagement and buy-in when moving to adopt a performance-based compensation system has been reiterated in the research literature on numerous occasions. For example, the Urban Institute's 1985 review of merit pay programs and the lessons learned from them concluded,

> The evidence available indicates that a number of characteristics are associated with positive consequences for monetary incentive plans. . . . [W]e make the following suggestions for school districts: Leave ample time to design and implement the plan, including time to gain teacher participation in its design. . . . Ensure substantive participation by teachers in the design, implementation, and monitoring of a merit pay plan. This is often recommended by researchers and school officials alike, but it is frequently violated by school districts wanting to move quickly to introduce the plan. (Hatry & Greiner, 1985, pp. 112–113)

The same message about the importance of teacher involvement in reform design has reappeared in the more recent wave of reforms. In *Meeting the Challenges of Stakeholder Engagement and Communication* (Koppich, 2010), a key finding emerged:

> Teacher Incentive Fund grantees have also found, often belatedly and unexpectedly, that effective stakeholder engagement and communication are challenging and essential to the success of their pay programs. Stakeholder engagement helps to create buy-in and initial acceptance of the TIF plan. It allows different voices and perspectives to be heard and recognized as new approaches to compensation develop. Communication provides the synergy to broaden buy-in and sustain support for the program. (p. 2)

One way to promote teacher engagement on the controversial issue of performance-based assessment for decisions about teacher pay is to frame the conversation around the many alternative forms of differential teacher pay that are more palatable to all parties. Although only (approximately) 50 percent of Gen Y teachers and 30 percent of non–Gen Y teachers think that paying teachers based on their performance would improve teacher effectiveness, a significant majority of teachers of all ages favor differential pay based on National Board Certification, putting in greater time and effort, and teaching hard-to-staff subjects or in challenging schools, as illustrated in Figure 2.5.

Publishing Teachers' Evaluation Scores in the Newspaper

Although publishing and ranking effectiveness ratings in the newspaper might sound absurd in any profession, freedom of information laws in some states permit the public to request and access teacher performance assessment information. Most states include exemptions for employment histories and personnel files but fail to define such terms, leaving it to state courts to balance public interests against potential invasions of privacy (Forman, 2012). Thanks to the buzz such information often generates, newspapers have a strong incentive to request and publish teacher effectiveness ratings. For some teachers, showcasing their effectiveness in this way is a plus; for others, public consumption of their performance appraisal information is humiliating, awkward, and stressful. In the worst

Figure 2.5. Teachers' Perspectives on Differential Pay

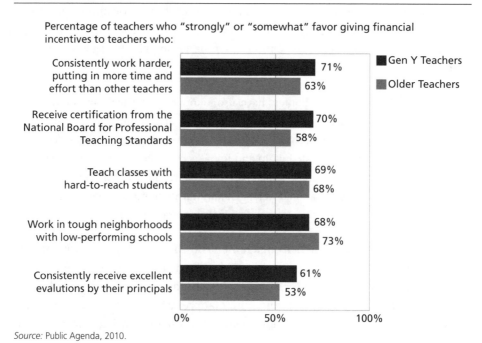

Source: Public Agenda, 2010.

cases, publication of evaluation ratings can act as "a Scarlet Letter policy" (Sandi Jacobs in Banchero, 2012), prompting evaluation reform advocate Bill Gates (2012) to write in the *New York Times,* "I am a strong proponent of measuring teachers' effectiveness. . . . But publicly ranking teachers by name will not help them get better at their jobs or improve student learning. On the contrary, it will make it a lot harder to implement teacher evaluation systems that work." Teachers have reported students taunting them in class about their low scores, and the suicide of a Los Angeles teacher was attributed to the publication of performance information (Zavis & Barboza, 2010). Treating measures of teacher effectiveness in this way can have devastating effects on some teachers, as well as negative (although manageable) outcomes for a large number of teachers. School districts can be inundated with requests from parents that their children be placed with the so-called top teachers, and the publication of these results can threaten the potential for a teacher evaluation system to systematically encourage teacher improvement.

On the flip side, parents will always discuss teacher quality. These discussions may be better informed if data and other information (aside from their children's opinion of their teacher) are available, and many believe that parents have the right to possess any available information about who is teaching their children. Taxpayers, who bear the burden of paying for public education, may also have a legitimate interest in teacher effectiveness data.

One potential solution is to limit the disclosure of teacher effectiveness data. After publication of teacher value-added ratings spurred controversy in February 2012, the New York State legislature approved a law that requires the State Education Department to post teacher effectiveness data on its website without teacher names. Parents are permitted to see the data on how their children's teachers performed, but they cannot see data on other teachers (Kaplan, 2012). This compromise provides parents and the public with more complete information about who is teaching their children without publicly shaming teachers who are labeled as low performing. In other states, including Massachusetts, state code specifies that information related to an educator's effectiveness is considered personnel information and is not subject to disclosure under public records laws (see, for example, Evaluation of Educators, 2011). Although striking the right balance between providing relevant performance information to stakeholders and publicly shaming low-performing teachers is often a state-level challenge, working with the media at the local level to inform how they present the data is an option for school districts and teacher leaders. Engaging parents directly in a dialogue about the publication of teacher effectiveness data and its benefits and drawbacks is also a promising solution to this concern. Strategies for parent and community member engagement on the use of teacher effectiveness measures are discussed in more detail in Chapter Eight.

Firing Teachers Who Receive Poor Effectiveness Ratings

Objectively speaking, dismissal is a legitimate outcome for an employee who consistently underperforms. Whether lack of effort, skill, or ability is to blame, it is hard to argue that a person *deserves* to keep a job he or she cannot do well—especially when the long-term consequences for children are so dire. Indeed, Public Agenda's national survey (2010) found that three-quarters of teachers believe that making it easier to terminate ineffective teachers would be a somewhat or very effective way to improve teacher effectiveness. Moreover, roughly eight in ten teachers believe that there are at least "a few" teachers in their school who fail to do a good job. As Figure 2.6 shows, about 20 percent of teachers think that there are more than "just a few" ineffective teachers in their school; 20 percent of teachers think that there are no ineffective teachers in their school.

Many members of the public assume—based on the low levels of student achievement that are reported nationally, and on their own experiences as students and parents—that there are ineffective teachers in the system who need

Figure 2.6. Teachers' Views on Ineffective Teachers

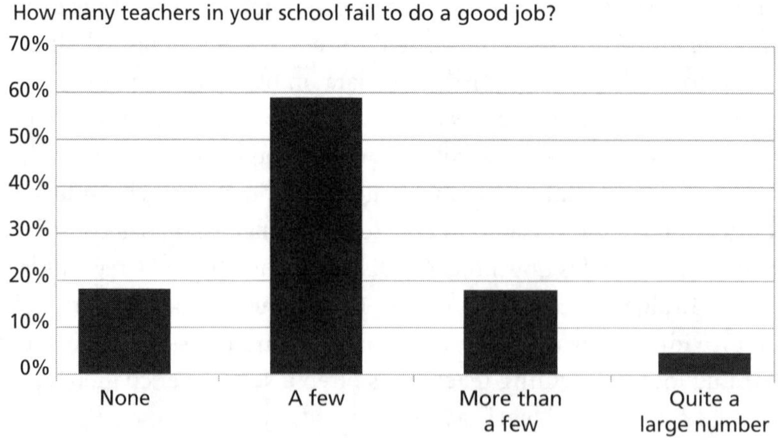

How many teachers in your school fail to do a good job?

Source: Public Agenda, 2010.

to be shown the door. Meanwhile, teachers' views on dismissing teachers based on their effectiveness will likely be colored by their views on the prevalence of ineffective teachers and the likelihood that evaluators will identify the right teachers as ineffective. Teachers who believe that all their colleagues are doing well (and particularly those who are fortunate to have a collegial school community) will have a harder time stomaching dismissals based on performance. Other teachers may fear the adverse incentive to unfairly fire older teachers— who tend to have higher salaries—as a means of cutting ever-tightening school budgets. Although this practice occurs in many sectors, it is especially problematic in schools where the pressures to keep the taxpayer burden low are constant. Most important, teachers' perceptions of the fairness of the measures used—including their trust in test scores and in the objectivity of administrators—may influence their receptivity to dismissal as an outcome of measuring effectiveness, making it all the more important for teachers to be involved in developing multiple valid and reliable measures. The model for school policy dialogue presented in Chapters Five through Eight helps depersonalize and depoliticize sensitive discussion topics like dismissal by focusing the conversation away from the current emotion-laden reality of a situation in a specific school and toward realistic hypothetical situations that could lead to dismissal.

Assigning or (Re)distributing Teachers Based on Their Effectiveness

Researchers have consistently found that by almost any measure conceivable, students in high-poverty and high-minority schools and classrooms are disadvantaged in their access to great teachers. They are less likely to be taught by highly qualified teachers; experienced teachers; and teachers with high valued-added scores, National Board for Professional Teaching Standards certification, high licensure test scores, and degrees from competitive colleges. Students from minority or low-income backgrounds are also more likely to be in schools with high teacher turnover (Allensworth, Ponisciak, & Mazzeo, 2009; Clotfelter, Ladd, Vigdor, & Wheeler, 2007; Glazerman & Max, 2011).

Inequitable teacher distribution was referred to by George W. Bush's secretary of education, Margaret Spellings, as education's "dirty little secret" (LaRock & Rodriguez-Farrar, 2005), but in recent years, this issue has become a federal priority. Proponents of using evaluation scores as a way to ensure that *all* students have an equal likelihood of being taught by the most effective teachers argue that redistributing teachers is in the best interest of the most needy students. Whether teachers are forced or incentivized through bonuses or other means, they argue that it is the responsibility of those leading the school system to ensure that high-poverty, low-performing students are not shortchanged in their education. However, some teachers argue that being effective in one type of setting does not necessarily translate to other settings, and forced reassignment may, in fact, result in effective teachers leaving the profession altogether.

With teachers at the table, informing the discussion of inequitable distribution, it is possible to create policies that will benefit the students most in need while also increasing teachers' morale, retention, and career satisfaction. Most teachers are concerned that students from at-risk backgrounds have excellent teachers. In fact, two-thirds of teachers stated that "putting underprivileged children on a path to success" was a major factor in their decision to become a teacher, and one-fourth of surveyed teachers said it was the *most* important factor (Public Agenda, 2010).

At the same time, many teachers are not interested in teaching in some of the most challenging schools. A survey conducted by the Illinois Education Research Council, for example, found that half of the state's teachers admitted that there were certain schools where they would refuse to teach (DeAngelis, Peddle, Trott, & Bergeron, 2002). Through teacher dialogue, this disconnect can be resolved. In the box "Common Ground and Common Goals," we describe how Teach Plus teacher fellows in Boston decided to get to the heart of what fundamentally made teachers hesitate to teach in the city's highest-need schools, and then to develop a completely teacher-designed solution. Brainstorming the different barriers, this bold group of teachers identified teacher turnaround teams ("T3s") as the "game-changer," whereby 25 percent of a struggling schools' teachers are brought in as part of a team and granted specific leadership responsibilities aimed at changing the school culture, as well as stipends to work together in the summer months toward targeting school turnaround interventions. Although the program is still in the early stages of implementation, it was seen as successful enough to implement statewide in Massachusetts and Tennessee.

Bringing the voices of teachers who would not teach in challenging schools together with the voices of teachers already in those schools is a smart way to identify the supports and resources that school and district leaders must provide to make teachers' and districts' *shared* goal of giving high-need students a great education a reality. Bringing the voices of parents and community organizations into the conversation can generate an even richer dialogue around the specific supports and resources that teachers find necessary to be successful in high-need settings. Teacher fellows at Teach Plus demonstrate what this process can look like.

Common Ground and Common Goals

Teach Plus Helping Teachers Teach Plus Get Involved in Policy

To get teachers involved in evaluation reform, "First, convince teachers that someone wants to hear what they have to say."

This is the advice of Maria Fenwick, a former teacher and current executive director of Teach Plus Boston. Fenwick became involved with Teach Plus through its fellowship because, as a teacher in Boston Public Schools, she wanted to find policy solutions to what she saw as systemic issues. She wanted to believe that all the teachers and administrators in her school were dedicated to providing a great education and improving opportunities for the students; unfortunately, her experiences in the classroom reinforced the belief that it wasn't about the kids. Although Fenwick knew many colleagues who shared her social justice orientation, "There seemed to be a widespread assumption by policymakers that strong teachers would not want to teach at 'hard to staff' schools."

Boston's Teach Plus fellows reached out to state policymakers in Massachusetts to explain that if the right conditions were in place, they could get great teachers in those schools. Fenwick and the other fellows designed a staffing model for urban schools that would create a tipping point of highly effective teachers—25 to 30 percent—supported through compensation, proven leadership, and like-minded peers. When Massachusetts passed school turnaround legislation mandating that 50 percent of teachers in the lowest-performing schools be highly effective, Fenwick and her colleagues had the perfect opportunity to suggest their staffing model. "We could really sell this as teachers because we lived this," she said, reflecting on how they presented the model and their impetus for creating it. Massachusetts adopted the staffing model, which has been incredibly successful in bringing highly effective, hardworking, and motivated teachers to struggling schools.

According to Fenwick, "It's easy for policymakers to see what's not working, but what they're really struggling with is how to solve the problem. I've never come across a policymaker who has said, 'Oh no, I don't value what teachers say.'"

In her current role with Teach Plus, Fenwick helps facilitate conversations between teachers and policymakers. Although she sees many challenges to creating teacher-led policy conversations, she has also identified a number of solutions that have proven to be successful. First, she has found that helping teachers find connections between their story—"which can seem very small and grounded in their personal experience"—and larger policy issues helps them realize that their story is worth telling. The most important thing, she says, is "being solutions oriented." What teachers need help with, she believes, is learning how to offer ideas rather than just telling their story. Organizations like Teach Plus are integral to helping teachers craft their stories so that they have a big impact on policymakers and to convincing teachers that policymakers truly want to hear what they have to say.

Source: Interview with Maria Fenwick, May 3, 2012.

Student Test Scores

Student growth on tests is probably the most controversial issue related to assessing teacher effectiveness. Many teachers do not embrace using student test scores to assess teachers. Their reasons are many, but to name a few, teachers are concerned that

- Tests capture only a small portion of what a teacher does.
- The tests often do not count for students' grades, so they are not taken seriously.
- Forcing a greater focus on test scores—in terms of the time spent preparing for and administering tests—will detract from teachers' efforts to meet other critical social-emotional and academic needs of students.
- Unintended consequences may surface; for example, teachers may unwittingly focus only on some students—be they low performing, high performing, or close to the cut-point in the middle—at the expense of the rest of the class.
- Some students are poor test-takers in general or "have a bad day" on the day of the exam.
- Not all grades and subjects are tested.

At the same time, those who favor including student test results as a measure of effectiveness tend to believe that

- Tests provide an indicator that is more objective than others.
- Tests measure part of what students are expected to learn and teachers to teach.

- Students should be "taught to the test" if it is a well-designed test that covers a range of important knowledge and skills that students are expected to acquire.
- Tests can encourage better instruction by providing teachers a benchmark by which they can see how much their students grow and can identify areas of weakness on which to focus or seek professional development.
- Tests can provide parents with an accountability tool and a benchmark for keeping track of their child's growth.
- Cheating or even unwanted teaching to the test can be monitored and addressed so that test results remain valid.
- By looking at *growth* in test scores (for example, how they change from the beginning of the year to the end of the year or from one year to the next), it is possible to give teachers credit for student improvement regardless of where the student started. For example, a teacher who brings his or her students up from a below-basic to a basic level receives credit for that growth, even though not all of those students have yet to reach proficiency.
- By looking at *subgroup breakdowns* of growth in test scores, it is possible to gain a sense on average of how a teacher has impacted low- and high-performing students and everyone in the middle, or to identify teachers who are particularly successful with, for example, English language learners or students with disabilities.

For these reasons, the current trend in the field is to require the inclusion of test scores as one measure of teacher effectiveness and then to pay attention to the quality and availability of tests, creating new ones as needed. Meanwhile, the field is developing new statistical methods for using test data in the most accurate and fair way possible. Chief among these techniques are growth and value-added measures (VAMs). Both include pre-test scores and a post-test score. Growth models refer to models whereby an expected amount of growth is established for each student based on his or her prior academic achievement. Student results are averaged to the classroom level, and a teacher is considered high or low growth depending on whether he or she "grew" his or her students more or less than expected. In that sense—and this is true of VAMs as well—teachers are compared to other teachers of students who are similar in terms of the factors included in the equation.

Growth measures may include nothing but prior scores, whereas VAMs generally include a number of other variables describing characteristics of students that are outside a teacher's control yet tend to affect students' academic growth. These factors might include limited English proficiency, low socioeconomic status, or special needs, among others. Statisticians are able to develop models that estimate what the expected growth of a student is, given these background characteristics and his or her pre-test scores. They then subtract this expected growth from the actual growth to calculate the "value added," or the amount of growth above what might be expected, presumably due to the teacher's effectiveness. The accuracy of these models improves with more data, so that expectations for student learning become more accurate as additional students are added to the equation and as additional years of data become available.

A number of leading scholars do not condone using VAMs to assess teacher effectiveness, whereas others in the field are highly supportive of the benefits of this approach. In a *Wall Street Journal* article, Harvard professor Thomas Kane went head-to-head with Stanford University professor Linda Darling-Hammond over the merits of using VAMs for evaluations that result in high-stakes decisions. On the one hand, Kane stated, "No information is perfect. But better information should lead to better decisions." Darling-Hammond, on the other hand, claimed, "Researchers who looked at the data found the ratings were enormously unstable" (Kane & Darling-Hammond, 2012). Researchers have found that when it comes to "top-performing teachers," principals' subjective ratings and VAM ratings were in agreement 52 percent of the time in reading and 69 percent of the time in math (compared to agreement rates of 14 percent and 26 percent, respectively, if principals assigned teacher ratings at random). This pattern holds true for teachers at the bottom of the performance spectrum too, although for teachers in the middle, there is far less agreement between principals' ratings and VAM scores (Jacob & Lefgren, 2005).

One key issue central to this debate is the tension between accuracy and transparency. In VAMs and other models of student growth, the statistical formula becomes more confusing to teachers as statisticians add layers of complexity to increase accuracy and fairness. These models are not simple formulas into which teachers can plug in their data (number of students, test scores, who is an English language learner, who is in special education, and so on) and calculate their value-added score on their own to make sure that the statisticians did not make mistakes. It is not the case that a person can look at student characteristics and test scores one day and calculate their expected score or growth a year from now, then wait one year and compare their expected growth to what actually happened. This is so because the statistical models require information on all students, at two points in time—including all pre- and post-test scores that go into the equation along with all the characteristics of all the students—to generate meaningful expected levels of student growth. Because no teacher (or, in fact, very few people, for obvious privacy reasons) has access to all that information, it is not possible for an individual to calculate his or her own scores. At the end of the day, much of the controversy stems from trust: there are those who trust that the policymakers and statisticians who collaborate to measure teachers' effectiveness will do so competently and those in Mark Twain's camp, who would rather put their trust in principals' judgment, believing "There are three types of lies: lies, damned lies, and statistics."

Regardless of *how* tests are used to measure teacher effectiveness, research suggests that most teachers are skeptical but, over time, are opening up somewhat to the idea of using test scores to assess effectiveness. Public Agenda and American Institutes for Research's research for the Retaining Teacher Talent project revealed that teachers view students' performance on standardized tests as the weakest indicator of their effectiveness, as illustrated in Figure 2.7.

Recent research by Education Sector, however, did find that the proportion of teachers who believe that measuring student progress over time is a good or excellent way to measure teacher effectiveness is on an upward trend, growing from 49 percent to 54 percent between 2007 and 2011 (Rosenberg & Silva, 2012).

As depicted in Figure 2.7, students' level of engagement was seen as superior to student test scores as a measure of one's success as a teacher. Although

Figure 2.7. Teachers' Views of Various Measures of Teacher Effectiveness

Measure of Teacher Effectiveness	Excellent	Good	Fair	Poor	Don't Know
How well the students perform on your district's standardized tests	12%	44%	30%	12%	2%
Whether the students are engaged in their coursework	46%	46%	7%	1%	0
The feedback you get from your principal and other administrators	20%	51%	22%	8%	*
How much your students are learning compared with students in other schools	26%	46%	21%	7%	1%

Note: *Less than 1 percent.
Percentages are rounded and may not sum to 100 percent.
Source: Public Agenda, 2010.

student engagement is not as easily or objectively assessed as student test score performance, it is on many districts' teacher observation rubrics. For example, the Danielson Framework described earlier in this chapter includes a component for classroom observers to assess student engagement (3c. Engaging Students in Learning).

For those interested in measuring student engagement alongside (or in lieu of) student test scores, surveys have begun to be created for this purpose. The Cambridge Education Tripod survey, which has been used by one hundred thousand students in the Bill & Melinda Gates Foundation's Measures of Effective Teaching initiative in New York City, Pittsburgh, Memphis, Tampa, Dallas, and Charlotte, North Carolina, surveys students to gauge their engagement with school and their perceptions of teacher effectiveness and school quality. The survey is based on "7 C's" of teacher effectiveness: (1) caring, (2) controlling behavior, (3) clarifying ideas and lessons, (4) challenging students to work hard, (5) captivating students, (6) conferring, and (7) consolidating what was learned. Research on the use of the survey in 141 classrooms was promising, finding that the survey data were reliable (there was a correlation of 0.80 across the different questions addressing a given concept); stable (there was a correlation of 0.70 to 0.85 between students' ratings of their teachers in one month and their ratings five months later); and valid, in that the survey results were correlated with other measures of teacher effectiveness (Bill & Melinda Gates Foundation, 2010). However, like the use of student test scores, the use of student perception data for the purposes of teacher evaluation is wrought with controversy.

◉

These issues of public debate—tying teacher effectiveness measures to teachers' pay, publishing results in the newspaper, using performance to dismiss teachers, and redeploying teachers based on data—drive much of the fear and trepidation teachers feel about evaluation reform. If the measures of teacher effectiveness could be trusted as 99.9 percent accurate, teachers might accept high-stakes outcomes, but it is precisely the existence of these high-stakes outcomes that makes it hard for them to believe that these measures will ever be free from cheating, favoritism, or teaching to the test.

The need to measure teacher effectiveness in ways that are valid, reliable, and fair creates a tremendous challenge for those charged with developing new evaluation systems. How all of these pieces come together into a coherent, comprehensive, and sustainable approach to teacher evaluation is discussed in Chapter Three.

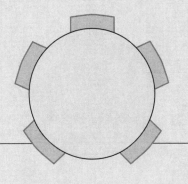

What We Know About Effectively Engaging Teachers

The Who, When, and How of Evaluation

Engaging Teachers on Issues That Matter

Like buying a house and getting a mortgage, successful teacher evaluation reform often requires attending to myriad unplanned details. For example:

- How frequently and for how many minutes should principals observe teachers in their classrooms?
- Through what processes should they document and communicate the results, including in-depth feedback for teachers to improve?
- How will principals' other duties be reassigned to accommodate these changes?
- Who else can help conduct evaluations, and what kind of training will they need?
- What will it cost to implement all this in practice?

Determining where to begin the overhaul of an existing evaluation system, or what steps to take in creating a new system, can be overwhelming. As a consequence, strategic decisions about when and how to include teachers (and the contributions of other stakeholders) are often afterthoughts. However, because teacher evaluation is so important to do well, it is critical that teachers are meaningfully involved at all stages. This chapter details the key decision points for teacher involvement in the design and implementation of new evaluation systems.

We address two forms of teacher engagement in this chapter:

1. Engaging teachers in the design of an evaluation system
2. Engaging teachers in the process of evaluating themselves, other teachers, and principals

TEACHER EVALUATION REFORM 101

Strategies for engaging teachers and other stakeholders are influenced by the steps involved in the larger reform process. To date, evaluation reforms typically originate with a state law or a local school board decision that requires a new approach to assessing teacher effectiveness—often specifying the types and mix of measures that must be included in the new approach. Most commonly, the state provides broad guidelines for districts to implement locally as long as certain requirements are met. New York State, for example, determined that certain measures—such as observation results and results of the state Regents exam—must be included in all districts' evaluation systems, but it has left some decisions to districts, including deciding which state-approved observation rubric to use and which local measures of student growth to include (New York State Department of Education, 2012). Similarly, Florida's teacher evaluation law requires districts to submit their locally developed plans to the state for approval (Personnel Evaluation Procedures and Criteria, 2012).

Alternatively, states like Massachusetts and Illinois are developing state-level models that districts are not required to adopt, as long as their local systems include all the required components (Evaluation of Educators, 2011; Performance Evaluation Reform Act, 2010). In other states, such as Delaware, all districts are required to adopt and implement the state model (Delaware Performance Appraisal System II, 2012). When the reform agenda is driven by a new state law, districts are typically given anywhere from one to four years to develop and implement a new teacher evaluation model; those receiving federal funding to support implementation tend to work within tighter timelines.

Given the overlap between efforts to reform teacher evaluation systems and other human capital issues that have historically been decided at the bargaining table—compensation, working conditions, and professional development— the role of unions has a significant impact on both the introduction and implementation of teacher evaluation policies in states with collective bargaining laws. As a result, in districts that are unionized, evaluation policies are often collectively negotiated through the teachers' union, as part of the teachers' contract.

These and other factors will have implications for how teacher evaluation reforms are introduced and approached at the district level and, as a result, will impact the ways in which teachers are engaged in the process. Nevertheless, the many experiments that are already in place around the country typically involve a set of steps that are similar to those outlined here to design a comprehensive teacher evaluation system:

- A committee or task force is established to make recommendations.
- This committee plans out its meeting and decision-making schedules and then tackles the many questions and considerations that are associated with the new policy.
- The recommended policy is communicated to all individuals who will be affected, in some cases with opportunities for two-way feedback.
- Ideally, the new policy is launched as part of a pilot, and some modifications are made.
- The new policy is adopted and implemented school- or districtwide.

In a best-case scenario, the following six key steps and the related tasks illustrated in Table 3.1 take place to guide teacher evaluation design:

1. **Prepare and Engage Leadership and Stakeholders.** Assess the current evaluation system and the strengths and weaknesses of existing tools, establish priority areas for reform, support the work of a steering committee, and establish a context-specific definition of teacher effectiveness.
2. **Develop a Vision and Plan.** Actively engage teachers and principals to develop a comprehensive plan for evaluation that addresses data needs and will demonstrate impact.
3. **Construct and Connect Tools, Training, and Infrastructure.** Develop appropriate performance management tools—including rating scales, protocols, and rubrics—and processes for successful implementation.
4. **Implement and Support the Evaluation System.** Launch the new evaluation system, provide relevant training, troubleshoot the system, and gather implementation feedback in close collaboration with stakeholders.

5. **Assess and Revise the System.** Determine the next steps for improvement, sustainability, capacity building, and the communication of impact and success based on data collected during implementation.

6. **Integrate and Enhance Talent Management Systems.** Ensure the integration of evaluation with other key components of educator talent management (for example, professional development, working conditions, and compensation).

Focusing more specifically on the Prepare and Engage Leadership and Stakeholders stage, this book recommends going beyond traditional approaches to

Table 3.1. Six Steps in Teacher Evaluation Design

Prepare and Engage Leadership and Stakeholders	Develop a Vision and Plan	Construct and Connect Tools, Training, and Infrastructure
Key Action: Establish evaluation priority areas to address the shared goals of the reform. **Other Actions:** • Identify a steering committee. • Identify stakeholder groups for ongoing engagement. • Complete a needs assessment and gap analysis of the current system. • Interpret needs assessment and gap analysis results. • Review examples of model teacher evaluation products and methods.	**Key Action:** Develop a comprehensive evaluation plan. **Other Actions:** • Designate existing and future communication methods and develop a communication plan. • Hold stakeholder meetings. • Review current data infrastructure system(s) and determine data infrastructure needs. • Confirm and document the preferred evaluation approach (for example, pilot, full-scale implementation, formative use only). • Determine the full set of multiple measures to use. • Identify how system impact will be measured.	**Key Action:** Construct evaluation tools (for example, rating scales, protocols, and rubric[s]). **Other Actions:** • Address any contractual obligations between the district and the teachers association. • Build solutions to data infrastructure challenges. • Develop an implementation plan and timeline. • Implement communication strategies. • Calibrate the evaluation tools to available state evaluation standards, professional standards, or both. • Test the developed evaluation tools.

Implement and Support the Evaluation System	Assess and Revise the System	Integrate and Enhance Talent Management Systems
Key Action: Launch the evaluation system. **Other Actions:** • Support the transition to new evaluation metrics, processes, and tools. • Conduct training activities for the new evaluation system for teachers, principals, and other evaluators. • Gather implementation feedback to recommend midcourse corrections.	**Key Action:** Determine next steps for improvement of the evaluation system. **Other Actions:** • Engage in thoughtful reflection on preliminary successes and areas for revision. • Examine evaluation system implementation and impact data. • Refine implementation structure (timeline, processes, leadership, tools). • Communicate and celebrate success stories, lessons learned, and next steps.	**Key Action:** Integrate additional educator talent management components to enhance the evaluation system. **Other Actions:** • Conduct a needs assessment and support integration of evaluation with teacher recruitment, hiring, induction, professional development, compensation, and working conditions.

Source: American Institutes for Research, 2012a. Reproduced with permission.

engaging and communicating with teachers, which may include using multiple venues (such as meetings, emails, websites, and newsletters) to let teachers know what changes a task force or committee (which typically includes only a handful of teachers) has decided to implement. Although these efforts are necessary, they are insufficient as a means of genuinely engaging teachers. The critical stages of teacher engagement, some of which are elaborated in great detail in Chapters Five through Seven, include

- Initially informing teachers of the opportunity to be involved in the design process
- Informing teachers about the changes being considered and the opportunities they have for weighing in
- Making sure that teachers are on the same page regarding key terminology related to teacher evaluation design
- Creating a culture that is conducive to open and respectful collaboration

- Identifying teacher leaders or others to facilitate constructive conversations on evaluation reform
- Initiating a districtwide dialogue on evaluation reform
- Fostering effective feedback loops that open the channels for ongoing communication about decisions as they develop

This may take many different forms, but the Center for Teaching Quality's New Millennium Initiative offers one innovative example of what such teacher engagement looks like in practice. The New Millennium teachers demonstrate how teacher leadership and teacher voice can be incorporated into decision making in the future if teachers harness their individual and collective power to influence the direction of the teaching profession.

The Center for Teaching Quality

Teacher Engagement in the New Millennium

Two teams of three face off at the bargaining table. Following precedent and protocol, representatives from the union and district negotiate the terms of a new teacher evaluation system. What is missing from this scenario?

According to Alesha Daughtrey from the Center for Teaching Quality (CTQ), districts and unions are valuable players in reform, but authentic conversations and the voices of teachers from across the district are often missing from the policy process: "In some cases the bargaining table is simply where conversations have always occurred, and it has not occurred to anyone that there are aspects that could happen in a non-bargained context. . . . The bargaining table is not [always] a good place for free-ranging conversations because there's just too much at stake."

CTQ taps the experiences and expertise of teachers, engages them in dialogue around reform, and, at times, shifts the arena where conversations occur. One effort of the organization, the New Millennium Initiative (NMI), brings together groups of early-career teachers to increase their shared knowledge of education policy and engage in education reform. Since CTQ launched NMI in 2009, the organization has worked with NMI teacher teams in six cities and states across the country. Staff from CTQ guide teachers through a curriculum that includes information about best practices for teacher evaluations. After completing the curriculum, the groups of teachers develop policy recommendations, create informational materials about policies for teachers, or meet with policymakers.

The Colorado Department of Education (CDE), for example, invited the teachers in the Denver NMI to review evaluation rules and legislation before they were publicly released. The teacher team offered suggestions to CDE and gave testimony at one of the legislative rule-making hearings held in Denver. Specifically, the group recommended wording changes around how observations would be conducted and how the Colorado growth score would be weighted in the evaluation. In May 2011, the group released a report, *Making Teacher Evaluation Work for Students: Voices from the Classroom,* which offered recommendations regarding the implementation of Colorado's new teacher evaluation system.

When asked to reflect on why CTQ's NMIs have been successful, Daughtrey immediately credited the teachers. NMI teachers aptly apply the practical knowledge acquired from working in the classroom to the policy implementation problems that districts are facing. They are able to provide an on-the-ground perspective, often noting that a policy idea may be "a truly excellent idea at the five-thousand-foot level but not in practice."

Source: Interview with Alesha Daughtrey, May 7, 2012.

The dialogue, feedback loops, collaboration, and communication should address *all* aspects of evaluation—from the highly politicized, controversial issues discussed in Chapter Two to the minute logistical details surrounding implementation. The next section focuses in on the most relevant decision points for teacher engagement.

DECISION POINTS FOR TEACHER ENGAGEMENT

Given teachers' limited time, it can be helpful to identify the key decision points that get the biggest bang for your buck. These are the issues that fundamentally shape what the evaluation system will look like, that tend to be open for deliberation rather than predetermined by state statute, and that teachers' expertise lends itself especially well to weighing in on. These are also issues for which research does not suggest a best practice and for which the particular context of a school or district—which can be judged only by teachers and other local stakeholders—will likely determine the "best" option.

A key first step to incorporating teacher input in evaluations is securing the commitment of those leading the system, be it the superintendent, school board president, or others who have the final say on policy matters. The commitment from local leadership to an inclusive approach to evaluation reform should

- Happen early (from day 1)
- Be announced publicly
- Specify exactly which decisions are open for discussion
- Be formally included in a strategic communication plan
- Be revisited frequently

It is important to ensure that the engagement is genuine—that is, that leaders sincerely want teachers' feedback. If teachers are led to believe that their voice matters but subsequently learn that it is being ignored or completely discounted, they will resent being misled and will be less inclined to trust leaders in the future. Most reasonable teachers will understand that, as is true of any job, not *every* decision is going to be open to discussion among employees. Sharing the decision points that are open for discussion and the details as to when, where, how, and by whom teacher input will be heard and how it will shape new policy and practice, and transparently communicating this information to everyone involved, are critical early steps in authentic teacher engagement. We explore this concept further in Chapter Five.

As noted, determining and clearly articulating the decision points that are up for discussion should occur early in the design process. These decision points will vary from setting to setting, but may include the following:

How will evaluation results be used? The primary goal of all evaluation systems should be to improve teachers' ability to help their students learn and to inform their own learning; but should performance data also be used to inform teachers' opportunities to advance their careers through mentorship, coaching, or other leadership positions? Should teacher pay be tied to performance? Should teachers with top ratings be encouraged to teach the students who are struggling the most? Should teachers' contracts be terminated or tenure denied based on these results, and if so, what degree of poor performance might lead to a high-stakes employment decision?

Who should primarily evaluate teachers? Most current reform efforts place the majority of responsibility for conducting observations of teacher practice on the principal. However, the principal is only one person, and he or she will not have expertise in every grade and subject area (especially in a middle and high school context). In fact, it may be the case that a principal doesn't have expertise in *any* of them. Determining whether the principal should be the primary observer of teacher practice depends largely on the size of the school, the principal's experience as an instructional leader, available resources to free up time for additional observers, and other factors.

Should experienced teachers conduct some observations for the purposes of evaluation? Experienced teachers are the primary participants in a formal peer observation system described in more detail later in this chapter, but they are often not included in a more traditional redesign approach to evaluation. Questions related to ensuring rater agreement and to identifying the necessary resources to cover teachers' time to conduct observations during the school day exemplify the complexity of this decision point.

How often should evaluations take place? Evaluating teachers more frequently means that the ratings are likely to be more accurate and holistic and that the feedback is likely to be more useful. However, frequent evaluations can also create extra stress for teachers, not to mention the time burden on evaluators. What is the right number of formal observations? Of informal walkthroughs? How often should teachers receive a final summative evaluation score? Should the frequency of these evaluations differ for more or less experienced teachers?

What constitutes a valid and reliable measure? There is little disagreement that a comprehensive teacher evaluation system should include multiple valid and reliable measures. However, the more rigorously each measure is employed to ensure its validity and reliability, the more time-consuming and expensive the evaluation system will be; this is an example of a trade-off that will need to be considered.

Should brief unannounced walkthroughs be counted as part of the formal evaluation? Although for some teachers unannounced walkthroughs will increase anxiety and potentially decrease their effectiveness, others—particularly younger, Gen Y teachers who are accustomed to regular parental and teacher progress monitoring—would like more regular feedback (Coggshall, Behrstock-Sherratt, & Drill, 2011). Further, regular walkthroughs may give evaluators a more honest picture of a typical lesson than the "dog and pony show" approach that typically accompanies formal, announced, and infrequent observations.

Should student surveys be part of an evaluation? In the states of Massachusetts, Georgia, and Hawaii, students are now required to complete surveys that will be aggregated and used as one component of a comprehensive teacher evaluation. Questions related to which grade levels to include in a student survey, how to fairly administer the surveys, and which aspects of teacher performance are suitable for student input will influence decisions about whether this is a useful measure in your local context.

How should student learning outcomes be incorporated? As discussed in Chapter Two, using student test scores in evaluations is an issue that continues to be hotly debated at every level of the education system. It is an especially sensitive topic among teachers, and explaining it in a way that all teachers will understand requires sufficient knowledge of the technical details, as well as sufficient time for discussion of the pros and cons of one technical approach versus another. Questions related to how much annual growth in student performance constitutes effectiveness, how growth is measured between different points in time, and how exceptional students' performance on tests might affect individual teacher scores are all fair game for teacher input.

◉

The decision points and sample questions included here are merely examples of the complexities involved in redesigning a teacher evaluation system. As a local school or district starts down this road, one cautionary tale is *not to get bogged down in discussion related to any one decision.* Early evidence from the field indicates that too often, leadership committees spend so much time deliberating over the first few decision points—such as defining effective teaching or determining appropriate measures—that they end up rushing through other equally important aspects of a comprehensive system. It is therefore important to set a long-term schedule of decision points to be covered and deadlines by which to reach consensus.

It is equally important to create business rules to keep the reform dialogue constructive and on track. A number of guidelines have been established and promulgated by national organizations to facilitate these highly charged reform conversations. The National Education Association's guidelines for developing teacher evaluation policy offer one such example (see box).

A number of resources have been developed to guide teacher evaluation system redesign. The Center on Great Teachers and Leaders Teacher Evaluation Models in Practice (TEMP) online tool is a useful resource to facilitate borrowing ideas from other districts; it provides detailed information about existing district teacher evaluation systems, including the types of measures used as well as details on other design and implementation features. At the time of writing, detailed reports describing the following district and state evaluation systems were available on the TEMP website (http://resource.tqsource.org/evalmodel/):

- Atlanta Public Schools, Georgia
- Austin Independent School District, Texas

- Chicago Public Schools, Illinois
- District of Columbia
- Montgomery County Public Schools, Alabama
- St. Francis Independent School District, Minnesota
- Tennessee

The TEMP resource allows users to search and compare particular aspects of multiple districts' evaluation systems, such as the evaluation system goals, evaluator selection and training, data infrastructure, system evaluation, and other components. It is possible to download a complete report about a particular school district's model or to view all of the district's tools, rubrics, and resources. Alternatively, it is possible to search for all processes, tools, rubrics, and resources related to a specific component (for example, evaluator selection and training or stakeholder communication and investment) for all districts. The searchable database provides examples of how some of the first redesigned teacher evaluation systems have taken shape, and it can be a useful starting point for teachers and other leaders around the country as they think about their own system. Other useful resources to stimulate reform-oriented discussions about teacher evaluation include the Center on Great Teachers and Leaders state teacher and principal evaluation policy databases and online Guide to Evaluation Products, the National Council on Teacher Quality's *State of the States* report, and the Aspen Institute's *Means to an End* report (see box).

ADDITIONAL USEFUL RESOURCES

State teacher and principal evaluation policy databases can be found at http://resource.tqsource.org/stateevaldb/. These resources allow users to search for a state's evaluation policies or to search for a particular aspect of evaluation policy (such as frequency of evaluations) and compare multiple states on that particular aspect of evaluation.

The **Guide to Evaluation Products** is an online, searchable database of more than one hundred existing tools and models for teacher and principal evaluation: http://resource.tqsource.org/GEP/

The **State of the States Report,** which summarizes and provides state-by-state information on recent policy changes and teacher evaluation system design components (such as frequency of evaluations), can be found at http://www.nctq.org/p/publications/docs/nctq_stateOfTheStates.pdf.

The **Means to an End** report can be found at http://www.aspeninstitute.org/sites/default/files/content/docs/pubs/Means_To_An_End.pdf. This report describes the components of evaluation systems focused on staff growth and development, offers examples of how districts are implementing policies of this type, and provides templates for districts to use in developing their evaluation systems.

DETERMINING DECISION POINTS WHEN PROGRESS IS UNDER WAY

In some cases, the evaluation reform process is well under way by the time teacher engagement in the process begins; Chapter Five offers strategies for making teacher engagement meaningful in these cases. In other instances, elements of a new evaluation system have been implemented while the complete system remains under development. If it is unclear where in the redesign process teacher dialogue should focus, or what level of investment in the reform effort is appropriate and sufficient for your school or district, consider taking the following self-assessment. The completed scorecard identifies whether your evaluation system is strong as it is, needs some tweaking, or requires a complete overhaul, and this will guide decisions about which topics are ripe for teacher engagement.

The AIR Performance Management Scorecard can be downloaded for free at http://educatortalent.org/scorecards. Similar scorecards for principal evaluation and for evaluation systems at the state level are also available.

The Teacher Performance Management Scorecard for Districts

This teacher evaluation system self-assessment identifies the areas where an evaluation system falls short of best practice, and may catalyze conversations around those areas.

Instructions: Please put a check in the box next to the statement that most closely describes the teacher evaluation system in your school district. There are no right or wrong answers to these questions. When you have finished, use the scoring guide at the end of this document to assess your system.

I. Defining Effective Teaching

1. Description of an Effective Teacher

☐ a. Our district does not provide or include a definition of an effective teacher as part of its evaluation system.

☐ b. Our district provides a definition of an effective teacher, but it is not tied to any state or research-based standards and focuses only on teacher practice or teacher outcomes, but not on both components.

☐ c. Our district provides a comprehensive definition of teacher effectiveness that is tied to state or research-based standards (or both). This definition describes the knowledge, skills, and practices a teacher must exhibit in order to improve student learning in the classroom.

II. Establishing the Purpose of the Evaluation

2. Use of the Evaluation System

☐ a. Teachers in our district are evaluated and are told their ratings or how they scored and why, but these evaluations are not tied to rewards for highly effective teachers, to sanctions for those who are found not to be very effective, or to meaningful opportunities for growth and professional development.

☐ b. Our district's teacher evaluations are detailed, but not to the extent that they are tied to incentives or other rewards (such as pay increases), sanctions, or meaningful professional development. Evaluations are not conducted widely, systematically, or with rigor.

☐ c. Detailed feedback from our district's teacher evaluation system is used throughout the year to make important decisions regarding professional development, tenure, promotion, dismissal, assignment, incentives, or other rewards, such as pay increases.

3. Criteria for the Evaluation

☐ a. Our district has adopted a set of professional performance standards for teachers. As written, the indicators are not observable or measurable.

☐ b. Our district has adopted a set of professional performance standards. As written, the indicators are observable and measurable. Our district has not developed or adopted a rubric, outcomes list, or formula to use when evaluating teachers.

☐ c. Our district has adopted a set of professional performance standards. As written, the indicators are observable and measurable. Our district has produced or adopted a rubric, outcomes list, or formula to use when evaluating teachers.

4. Diversifying Evaluations for Different Types of Teachers

☐ a. In our district, all teachers are evaluated using the same general methods and the same instruments.

☐ b. In our district, teachers are evaluated using the same general methods and the same evaluation instruments, with minor adjustments for some job-alike groups.

☐ c. In our district, evaluations are tailored to the specific nature of the work of different types of educators, including core content teachers, English language learner (ELL) teachers, special education teachers, instructional coaches, librarians, and guidance counselors.

III. Quality of the Performance Evaluation System

5. Comprehensiveness of the Evaluation System

Here is a list of teacher performance measures:

- Student performance on annual standardized achievement tests, measured by either growth or value-added calculation
- Student performance on classroom tests (for example, curriculum-based measures)
- Student performance measured against learning objectives
- Evaluation of student artifacts and work judged according to rubrics
- Unique assessments for teachers in nontested grades and subjects
- Review of teacher portfolios
- Student surveys
- Parent surveys
- Self-report measures
- Goal-driven professional development
- Classroom observations

   ☐ a. Our district relies on only one of the above measures to assess teacher performance.

   ☐ b. Our district relies on two or three of the above measures to assess teacher performance.

   ☐ c. Our district relies on four or more of the above measures to assess teacher performance.

6. Tying Evaluation to Student Performance

   ☐ a. Our district's teacher evaluations do not consider student performance.

   ☐ b. Our district's teacher evaluations do include some student performance measures, mainly those tied to increases in student test scores over time.

   ☐ c. Our district's teacher evaluations include several student performance measures. Growth or student measures based on state test scores are included, and other measures of student performance (for example, on-time graduation rates) also are included, as are several district-determined measures of student growth.

7. Validity of the Evaluation System

   ☐ a. Our district does not gather data to systematically evaluate the quality and implementation fidelity of the teacher evaluation system.

   ☐ b. Our district collects minimal data about the implementation and quality of the teacher evaluation system.

☐ c. Our district collects and reviews data about the quality of the teacher evaluation system, and data collected from these system reviews are used to make adjustments or improvements to the system.

8. Frequency of the Teacher Evaluations

☐ a. Nontenured teachers are evaluated frequently, but tenured teachers are not routinely evaluated. It is generally assumed that the tenured teachers have mastered their practice.

☐ b. Tenured and nontenured teachers are evaluated at least annually.

☐ c. By policy and in practice, all teachers are formally evaluated at least once a year, and informal evaluations take place much more frequently so that teachers receive regular feedback on their practice.

IV. Quality of Training and Reliability of Evaluators

9. Selection of Evaluators

☐ a. Evaluators tend to be people with authority in the district, but they do not necessarily have experience in the classroom or content knowledge in the same area as the teachers they are evaluating.

☐ b. Evaluators may include a mix of individuals from within or outside the school or district. Although they have classroom experience and are trained in conducting evaluations, they may not have relevant content knowledge or experience in the subject area or grade level being evaluated.

☐ c. Evaluators have significant classroom experience, are highly trained as evaluators, and are carefully selected to ensure that they have relevant content knowledge and experience in the subject area or grade level being evaluated.

10. Evaluator Training

☐ a. Evaluators do not receive training. It probably would not be fair to tie any high-stakes decisions (for example, teacher pay, advancement, dismissal) to evaluation results because they typically reflect just one observation on one day and are trustworthy only to a certain degree.

☐ b. Evaluators receive some training initially, but they do not receive ongoing training. Teacher evaluations are almost always based on more than one observation.

☐ c. New and seasoned evaluators receive initial and ongoing training on evaluating objectively. Teachers are observed on multiple occasions, including both announced and unannounced visits, by multiple observers.

11. Evaluator Interrater Reliability

☐ a. Rater agreement is not established or analyzed; therefore, no method is available to determine whether evaluators are scoring teachers differently. Trends in teacher ratings over time are not compared districtwide or by individuals.

☐ b. Little to no rater agreement testing occurs to ensure that evaluators rate teacher performance similarly. Trends in teacher ratings over time are not compared districtwide or by individuals. Evaluators do not receive data or feedback on their practice to ensure that all teachers are similarly evaluated.

☐ c. Rater agreement is checked regularly. Trends in teacher ratings are reported to evaluators districtwide and by individuals for the purpose of improving evaluation practices. Evaluators receive feedback and professional development on their work in an effort to ensure that all teachers are similarly evaluated.

V. Using Results of the Evaluation

12. Addressing Ineffective Teaching

☐ a. Our district does not formally identify persistently ineffective teachers and does not have courageous conversations with teachers who appear to be persistently ineffective.

☐ b. Our district often encourages ineffective untenured teachers to leave, or the majority of ineffective untenured teachers leave of their own volition. Our district makes little effort to address ineffective tenured teachers because they are too much of a challenge.

☐ c. Our district has both a formal and informal dismissal process in which even tenured teachers who are found to be persistently ineffective are asked to leave. The district tracks the percentage of teachers who exit through this route.

13. Evaluation and Teacher Retention

☐ a. Our district is not able to identify which teachers are most effective at improving student performance.

☐ b. Our district does identify top-performing teachers and keeps track of whether the teachers who are most effective at improving student performance are teaching in hard-to-staff schools. However, the district does not capture the reasons these teachers may be leaving the district.

☐ c. Our district does keep track of whether highly effective teachers are continuing to teach in hard-to-staff schools or are leaving their schools or the district, and why these teachers say they left.

14. Use of Performance Evaluation Results

☐ a. Our district does not have policies or other guidance on whether results from the teacher evaluation can be used to inform retention, promotion, incentives, or dismissal decisions.

☐ b. Our district has limited or vague polices or other guidance on whether results from teacher evaluation can be used to inform retention, promotion, incentives, or dismissal decisions.

☐ c. Our district provides explicit policy and guidance on whether results from the teacher evaluation can be used to inform retention, promotion, incentives, or dismissal decisions.

VI. Quality of Professional Growth

15. Professional Growth Opportunities

☐ a. Our district does not provide teachers with access to supportive provisions of coaching, mentoring, observations of colleagues and their mentors, and other professional growth and learning opportunities (for example, courses, conferences, webinars).

☐ b. Our district provides teachers with access to supportive provisions of coaching, mentoring, observations of colleagues and their mentors, and other growth and learning opportunities, but these offerings are not connected to or informed by the results of a teacher's evaluation.

☐ c. Our district provides explicit strategic support, informed by teacher evaluation results, for teachers to access provisions of coaching, mentoring, observations of colleagues and their mentors, and other professional growth and learning opportunities.

Scoring

Assign your district's teacher evaluation system 0 points for each "a" response, 1 point for each "b" response, and 2 points for each "c" response.

Add up these points to get an overall score.

Your score is _____.

If your score is 0 to 9: The students in your district are not benefiting from policies that would ensure that their teachers are effective. Teachers are not receiving the feedback and support that they require to improve their work. Developing a stronger evaluation system would show both students and teachers that the district is deeply concerned about the quality of teaching.

If your score is 10 to 19: Although some elements of a strong evaluation system exist in your district, many elements still are missing, and the evaluation function is not part of a connected, aligned system of performance management. Creating a stronger system would allow you to recruit and retain more effective teachers who can help more students achieve to their highest potential.

If your score is 20 to 30: Congratulations! Your district's teacher evaluation system is strong and is well connected to the larger system of performance management strategies, including recruitment, hiring, induction, professional development, preparation, and compensation and incentives. Continuous assessment of the teacher evaluation system and further refinements will allow you to build on the strengths of the system and determine its impact on teachers and students.

Reflection Questions

1. What are the "assets," or high scores, as indicated by the scorecard?
2. Do you agree that these are actually assets of your current system?
3. What are the "gaps," or low scores, as indicated by the scorecard?
4. Do you agree that these are actually gaps in your current system?
5. How similar is your perspective to the perspectives of other leaders in your district?
6. What can you do to build on assets and address gaps?

Source: American Institutes for Research, 2012b.

TAKING THE TIME TO MAKE TEACHER EVALUATION MEANINGFUL

A common source of tension related to reforming teacher evaluation is the time needed to do teacher evaluations well. In addition to the time required in the planning and design phases to create a well-thought-out model that includes all relevant stakeholders' input, the execution of the evaluations themselves can be incredibly time-consuming; and time, as any teacher or principal knows, is in limited supply.

Both teachers and principals need to spend time preparing for evaluation activities, completing evaluation activities, and reviewing evaluation results. For teachers, these activities may take anywhere from two to five hours per evaluation cycle. If self-evaluations, collection of artifacts or creation of portfolios, or formal pre- and post-observation meetings are involved, the time required of teachers will be greater. In districts where teachers check complicated formulas (that assign weights to the various measures that make up their score) and confirm their classroom roster to ensure that the correct students' test results were used in their evaluation, the process of data checking alone can take as many as ten hours per evaluation cycle. If there are problems and a review or appeal must be requested, the hours spent on evaluation activities increase further. In addition, time needs to be set aside to train new teachers and principals on the evaluation system requirements and processes. Principals who have many teachers to evaluate each year may find that spending this much time evaluating teachers is simply impossible.

When new state policies are enacted requiring evaluations that are more frequent and rigorous, the design and implementation process often includes a number of time-intensive steps. In one district that implemented a promising (though intensive) new teacher evaluation system, principals reported spending twelve to twenty-five hours per teacher per year on evaluations, not including time spent in evaluator training or time spent on their own evaluations. In total, principals spent approximately 50 to 60 percent of their time on activities related to teacher evaluation. The following activities were included:

- Formal observation 1:
  - Pre-meeting (30 minutes)
  - Observation (45 minutes)
  - Observation write-up (60 minutes)
  - Debriefing (30 minutes)
- Formal observation 2:
  - Pre-meeting (30 minutes)
  - Observation (45 minutes)
  - Observation write-up (60 minutes)
  - Debriefing (30 minutes)
- Eight unannounced spot observations plus 5-minute debriefs (2.5 hours)
- Final summative write-up (4 hours)
- Additional hours spent providing feedback to teachers who need support

There is an inevitable trade-off between time and quality in conducting teacher evaluations. If the principal eliminated or shortened any of the aforementioned activities, there would be less confidence that he or she had accurately captured a teacher's instructional practices, and the quality of feedback would be lower. Yet devoting so much effort to evaluating teachers takes up time that principals already do not feel they have. A significant reshuffling of responsibilities must take place to accommodate the time needed for thoughtful, accurate, high-quality evaluations if principals are not to burn out from the responsibility.

The most obvious people to turn to for support with some principal duties are teachers with an interest in exploring new responsibilities and opportunities outside the classroom, and this brings us back to the topic of teacher leadership, covered extensively in Chapter One. Teacher leaders can assume new responsibilities and provide principals with more time to be instructional leaders, including conducting meaningful, high-quality teacher evaluations. The following section discusses several approaches to engaging teachers not so much in evaluation reform but in the evaluation process itself.

INVOLVING TEACHERS AS EVALUATORS

Thus far, this chapter has focused on teacher engagement in the *design* of an evaluation system, but opportunities for teacher engagement extend to the evaluation process itself as well. Creating more avenues for teachers to be actively involved in evaluations as leaders and reflective practitioners provides meaningful leadership and growth opportunities and, if done well, can lend greater legitimacy to the evaluation system.

Peer Evaluation

Teacher leaders can provide input into evaluations as evaluators of other teachers. A popular and proven approach to teacher-led evaluations is *peer assistance and review* (PAR). PAR involves experienced and effective teachers—often referred to as "consulting teachers"—who leave the classroom for a specified period of time, usually between one and three years, to observe and intensively support beginning and low-performing teachers. Their rotation in and out of the classroom ensures that they will continue to be perceived as peers rather than administrators. They analyze each participating teacher's strengths and weaknesses and develop a targeted annual program to help each teacher grow professionally. These peer-led activities are well documented and are used in final summative evaluations, which can be conducted by these consulting teachers or by PAR panels that are composed of equal numbers of peers and district administrators, and which determine a teacher's final evaluation rating and supports. In comparing the quality of the performance appraisal notes of principals to those of these full-time peer evaluators, researchers found the latter to be far more comprehensive (Humphrey, Koppich, Bland, & Bosetti, 2011).

Student Learning Objectives

A second approach to teacher engagement in the evaluation process is through *student learning objectives* (SLOs). This approach is quickly gaining attention in the field as a means of assessing student achievement gains that goes beyond the simple use of standardized tests. SLOs represent a participatory method of setting measurable goals or objectives based on a teacher's particular students, subject, and grade, and of determining possible ways to measure student growth in light of these. An SLO might specify that 80 percent of students in a given class will improve their exam scores, as measured by a pre- and post-test. SLOs might use standardized tests, or they might rely on teacher-developed or other classroom assessments, as long as they are considered rigorous and comparable across classrooms. A key challenge is ensuring that the objectives set high but attainable standards and that they serve as a source of motivation for teachers to reach their maximum potential with their students (Lachlan-Haché, Cushing, & Bivona, 2012). A key aspect of this model is that teachers develop their own student growth goals—often in collaboration with their principal and with support from district instructional leaders—a process that yields goals that are more meaningful to them.

Teacher Self-Evaluation and Goal Setting

A third way to bring out teacher voice through evaluations is to include teacher self-evaluations in the process. Teacher self-evaluations typically take place as a first step in evaluations. Using the same rubric that their evaluators use, teachers assess themselves in a variety of competencies, identify their own perceived areas of strength and areas in need of growth, and request resources and supports to help them develop their practice. These self-ratings can then be used in various ways to facilitate professional learning.

For example, the self-evaluation may be used at the start of the school year to reflect on progress made over the previous school year and to set goals for the current year. Alternatively, teacher self-evaluations can be compared against their evaluators' ratings; this promotes a more meaningful discussion about the teacher's performance by focusing the conversation around areas of agreement and discrepancy. Teachers can provide self-assessments both on the final summative rating rubric and on any separate templates for rating individual observations. These templates may ask, for example, what went well or poorly in a particular classroom lesson, and teachers' self-ratings can again be used to foster more productive discussions with their observers about the lesson. Self-evaluations can then inform goal setting to promote teachers' ongoing growth and development. In Massachusetts, for example, teachers are required to complete a self-assessment based on a comparison of their own practice with the performance levels on the rubric and to conduct an analysis of student data prior to setting their professional goals (which can include both individual and team-based goals).

Professional Dialogue in Meetings Between Teachers and Their Observers

A fourth approach to teacher engagement in the evaluation process is to include multiple formal meetings (for example, pre- and post-observation debrief meetings, beginning-of-year meetings, end-of-year-meetings, or midyear check-ins) and to structure those meetings so that a meaningful, two-way, professional dialogue takes place. These meetings may include conversations between teachers and their evaluators or conversations between teachers and nonevaluating observers (or both). Teacher leader and blogger Anthony Cody (NBCT) describes what this process might look like:

> A teacher meets with his or her evaluator. They review the professional standards in use, and look for areas in need of growth. Maybe it is a focus on literacy and writing skills. Maybe it is bringing the English learners' level of engagement and participation up. They discuss strategies the teacher might try to address these things, and they also discuss the forms of evidence they will look at over the year to see what is happening in this area. Assessment, especially of the classroom-based formative sort, is a powerful tool. How is a teacher assessing his or her students' abilities? How are they using that information to give feedback and give the student appropriate, challenging work? This is where teachers use genuine assessment grounded in their understanding of their students. When this sort of assessment data is shared with an evaluator, a comprehensive portrait of how this teacher is helping students to grow can emerge.
>
> Once an area of focus has been defined, the teacher and evaluator find some professional development resources that might help as well—maybe a conference to attend, some books that might be read, a grade-level team that might come observe a lesson here and there and offer feedback, a colleague that is expert in this area to go observe. Then over the year, the teacher collects student work samples that provide evidence of learning. They document how they have designed instruction to help students learn, and show where they have provided feedback. The evaluator observes, a few times at random, and a few times by request, to see particular lessons. This evidence would be appropriate to the goal that has been set. It could include some test data, but test data would just be one source of evidence among many. (Cody, 2012)

Giving Teachers a Stake in Evaluating Principals

A fifth way to engage teachers in evaluation is to give them a stake in evaluating principals, specifically through 360-degree performance assessments; 360-degree principal evaluations survey all teachers in a school regarding the principal's effectiveness. The model of 360-degree principal evaluations is derived from systems used extensively in the private sector (for example, at Microsoft, General Electric, and in other companies) to incorporate employee input into company leaders' evaluations as a way to provide valuable feedback, increase support of the evaluation process, and reinforce company values.

Probably the most widely used evaluation instrument for school principals—and the only teacher survey that is intended to be used for summative evaluations of principals (as opposed to feedback only)—is the Vanderbilt Assessment for Leadership in Education (VAL-ED). The 360-degree survey was developed by researchers at Vanderbilt University, University of Pennsylvania, and Arizona State University, and it includes surveys of principals, teachers, and principals' supervisors. It focuses, in particular, on the instructional leadership that principals provide teachers (Condon & Clifford, 2012). The Balanced Leadership Profile from Mid-continent Research for Education and Learning also surveys principals, teachers, and principals' supervisors; it includes a focus on leadership for school change, but is only intended to help principals identify areas of strength and areas for growth. (More information about engagement in principal evaluations is provided in Chapter Eight.)

⊙

There clearly are many entry points for teacher engagement in evaluation—from influencing the design of a new system to providing input at various stages of implementation to meaningfully participating in the evaluation process itself. In the next chapter, we describe how to ensure that teacher engagement in evaluation is authentic.

CHAPTER
FOUR

The Elements of Authentic Engagement

When the Los Angeles (LA) school district was looking for input from LA teachers on an evaluation redesign for the city—seeking answers to such questions as What are the critical elements? and What should the weight of those elements be?—Teach Plus Los Angeles helped facilitate the feedback process. Working groups from the organization's Teaching Policy Fellowship engaged the larger population of LA teachers.

As in many cities, the teacher evaluation conversation in LA is highly charged and often political. Teach Plus sought a way to depoliticize the conversation so that teachers could have an honest and productive dialogue about their priorities. Teach Plus fellows—all active teachers—used the nonpartisan deliberative materials from Everyone at the Table to moderate structured dialogues and gather accurate qualitative research. During these dialogues, LA teachers shared their thoughts on what a general evaluation plan should look like, unencumbered by politics. Teach Plus fellows facilitated multiple discrete focus groups, as well as breakout sessions at a larger event, and articulated the findings in an interim memo to the district.

John Lee, director of Teach Plus Los Angeles, said that the framework of the dialogues—facilitated by trained moderators and structured using neutral discussion materials—enabled the teachers to have robust, depoliticized conversations, and the meetings provided a safe space for teachers to thoughtfully and efficiently weigh in. Teach Plus shared the LA teachers' feedback at a large meeting with district and union officials, and the feedback will ultimately contribute to an end result for the district.

◉

All too often, education leaders present their newest policy decision and open it up to a half hour of questions or invite teachers to attend board of education meetings, and they presume that these gestures are sufficient to give teachers a voice. They are not. Leaders often push back against a fuller and more in-depth approach to engagement with teachers (as well as with parents and other education stakeholders) for a number of reasons. The process may seem too time-consuming, especially when policy change is on a fast track, as it often is for evaluation reform. These leaders may never have seen a well-designed process and may fear that engagement will lead to counterproductive venting and criticism, opening a Pandora's box of conflict and acrimony. They may think that they have access to more knowledge, or perhaps a bigger picture, than teachers and are therefore in the best position to make decisions anyway. Or they may fear that teachers will voice ideas that are counter to the policies they want to pass, and will then be even angrier that the administration went ahead with a policy despite clear teacher opposition.

Bringing a group of teachers together to talk productively about a contentious issue like teacher evaluation will never be effortless. But creating sustainable teacher evaluation policy will require honest and creative collaboration. We've explored earlier in this book the myriad reasons *why* this is the case. This chapter explores *how* to design a teacher engagement initiative that is meaningful and productive and that leads to solutions.

Tantamount to successful, solutions-oriented inclusion of teacher voice in evaluation reform is *authentic* engagement. Authentic engagement describes the process of

- Helping people grapple with complex issues that involve conflicts of competing values or priorities
- Developing a more mature, stable perspective on the issues
- Building common ground, in spite of differences, on the best way to move forward

Authentic engagement arises from thoughtfully designed and well-facilitated processes which ensure that teachers have a seat at the table when decisions are being discussed. It involves much more than a few public hearings, an occasional survey, and cursory lip service to the attitudes of teachers. This chapter explores some of the most important elements to include when authentically engaging teachers, including discussion materials that help defuse the politics around the issue and skilled facilitators who help structure the conversation and create dialogue. Although supportive leadership and a culture that is amenable to teacher voice and leadership are helpful, their absence does not render an authentic engagement initiative impossible. In fact, such an initiative can actually build support from leaders and foster a culture of engagement.

Finally, engagement is not a one-time event. Both during design and throughout implementation, there are ongoing opportunities for *all* teachers (1) to have a forum to share their ideas and concerns and (2) to know that they were genuinely considered when decisions were made. This chapter also explores ways to build ongoing and sustained teacher engagement into the overall decision-making process of a school or district.

THE LEARNING CURVE: HELPING PEOPLE WRESTLE WITH TRADE-OFFS AND MOVE TOWARD WISER JUDGMENT

Engagement helps people grapple with complex issues that often involve considerations and values that are in tension. Through engagement, they are able to develop the more thoughtful, stable perspective needed to build sustainable policy related to the issue. The approach we describe in this book is a good framework for helping people in this process. Derived from Public Agenda founder Dan Yankelovich's view of public judgment, the *Learning Curve* is a pragmatic theory of how people engage with difficult issues, work through the values conflicts and trade-offs inherent in those issues, overcome wishful thinking, and come to a realistic and responsible judgment as to how to move forward (Yankelovich & Friedman, 2011).

Yankelovich has spent decades examining how people think through tough issues and form more stable judgments about them. He explains that people advance through different stages on their Learning Curve (illustrated in Figure 4.1) as they learn about an issue and as their thinking on it evolves.

The Learning Curve is segmented into three distinct phases:

1. **Consciousness-raising.** People become aware of an issue and start taking it seriously; this stage is typically media driven.

2. **Working through.** People begin to confront the need for change, consider the pros and cons of proposed actions, and wrestle with trade-offs. In this stage, people also struggle to reconcile their core values with their positions on

Figure 4.1. The Learning Curve

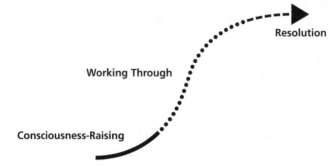

Resolution

Working Through

Consciousness-Raising

Source: Public Agenda, 2010.

issues. In this sometimes stormy process, values and emotions play a major role, along with objective analysis and deliberation.

3. **Resolution.** Having worked through their emotional resistance and cognitive weighing of pros and cons, people choose a course of action and are prepared to accept its likely consequences.

The amount of time that is required for opinion to evolve depends on the issue and can vary enormously. Some issues require just months, especially in a limited context like a school district. Others can take decades, especially across society as a whole. Yankelovich also explains that developing a better understanding and wiser judgment around an issue requires much more than just knowing the right information; information is valuable, but it is not enough. The way people think about a complex issue is often deeply affected, and even derailed, by values conflicts, anxiety about change, and lack of trust. Taking the appropriate action when it comes to a complex issue often requires sacrifice or a change in behavior, and people need to be ready to accept this to move forward. For example, this may help explain why, even when faced with ever-increasing scientific evidence on climate change, people find it difficult to stand behind a specific energy policy. Before people can truly embrace an acceptable pathway forward, they must come to terms with it both intellectually and emotionally.

The evolution of public thought can occur naturally—for example, people have grown from rejecting to accepting things like the role of technology and the Internet in classrooms and the notion that most people need some kind of postsecondary education credential to be able to make a decent living. Such evolution, however, can be slow and incomplete. A well-designed and well-facilitated process of authentic engagement can accelerate this evolution and move people to a stage of thinking where they are more ready to make a stable decision and embrace change. For example, Public Agenda conducted qualitative research into citizen forums on the national debt; these forums were structured to help participants develop more stable judgment. We found that providing critical bits of information and giving participants a chance to talk through the options resulted in their very quickly becoming quite realistic and pragmatic about some of the essential ingredients for addressing the debt.

One of the purposes of the *Everyone at the Table* activities outlined in Chapters Five through Eight is to accelerate the Learning Curve of teachers, principals, and other stakeholders on evaluation reform. This is not to say that the process in any way helps persuade teachers to embrace one point of view or another. In fact, the process does the exact opposite: in exposing teachers to viewpoints that are divergent from their own, it helps them work through all of the possible trade-offs involved in any potential solution, break down the wall of dichotomous thinking, realize that there is no magic bullet, and make the most stable judgment as to what process would best lead to continuous improvement in their instruction and their students' learning.

PRINCIPLES OF SOUND ENGAGEMENT

There are a number of core principles that help enable productive engagement that leads to collaborative problem solving and sustainable policy solutions. Adapted from those described in *Public Engagement: A Primer from Public Agenda* (Center for Advances in Public Engagement, 2008), these principles were developed through years of engagement in multiple fields.

Beginning by Listening

Listening to teachers before talking to them will facilitate meaningful engagement that takes teachers' interests, concerns, and natural language into account. Understanding where teachers are coming from, their entry points into the conversation, and how they interpret the language of reform helps uncover both potential stumbling blocks and opportunities for common ground. In its higher education engagement work, for example, Public Agenda spoke to college adjunct and full-time faculty and discovered, through careful listening, that one term that triggered dissent was the word "productivity." For institutional leaders, productivity represented the idea of helping more students earn a meaningful credential more efficiently and at a lower cost (for students and taxpayers alike), but the same word had very negative connotations for faculty members, for whom it conjured images of assembly lines. For advocates of productivity, attempts at constructive dialogue with faculty on the topic were immediately stymied on account of a word—even when research revealed shared goals and sense of purpose among productivity advocates and faculty members. Framing the conversation in a way that emphasized measures of productivity without using the word itself—for example, reducing student debt, experimenting with technology within a classroom to transform the learning experience—helped participants identify common ground and stimulated much better conversations between institutional leaders, policymakers, and faculty (Kadlec & Friedman, 2010).

In a similar way, understanding teachers' starting-point values and opinions when it comes to measuring their own practice, and identifying the best ways to communicate with and engage teachers on tough issues, will improve communication and problem solving among teachers and education leaders. Through a careful and systematic process of listening, leaders in the engagement effort are able to speak teachers' language and acknowledge their concerns.

In practice, this means that anyone leading an engagement initiative must be alert to the issues that teachers care about, the language they use to discuss those issues, and their concerns, aspirations, knowledge base, misperceptions, and initial sense of direction with respect to solutions. Leaders should take care to translate any expert-speak into language that typical teachers use and should address common teacher concerns. Doing so minimizes potentially counterproductive jargon and faulty assumptions about teachers' positions. Leaders also need to tailor their communication with teachers to fit teachers' level of knowledge around evaluation. Although it may be the case that a majority of teachers are already knowledgeable about the issue of evaluation, assumptions should never be made; research from Public Agenda and AIR for the Everyone at the Table project suggests that teachers are much less familiar with the issue than many leaders presume.

Framing for Deliberation: The Power of Choicework

Framing for deliberation means structuring a conversation in a way that makes it clear that there are no easy answers and that many points of view are welcome and essential to the discussion. In the approach described in Chapters Five through Eight, we use what we refer to as Choicework discussion starters. These discussion starters are based on the theory and practice of Dan Yankelovich and are one practical approach for framing a conversation for deliberation. The box "Choicework Discussion Starters" includes an example of Choicework.

CHOICEWORK DISCUSSION STARTERS

The section "Three Scenarios for Teacher Evaluation" in Chapter Six is one example of Choicework. The following is another, an abridged version of Public Agenda's *Education: A Citizens' Solutions Guide,* in which the pros and cons of varied approaches to improving K–12 education in the United States are distinctly laid out. The full document includes specific policies and actions for implementing each approach and three or four pros and cons per approach. You can view the entire document at http://www.publicagenda.org/pages/csg-education.

Approach One
Set high standards and hold schools, teachers, and principals accountable for helping all children meet them.

Arguments for:
- Almost every other advanced industrial nation has an agreed-on core curriculum that specifies what students are expected to learn at each grade level. That system has produced higher and more equitable academic achievement than our own.

Arguments against:
- This approach puts too much emphasis on testing. Standardized tests have a role, but they shouldn't be used as a central basis for determining whether teachers are effective or whether students are really learning.

Approach Two
Give parents more choice about the schools their children go to.

Arguments for:
- Parents could choose the school that is best suited to their children's needs and interests. This gives average Americans an option that wealthy families have long enjoyed.

Arguments against:
- Research shows that students in public schools often outperform those in charter and private schools, and some districts have had to close charter schools because they were so ineffective. Choice is not a surefire recipe for improving student achievement.

Approach Three
Give public schools the financial and community support they need to help all children learn.

Arguments for:
- No school reform can succeed until schools have sufficient resources to provide a rich, high-quality educational environment for every child. Public schools need more money to do the job right.

(continued on next page)

(continued from previous page)

Arguments against:

- This approach will cost an enormous amount of money, and the federal government and many state governments are already operating in the red. There's no way to pay for all of this without raising taxes, which is politically difficult and economically questionable in a poor economy.

Approach Four

Make sure every school has a talented, committed principal who will work closely with teachers to transform what happens inside the school every day.

Arguments for:

- Effective principals are the single most important factor in creating a school climate that clearly emphasizes learning as priority number one. Principals establish the sense of mission and an environment in which teachers can teach and students can learn.

Arguments against:

- This approach places too much of the responsibility on principals, and even the best ones can't be effective without strong financial, parental, and community support.

The "Three Scenarios" Choicework used in *Everyone at the Table* does not explicitly lay out pros and cons; rather, it is up to the moderator to tease them out. For other examples of Choicework discussion starters, visit http://www.publicagenda.org/pages/discussion-starters.

Choicework enables participants in an engagement process to confront the fact that there is no magic bullet. These materials lay out three or four potential approaches to a problem at hand, while also making it clear that there are trade-offs regardless of the preferred approach. Considering choices arrayed side by side obliges people to look at different ideas for addressing an issue, and it helps them break out of an either-or pattern of thinking. Through years of practice, we have found that people cannot begin the process of deciding what matters most on complex issues and what trade-offs and compromises might be necessary in resolving them until the credible choices they have to work with have been made clear.

Perfect solutions to policy problems are rare, but Choicework engenders a more practical frame of mind and can move people beyond polarizing, zero-sum arguments and toward productive, realistic, solution-oriented dialogue. This approach to framing gives people context, focuses their attention, and staves off repetitive venting. Choicework also builds common ground by drawing out the common values that participants share. Furthermore, it helps people with very different levels of expertise engage both with the issues and with one another more effectively than in a wide-open, unstructured discussion.

The concept of Choicework is explicitly incorporated into the main **Dialogue Focus Group** activity of *Everyone at the Table* (see Chapter Six), which frames a discussion around three potential evaluation scenarios for teachers to consider, each of which has potential trade-offs, pros, and cons. Participants are not meant to choose one of the three scenarios in its entirety; rather, we frame the choices as a discussion starting point that represents a wide range of values. Choicework is especially critical in discussions around issues that have very real political implications, such as teacher evaluation. Indeed, people who have used the materials in this book with teachers in LA told us that the Choicework scenarios and the structure of the conversation helped depoliticize the issue, enabling teachers to have a conversation that drilled down to the real issues at hand.

The Importance of Facilitation

Productive engagement often hinges on how it is facilitated. An effective moderator is critical to fostering an open, inclusive, and productive conversation on tough, emotionally wrought issues. One of the biggest challenges to an engagement initiative is the risk that the conversation will disintegrate into a session for gossiping, venting, blaming, or arguing. This can happen at the best of times, but it is a particular threat for conversations around a sensitive topic like teacher evaluation. The right moderator will guide the conversation, keep it on a productive path, and maintain a focus on developing solutions.

A successful moderator is comfortable with the goal of an open dialogue without a preset conclusion. For the engagement event to be credible, moderators need to be—and to be viewed as—neutral and unbiased. Moderators are like skillful hosts who keep the party lively without themselves becoming the center of attention; they must not allow their own opinions and voices to overwhelm or redirect the natural flow of the conversation. It is not their goal to lead anyone toward a "correct" answer, and this is not a role for someone who feels that they are unable to be objective, who often gets defensive, or who grows impatient with "wrong" answers. For these reasons, moderators need to be chosen and trained with care. In the section "Understanding the Role of Moderators and Recorders" in Chapter Six, we examine in depth the qualities to look for and encourage in a moderator.

The Role of Dialogue

Engaging teachers in a way that promotes evolution of judgment and collaborative problem solving requires a very specific kind of communication: dialogue. Unlike debate or negotiation, dialogue is not intended to settle a matter, bargain, conciliate, win an argument, or vanquish an opponent. Instead, dialogue helps people uncover and confront assumptions, wishful thinking, and value differences; broaden perspectives; build trust; and find common ground. The process encourages a teasing out of the multiple complexities behind a problem so that people are better positioned to advance toward an empathetic exchange of differing ideas and viewpoints and, ultimately, to reach mutual understanding and common ground.

Dialogue can be a truly transformative experience. As Public Agenda senior fellow Jean Johnson writes in her book *You Can't Do It Alone,* dialogue "helps people feel less like victims and more like colleagues" (2012, p. 34). When teachers engage in dialogue with one another, Johnson continues, it helps them "work through their own ambivalences and conflicted feelings. It can help dissolve some of the mistrust and resentment teachers feel at the changes 'being forced on them.' And dialogue conveys one extraordinarily crucial message—that teachers' views are important and that school leaders want to hear and consider them" (p. 34).

In theory, understanding the difference between dialogue and other forms of discussion, such as debate or negotiation, seems easy to grasp. In practice, participants often find themselves gravitating toward debate, as it can feel more natural to defend one's position rather than explore the other side. Adapted from Dan Yankelovich's book *The Magic of Dialogue* (1999), the following principles that differentiate dialogue from debate can help participants distinguish between the two in practice:

- Dialogue is collaborative; participants explore areas of common ground and work together toward common understanding. Rather than attempting to prove the other side wrong, the intent is to discover together what's right or, perhaps better, what works. In dialogue, participants assume that many people possess parts of an answer, and work together to build a solution. They don't assume that there is one right answer in the possession of one person.

- Dialogue participants listen to each other to understand where others are coming from and search for the strengths in others' thinking. They don't listen to each other to identify flaws in an argument and craft a defense.
- In dialogue, participants understand that the thinking of others can improve and sharpen their own thinking. They don't defend their own views at the cost of others'.

When done well, dialogue is a unique opportunity for dissolving long-standing disagreements, overcoming mistrust, gaining new perspectives and insights, building shared purpose and understanding, stimulating creativity, strengthening bonds, and building common ground, but dialogue does not just happen. Unfortunately, examples of dialogue have become much harder to find, whereas examples of polarized, and often angry, debate (among politicians and leaders and in the media) are increasingly common.

Transforming a regular conversation into dialogue takes deliberate effort and such skills as active listening. Nonpartisan discussion materials like Choicework and the assistance of a skilled facilitator can help. In *The Magic of Dialogue,* Yankelovich (1999) highlights two other important features that distinguish a normal discussion from dialogue.

Equality and Trust as a Foundation

We don't live in an ideal world, and it's not always the case that teachers and education leaders operate in an environment of trust. It's also important to note that if trust and equality are not optimal within a school or district, dialogue can lend a hand in building up that trust.

However, without at least a minimal amount of mutual trust among participants, dialogue is not possible. To help engender trust, teachers should come into a dialogue as true equals, shedding any literal or figurative badges of authority. First-year rookies and thirty-year veterans, teachers who actively participate in policy discussions and those brand new to the debate, department heads and union reps, art teachers and math teachers—everyone should participate on an equal footing. In genuine dialogue, teachers do not pull rank, twist anyone's arm, hint at sanctions for specific opinions, or use coercive influence.

Distinguishing Real Differences from the Trivial Ones

Dialogue helps people distinguish and move past differences that are trivial, while also illuminating the real differences that people will need to work through and negotiate in order to make progress. Differences of opinion are often vastly exaggerated; all too often, we assume that if someone does not support what we stand for, it must mean he or she rejects it outright. It is more often the case that we have many values in common when it comes to a complex issue like teacher evaluation, but we rank them differently. It is safe to say, for example, that the majority of people—teachers, parents, education leaders, and policymakers alike—would agree on certain underlying values of teacher evaluation: evaluation should be comprehensive and consistent; evaluation should be fair and flexible; we should have high, yet reasonable, expectations for our teachers; the evaluation process should be efficient in time and cost; the evaluation process should be collaborative and should help build community and advance learning and practice. It is unlikely that anyone would argue against any of these values, but different people can—and do—rank them in different ways.

Conflicts and differences of opinion are natural and are a healthy part of a collaborative problem-solving process. It is okay for people to disagree—differing opinions and viewpoints can often lead to better decision making—but disagreements ought to be productive. We all must take care to prevent trivial differences from becoming pernicious and destructive. Dialogue itself can help surface those differences that are less divisive than we assumed; actions on the part of participants can also help. For example, participants should be active and empathetic listeners. It is important that participants do not simply fight blindly for their own convictions. A moderator can help participants acknowledge the viewpoints of others and attempt to understand those viewpoints from their colleagues' perspectives. Thoughtfully examining assumptions and making them explicit to their colleagues also help minimize destructive conflict, even if disagreement and tension still exist. When we examine our assumptions, we are far less likely to misunderstand one another or to make errors in judgment, and we are better able to view one another as human beings rather than as ideologues.

Of course, some of our differences are real and must be understood and negotiated to facilitate better decision making. As a whole, the engagement initiative itself helps people accept these differences, work through conflict, and build practical pathways forward in spite of divisions and differences. In the section "Strategies for Overcoming Obstacles and Troubleshooting" in Chapter Six, we discuss specific interventions and suggested actions moderators can take when they experience conflict during an engagement activity.

COMMON MISTAKES TO AVOID

When leading an engagement initiative, even the most well-intentioned organizers and moderators can make mistakes. Here are some common missteps, along with how to avoid them:

Cross-talk: starting the conversation where leaders and experts are, rather than where participants are. Make sure participants understand the problem that the initiative is trying to address by, for example, providing them with the essential facts they need to understand its complexities.

Expert speak: using jargon or unfamiliar concepts. This can be off-putting, so use plain, accessible language instead.

The data dump: providing more data than people need or can cope with for a given question and conversation. Instead, provide only the critical information that they need to grasp the issue's complexity and weigh the trade-offs.

Poor meeting design: long-winded expert panels or public-hearing-style gripe sessions. These types of meetings do not lead to productive, solutions-oriented dialogue. The process outlined in this book may take more planning, but it is well worth it.

Selling rather than engaging: coming in with "the" answer and expecting participants to buy it. Instead, come with the problem and work on answers together.

Framing for persuasion, not deliberation: defining an issue to one's advantage in the hopes of getting an audience to do what you want. Instead, offer people a range of options to choose from to jump-start their thinking.

Partisan facilitation: using facilitators who have, or are perceived to have, a stake in the issue. Recruit moderators and recorders who are trusted by participants as neutral and nonpartisan.

Rigged game: having made decisions before the engagement initiative begins. Instead, engage teachers to help make decisions and begin when there are decisions to be made.

Poor follow-through: talking without any action. This frustrates participants. Instead, have a vision and a real plan for how to follow up on the meeting.

Failure to communicate: not letting participants know about subsequent follow-through. Instead, let participants know about any outcomes of subsequent steps that stemmed from the dialogue.

EMBEDDING ENGAGEMENT IN THE LOCAL CULTURE: BRIDGEPORT, CONNECTICUT

Inviting those who will be most affected by policy decisions to have a seat at the table during the decision-making process is not a new phenomenon. Policy organizations, democratic theorists, and various education experts have argued that when leaders listen to and consider the insights and concerns of those who will be affected by an outcome, they make better decisions and create programs and policies that will actually stick. Engagement can truly transform public life, as illustrated by the story of Bridgeport, Connecticut (summarized in the chapter "Working Toward Public Judgment at Public Agenda" in Yankelovich & Friedman, 2011).

In 1997, Public Agenda—with the leadership and support of the William Casper Graustein Memorial Fund and along with the Institute for Educational Leadership, the Connecticut League of Women Voters, and the Bridgeport Education Fund—embarked on a project to engage community members on school improvement through a series of Community Conversations, a signature Public Agenda methodology.

Community Conversations are large-scale facilitated dialogues with diverse members of the community; they foster productive and inclusive deliberation and generate solutions. The conversations are planned and sponsored by local, community-based, nonpartisan organizations and institutions in order to encourage the involvement of a broad cross-section of participants and to facilitate follow-up that leads to results. Generally, Community Conversations include many participants, sometimes hundreds. Following an opening session, participants break into small, diverse groups with trained moderators and recorders. The discussion is structured using unbiased Choicework materials. Each Community Conversation is part of a broader process in which conversations are connected to action and follow-up (Public Agenda, 2012a).

Residents of Bridgeport initially came together in Community Conversations to address problems in education and school reform—for example, ensuring school safety, closing achievement gaps, and preventing bullying. Since the Bridgeport initiative started, local community leaders have used the Community Conversation model scores of times to create common ground and forge new partnerships on a wide variety of issues affecting the Bridgeport community. Thousands of parents, educational professionals, students, local policy and business leaders, seniors, and others have gathered for dialogue on bullying, children's mental health, family violence, corruption, employment needs, housing, economic development, and more. A Harvard research team called the experiment a sterling example of public engagement becoming embedded in a community (Friedman, Kadlec, & Birnback, 2007).

In Bridgeport, the inclusion of a wide variety of the voices most directly affected by policy change related to some of these incredibly tricky and often divisive issues led to concrete improvements. In interviews with local leaders who had participated in the Community Conversations, the leaders pointed to a variety of programs and policies that aimed to improve the education and lives of the state's children, as well as to individuals who had chosen to take an active role in improving education for the community's children. These policies, programs, and people had emerged out of the engagement work and include

- Mentoring from area colleges for the city's high school students
- Individual volunteers who read to public school children following an education summit
- An antibullying policy adopted by the school district
- A reduction in class size in the school district
- School leadership teams that give parents a voice in education policy

There is also significant evidence that the engagement effort and ensuing programs had a positive effect on student outcomes:

- Due to gains in student achievement, five city schools have recently moved off a list of poorly performing schools.
- Among students who had been matched with a mentor in the year and a half following an education summit, 90 percent showed improved attendance and higher grades in mathematics and social studies.
- Bridgeport was a finalist in 2006 and 2007 for the Broad Foundation Prize for Urban Education—a prestigious national prize for urban school districts that is awarded for the greatest overall performance and improvement in equitable student achievement.

THE IMPORTANCE OF CULTURE

For engagement to have a lasting impact, schools must adopt an evolving set of practices and habits among education leaders and other stakeholders, including teachers, that become embedded in the life of the school and community. Engagement should become an integral part of a culture in which schools and districts build common vision and common ground. Within this culture, different kinds of people, with different interests and experiences, work together to make headway on common problems. A culture of engagement is one in which engagement practices become ongoing and even habitual and are not just isolated exercises in collaborative problem solving. Each round of teacher engagement, when effective, will set the stage for broader and deeper engagement throughout schools and districts in the future.

Ideally, an engagement culture integrates a loop of reflection and feedback on the part of all stakeholders, one that leads to better decisions, communications, and collaborations aimed at improving results for students. A culture of engagement can be seen as a continuum of events, activities, attitudes, and opportunities—from spontaneous conversations that last only a few minutes to formal dialogues that are planned in advance and take place over a series of weeks or months, in which meticulous attention is given to setting, composition, and agenda.

It is particularly important that leaders and decision makers engage teachers continually, throughout decision making. A culture in which teacher engagement occurs not just at the beginning of evaluation policy formation and during action planning but also (indeed, particularly) during implementation will help ease the transition that implementation entails. After all, even in the best of circumstances, when teacher voice has played a significant role in decision making and crafting policy, transitioning from designing policy to making that policy come alive within a school can, and often will, be a bumpy road. Ongoing engagement can make the ride smoother.

A school and district culture that is amenable to including teachers in decision making obviously helps in getting an engagement initiative off the ground. At the same time, the absence of such a culture does not mean engagement is impossible. If the culture doesn't exist already, it can be developed. Opportunities for nourishing a culture of engagement are many and varied. On its own, the process described in Chapters Five through Eight can help foster such a culture. Supportive leadership and the existence of trust both contribute to and are nourished by a culture of engagement. Finally, technological advances and online communities help make engagement broader and more accessible than ever.

Leadership

Leadership can be key in the engagement process. Leaders catalyze activities, help build trust, and drive change. In Chapter One, we discussed how teacher leadership can promote teacher dialogue and voice in teacher evaluation. But leadership—from teachers and principals alike—also contributes to a culture of trust that fosters authentic engagement. In this context, we are referring to leaders on multiple levels, from superintendents to principals to teacher leaders, as well as community leaders who may be working with the schools. Ideally, school and district leaders—principals, superintendents, and union leaders—support and inspire the engagement effort. In our experience, in most cases of successful engagement efforts—in the education arena and elsewhere—the charge was supported by strong institutional leaders with a clear vision of the need for change and an appreciation for the importance of broad-based engagement to help bring that about.

Through extensive research and experience with engagement efforts in higher education, Public Agenda has identified other engagement-supporting leadership qualities for institutional leaders (for example, principals and department heads) (Public Agenda & Achieving the Dream, 2011). These qualities should be nurtured and encouraged in the hiring process. Such qualities include

- The ability to communicate a vision for change in a compelling and inspiring way and to connect the dots among the steps in that change process. This quality tends to reduce the sense of reform fatigue, initiative overload, and mission creep that can occur.
- The ability to establish an atmosphere of collaboration and co-ownership by approaching teachers with questions—rather than with decisions and answers—and viewing teachers as resources for problem solving.
- An appreciation and respect for the knowledge, expertise, contributions, and commitment of teachers.
- An inclination to publicly recognize the accomplishments and contributions of teachers.
- Taking the time to listen to, understand, and appreciate where teachers are entering the conversation (their starting-point attitudes) in order to understand how to frame and facilitate productive, problem-solving conversations.

Sadly, some schools and districts are not receptive to teachers having a say in evaluation. One district administrator with whom we spoke, for example, was concerned that the trust they had worked so hard to create with teachers would be broken if the district was not able to provide the system teachers requested. Another district administrator was skeptical that discussions of this nature were a good use of teachers' time, which should be focused more exclusively on instruction. A third administrator was forthright in saying that, aside from the opinion of the six union officers at the bargaining table, the opinion of other teachers was frankly not of interest to him.

It is worth noting that in such situations, it is possible (though more difficult) for teachers to try to create a culture of engagement on their own, and a teacher-initiated process using the strategies outlined in this book may be a useful step toward transforming a school or district culture into one that is more inclusive of teacher voice. We return to this point in the section "Engaging Teachers When Progress Is Already Under Way" in Chapter Five. Sometimes, school leaders supportive of teacher engagement may find themselves in a position where district leaders do not share their view. In this case, leaders will need to be willing to take a risk and endure some possibly uncomfortable conversations in the short term in order to create stronger conditions that support engagement in the long term.

Fortunately, in the large majority of schools and districts, administrators, many of whom were teachers themselves, appreciate what teachers can bring to the discussion of policies that affect them. When this appreciation of teacher voice exists, it is important that it be conveyed to all teachers so as to cultivate this culture of engagement.

To develop a leadership system that embraces engagement, district and school leaders should focus on hiring practices, professional development, and incentives that support a culture of engagement. At individual schools, an effort should be made to recruit and hire principals with an engagement mind-set—one that establishes an atmosphere of collaboration and inspires constructive inclusion of teachers in the decision-making process—as well as teachers oriented toward a collaborative mode of problem solving. Efforts should also be made to cultivate and provide support for those teachers who are willing to be early adopters and champions of engagement.

Trust

When a school culture creates trust and opportunities for meaningful feedback from all teachers, it allows them not only to engage productively in the policy-making process but also to engage with the system in an ongoing manner, as evaluators. When this trust is lacking, there is only one thing to do: (re)build a positive, productive, and constructive school culture.

Engagement itself can help (re)build trust and heal the alienation and confusion that past reform efforts may have wrought. After all, by including teachers in the decision-making process and by ensuring and demonstrating that they are being heard, education leaders demonstrate their recognition that teachers are important and that their views have merit. This active recognition on its own can heal wounds. School leaders and teachers can help (re)build trust within their schools by encouraging and modeling such behaviors and qualities as transparency, sharing of data, candid communication, good listening, real collaboration, holding high expectations while providing real support, leading by example, and celebrating success (Covey, 2006; Hagelskamp & DiStasi, 2013).

Focusing on their extensive engagement activity in higher education, policy researchers at Public Agenda & Achieving the Dream (2011) found that the following tips can help leaders build trust:

- Begin by acknowledging the positive engagement, input, and collaboration that is already taking place.
- Focus on the system first, as opposed to issues of instruction and its quality.
- Acknowledge staff concerns and focus on the topics that are of interest to them.
- Provide support and incentives to allow staff to meaningfully participate in the engagement activity.

Creating the cultural conditions that enable the engagement of teachers in evaluation, including supportive leadership and a foundation of trust, is not impossible; they already exist in many schools. Still, situations are rarely ideal, and it is often the case that schools and districts lack supportive leadership at all levels or operate without a foundation of trust. Strengthening these qualities where they exist can help create a collaborative culture where meaningful and embedded engagement leads to better decisions and sustainable solutions.

Technology and Online Engagement

We would be remiss if we did not mention the positive contributions that the Internet and technology are making to help build a culture of engagement—one that crosses schools, districts, and even countries. Increasingly, engagement culture is manifested online. Technology and the Internet are opening new doors to the practice of engagement. There is a huge community of people online who are engaged in the conversation about education reform, and policymakers, advocates, activists, parents, and teachers are all included in online conversations about policy in a variety of ways. Although we have not yet found that technological tools are effective at replacing face-to-face engagement (Bittle, Haller, & Kadlec, 2009), it is the case that such tools—including Twitter,

Facebook, other social media platforms, webinar technology, and interactive games—can complement engagement practices and help foster an environment where dialogue is continuous and teachers can deliberate the issues outside of face-to-face meetings.

Advocates and teachers alike will freely admit that one of the greatest challenges in involving teachers in policy is not having sufficient time. One of the strengths of online engagement is that it facilitates access to the dialogue for those teachers who may not otherwise have the time to participate in or learn about policy discussions. Social media can also create a more direct avenue for teachers to communicate with each other and with policymakers and education leaders. Such informal exchanges of ideas among teachers can also foster an environment of learning and mutual understanding and give teachers the confidence to have a greater voice in the policy debate that is taking place in their school or district.

Getting online to speak and collaborate with other teachers may also be the only opportunity for some teachers to engage in this manner, particularly those whose school environments are not supportive of teacher voice. As Cass Daubenspeck, former teacher and part of the social media team for Everyone at the Table, noted, "If those [supportive] relationships don't exist, which in some public schools they don't . . . get online—that's the alternative."

Most important, online conversations and communities can help teachers escape the isolation of the classroom and discover a community where teacher voice is prevalent. Online forums create a community where teachers can be less isolated. Speaking up online, where teachers can be anonymous and connected to a variety of other educators across the country, may be a great way for teachers to find their voice and begin to feel empowered.

The community of teachers online—using social media like Twitter, LinkedIn, Facebook, and Pinterest—is large and diverse, and it is continuing to grow as organizations like Hope Street Group and Educators4Excellence train even the most veteran of teachers in the ways of social media. VIVA Teachers has seized the concept of online engagement as a way for busy teachers, with barely minutes to spare, to have an easily accessible platform for collaboration; it provides teachers with online channels to participate in problem solving on issues in education and brings their best ideas to policymakers and legislators.

VIVA Teachers

Amplifying Professional Voices Through Online Collaboration

During a decade spent as an education policy advocate, Elizabeth Evans noticed a consistent theme: "I realized teachers were never in the room . . . and the people in the room never stopped asking, 'What would a teacher think?' I wanted to hear from teachers." Evans began floating the idea of a new approach to bringing teacher voice more directly into the policy development process. The response? "It's too hard to authentically engage a busy, overstretched, classroom-based workforce in a way that can influence policy."

In 2010, Evans put this skepticism to the test and founded New Voice Strategies. The nonprofit operates VIVA Teachers (VIVA stands for Voice Ideas Vision Action), a completely new approach to bringing passionate, committed, and interested classroom teachers into the policy conversation, even if they have only a few minutes to contribute. VIVA Teachers provides classroom professionals with a secure, online "idea exchange" platform to engage in a professionally moderated conversation on a carefully selected, focused question with direct relevance to their classrooms. According to Evans, the online format "take[s] away the pressures of time and place, which are two huge barriers for teachers in being able to connect their practice to the policies that inform their practice." Through an efficient three-phase process, VIVA Teachers enables participants to move from ideas and brainstorming to a final report that puts forward realistic, actionable recommendations that participants present directly to policymakers at an in-person meeting.

In January 2012, for example, VIVA Teachers collaborated with the Minnesota Department of Education and Education Minnesota (the statewide teachers' union) to convene teachers for a VIVA Idea Exchange about new principal evaluation system designs. In phase one, any Minnesota public school instructional professional could join the secure conversation online by signing up and contributing an idea, commenting on other teachers' ideas, or voting for specific ideas put forward in the conversation. During the cold Minnesota winter, nearly six hundred teachers put forward 129 ideas and posted hundreds of comments as part of the moderated conversation over a two-week period. In phase two, VIVA Teachers used the technology built into the online platform to identify twelve "thought leaders," based on both the quantity and quality of their contributions to the VIVA Idea Exchange. The thought leaders were invited to form a writing collaborative that was charged with spending four weeks translating the ideas generated by the online exchange into actionable recommendations. The report writers also had access to experts and key research as they worked. In phase three, members of the writing collaborative presented their recommendations to Mark Dayton, the governor of Minnesota, and Education Commissioner Brenda Cassellius at an in-person meeting and discussed the findings. VIVA Teachers is returning to Minnesota to run a second VIVA Idea Exchange, this time asking teachers for their input into the design of a teacher evaluation system.

The average length of a VIVA Idea Exchange, from phase one through presentation of the final report, is approximately three months—a timeline that is possible only through the online format. In 2010, VIVA Teachers used this format to hear from teachers across the country about national education policy. The project resulted in a report called "Voices from the Classroom," which was presented to Secretary of Education Arne Duncan. Since that first national project, VIVA Teachers has hosted platforms on pressing policy issues in Chicago Public Schools (length of the school day), New York State (teacher evaluation), Arizona (common core implementation), Massachusetts (closing the achievement gap), and New Jersey (character education).

The VIVA Idea Exchange is actively facilitated by a professional moderator who ensures that the conversation is respectful and focused on the question at hand. "We have a specific focus for the discussion and clear outcome at the beginning. . . . It's a very clear and important part of our process—that the rules of the game are known, and you know that you have to follow them; it builds trust among all the participants."

The final key condition is ensuring that participants know that the outcomes of the VIVA Idea Exchange will be heard by policymakers. "In order to really build the trust on the teacher side, we've got to be able to legitimately convey the expectations and the level of interest that the public official has placed on hearing their opinions and recommendations." VIVA Teachers addresses this challenge in its work by meeting and collaborating with public officials before initiating an Idea Exchange to ensure clarity of expectations on both sides. Evans notes that "if we can't explain to the teachers in the beginning what hearing they are going to get (and I don't mean just a meeting), or how their ideas are going to be considered in the process," then the project does not move forward.

VIVA Teachers has completed six online platforms in its first eighteen months, and Evans has seen the aspirational goals of the project produce dramatic results. "I think VIVA Teachers has begun to prove, and I'm totally confident that it will prove over time, that education systems can get much stronger if they actually do incorporate the professional voice of the workforce in a more meaningful way."

Source: Interview with Elizabeth Evans, May 23, 2012.

Authentic engagement takes more than just the right tool or the right logistics. This chapter examined the critical role that leadership, trust, culture, dialogue, facilitation, and listening play in authentic engagement. It is important to always have these principles of authentic engagement and dialogue at the forefront as the engagement process unfolds. Using these principles as a platform for all efforts to bring teacher voice to the policy table, the next three chapters will walk you through logistical planning considerations and specific suggested activities to make this new approach to policymaking a reality.

PART THREE

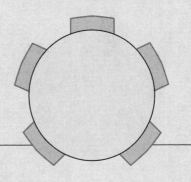

The Engagement Process

Planning

Steps for Engaging Teachers

Authentically engaging teachers requires a lot of logistical preparation. Who will organize the engagement events? Who will you invite? Where will they take place? How many meetings should you plan? How long will it take? How can you bring more teachers to the table and fully engage them? What do you do with teachers' feedback? How will you share it with education leaders and connect it up to the evaluation process?

Planning a teacher engagement initiative may seem daunting, but this chapter will help both those doing the granular planning and those overseeing the effort from afar think through these questions and others. It provides model plans and frameworks to help you think through and answer questions about expectations and the timeline, as well as potential strategies for implementing teacher engagement. The end of the chapter offers a series of vignettes featuring successful teacher engagement in action—both with the *Everyone at the Table* materials and otherwise—to demonstrate that this process *can* be done and to illustrate what the process can look like in a school, district, or state. Regardless of the chosen approach, it must be well developed, fully planned, and clearly communicated in advance.

BEFORE YOU BEGIN

Before examining questions having to do with which activities to include and the number of meetings to plan, those leading the process must decide how teacher input will be used to inform teacher evaluation reform. If the teacher feedback gathered from this initiative is meant to impact evaluation policy at the district or state level, it is important to communicate information about the initiative and intended outcomes with *all* district officials, task force leaders, and others who are heavily involved, especially in smaller districts. Initiative leaders must also determine the decision points available for teacher input as well as how, specifically, the information gathered from teacher conversations will be relayed to decision makers. Please refer to "Decision Points for Teacher Engagement" in Chapter Three for a discussion of common decisions available for teacher input.

Teachers need to have clear and realistic expectations about the results of their effort—and the time they invest. Be specific and direct with teachers from the beginning about how their input will be shared, and indicate the precise ways that their feedback will be presented to, for example, the district task force charged with evaluation reform, the principal and superintendent, or other decision makers.

Engagement Teams

In any engagement initiative, establishing engagement teams should be the first step. Engagement teams provide a forum for knowledge-sharing and an organizing platform for the teachers leading the actual engagement effort. They are responsible for organizing the engagement events and making sure that the appropriate follow-up takes place in a timely manner. These teams are a necessary part of any formal teacher engagement process, whether the engagement strategy is short term or long term and teacher led or leader led. Members of the engagement teams will liaise with school, district, and state leaders, where applicable, at different stages in the process; arrange logistics for engagement events (venue, food, audiovisual equipment, and so on); recruit participants for conversations; manage moderators and note-takers; and coordinate follow-up with decision makers.

Members of the teams do not have to agree on the best way to approach teacher evaluation, as long as they agree that dialogue with teachers is an important way to tackle the challenges of teacher evaluation. The membership of teacher engagement teams need not be static; teachers can be part of the team for a term and then help orient new members. The process of assembling engagement teams should be a deliberate and thoughtful one. When creating these teams, it is important to make a conscious effort to include not only the "usual suspects"—those teachers who tend to frequently have an active voice in decision making at the school or who serve on the task force—but also the wider population of teachers who have not been especially active in policy discussions, as well as others affected by the reforms. This will allow a more inclusive and diverse cross-section of teacher voice to emerge.

If a state or district has a task force in charge of decision making on evaluation, teachers on the engagement teams should be on it. Engagement team members who work with a task force to create evaluation policy are charged with sharing outcomes of the teacher engagement process with that task force. In addition, they can (and should) share the results from these conversations with the broader teaching community at the school or within the district.

Some teachers on the engagement teams can also serve as moderators during the engagement events, although not all have to, and we encourage recruitment of moderators from outside the team as well. Not all moderators will be a good fit for leading planning of the engagement effort, and not all planning leaders will be good moderators.

The size and number of teacher engagement teams that are formed, and their makeup, depend primarily on the scale of the engagement initiative. If the initiative is districtwide, the geographical size of the district and the number of teachers in each school will be factors in deciding the makeup of teams. A district might consider convening one teacher engagement team per school (which is usually sufficient), and more can be formed in large schools. The sample plans in this chapter will better help you envision the best strategy for integrating teacher engagement teams into your approach. We also revisit the topic of teacher engagement teams in Chapter Six.

Once convened, these engagement teams can also foster dialogue and arrange communication and consensus-building activities around issues other than evaluation, such as length of the school day, professional development, compensation, and student technology policies. Using engagement teams in this way will contribute greatly toward building a culture of engagement within a school or district. More information on modifying these materials to facilitate meetings on diverse topics can be found later in this chapter, in the section "Engaging Teachers When Progress Is Already Under Way."

Timeline

The suggested engagement approach recommended in this book consists of three central activities to engage teachers on evaluation, as well as a number of optional activities that can further enhance the process. Chapters Six and Seven explore each activity in turn and describe how they uniquely contribute to the process of engagement.

A teacher engagement initiative incorporating these activities can occur under a number of scenarios and along a variety of different timelines. For example, it can be a large-scale, long-term process in which hundreds of teachers participate in multiple meetings. Such a scenario may determine evaluation policy in coordination with the state or district. Or the initiative can comprise a single meeting in a single school, with twenty teachers, to open the conversation and start building a culture of engagement. The engagement activities we describe in this book can fit either of these scenarios or any scenario in between.

The scenario you choose (or have capacity for) will determine the makeup of your teacher engagement team(s), the number of teachers you invite to the engagement events, your timeline, and your menu of activities. In the following section, we lay out three sample plans for planning the teams, to help you better envision the process.

THREE SAMPLE PLANS FOR TEACHER ENGAGEMENT

The engagement activities in this book are flexible and can be used whether your timeline is rushed or unhurried. The following sample plans are general guides to help elucidate some practical options for using the activities in this book.

Sample Plan 1: Multiple Conversations at the Table

This plan is best suited to a school or district that can dedicate at least a semester, if not a year or more, to teacher engagement. With so much time invested by teachers, it's advisable that, under this scenario, teacher input be very strongly considered in the school or district's evaluation policy planning. The engagement initiative should begin well in advance of the key decision-making period, and there needs to be a clearly determined plan for how insight gathered from participating teachers will be shared.

Ideally, the teacher engagement team should consist of between ten and twelve teachers. Considering that there will be many meetings, there will be a lot of logistics to consider, from inviting teachers to choosing locations to arranging for food to finding and training moderators. The team should divide up responsibilities as they see fit, and can even assign people to separate committees.

Depending on the size of the school or district, when all is said and done, it's possible that one hundred or more teachers would attend the different engagement events under this scenario. Regardless, there should be a core group that attends as many events as possible.

As shown in Table 5.1, this plan incorporates all of the Everyone at the Table activities suggested in this book. In between each activity, the engagement team should prepare for the next session and actively engage with key district decision makers to bring the voice of teachers to the policymaking table.

Table 5.1. Sample Plan 1: Multiple Conversations at the Table

Suggested Timeline	Duration	Activity and Description
Weeks 1–4	Ongoing	**Teacher Recruitment** During this time period, the teacher engagement team reaches out to all teachers in the school or district. The team works with their schedules, determines a calendar that provides enough time for ample discussion, and shares with teachers the plan for using their insight.
Weeks 1–4	Ongoing	**Moderator Selection and Training** The engagement team will select a moderator or moderators and provide them with any necessary preparation. (The number of moderators will depend on how many teachers sign up to participate. There should be one moderator per ten to twelve teachers.)
Week 5 or 6	1 hour	**Taking the Temperature Part 1: Consensogram and Taking the Temperature Part 2: Viewing the "Foundations of Evaluation" PowerPoint presentation** *Note*: this activity, and all subsequent activities, are best conducted with twelve to fourteen teachers. If more teachers sign on, you can lead different breakout groups, each group with its own moderator. These preliminary "taking the temperature" exercises will introduce the concept of engagement to participating teachers and determine the starting points in their knowledge and awareness of teacher evaluation.
Week 6 or 7	2 hours	**Dialogue Focus Group** (which includes viewing the "Engaging Teachers in Evaluation Reform" video) This focus group protocol presents three different scenarios for teacher evaluation. Each scenario contains different elements in different combinations, none of which are fully right or wrong. This approach offers a starting point for conversations about what an effective evaluation system might look like in your school or district. Teachers will work to build consensus, although it is okay if not everyone agrees and no final consensus is reached.

(continued on next page)

Table 5.1. *(continued from previous page)*

Suggested Timeline	Duration	Activity and Description
1–4 weeks later	75–90 minutes	**Interview** In this multistep exercise, each participant collects information about teacher evaluation in a fast-paced series of interviews with at least four other teacher participants.
1–4 weeks later	45–90 minutes	**Additional Resources and Jigsaw** This cooperative learning and reading exercise brings research-based findings to the table as teachers weigh in on the ideal evaluation system. Using a "divide and conquer" approach, teachers read different resources prior to the meeting in order to develop or build on expertise in a particular aspect of a topic. They then relay the key takeaways to the rest of the group in pairs and small groups, and then to the entire group.
1–4 weeks later	45–60 minutes	**Build Your Own Evaluation: Part 1** Drawing on Dialogue Focus Group discussion and materials, teachers build a consensus about which features should be included in the evaluation plan for a state or district. The results are compiled in **Build Your Own Evaluation—Group Handout 1** and **Build Your Own Evaluation—Group Handout 2.**
1–4 weeks later	45–60 minutes	**Build Your Own Evaluation: Part 2** The moderator brings printed copies of the **Build Your Own Evaluation—Group Handout 2** and shares them with the whole group. Additional teachers may be invited to this meeting. For further clarification, the group may wish to complete **Build Your Own Evaluation—Group Handout 3.** Depending on the reactions of the group, the moderator makes any necessary modifications before sharing the "ideal" evaluation system with the task force or committee, or with other leaders in the reform.

Sample Plan 2: A Few Key Conversations at the Table

This plan is best suited to a school or district that is able to dedicate several months to the process of engaging teachers on a teacher evaluation plan. Although a few months is not a great deal of time, it is enough to include a few key activities. The process should still begin well in advance of the decision-making period, and there should be a clearly determined plan for how the insight from participating teachers will be shared.

As this is a mid-scale initiative, the size of the planning team should be between six and twelve teachers. Table 5.2 shows what activities can be included and the timeline for the process.

Table 5.2. Sample Plan 2: A Few Key Conversations at the Table

Suggested Timeline	Suggested Time	Activity and Description
Weeks 1–2	Ongoing	**Teacher Recruitment** During this time period, the teacher engagement team reaches out to all the teachers in the school or district. The team works with their schedules, determines a calendar that provides enough time for ample discussion, and shares with teachers the plan for using their insight.
Weeks 1–2	Ongoing	**Moderator Selection and Training** The engagement team will select a moderator or moderators and provide them with any necessary preparation. (The number of moderators will depend on how many teachers sign up to participate. There should be one moderator per ten to twelve teachers.)
Week 3 or 4	1 hour	**Taking the Temperature Part 1: Consensogram and Taking the Temperature Part 2: Viewing the "Foundations of Evaluation" PowerPoint presentation** These preliminary "taking the temperature" exercises will introduce the concept of engagement to participating teachers and determine the starting points in their knowledge and awareness of teacher evaluation.
Week 4 or 5	2 hours	**Dialogue Focus Group** (which includes viewing the "Engaging Teachers in Evaluation Reform" video) This focus group protocol presents three different scenarios for teacher evaluation. Each scenario contains different elements in different combinations, none of which are fully right or wrong. This approach offers a starting point for conversations about what an effective evaluation system might look like in your school or district. Teachers will work to build consensus, although it is okay if not everyone agrees and no final consensus is reached. (You may also conduct a single, longer meeting combining the "Taking the Temperature" activities with the other key activities.)
1–4 weeks later	45–90 minutes	**One activity chosen from Chapter Seven, "Optional Activities for Teacher Engagement in Evaluation Reform"** The engagement team or the moderator chooses the optional activity that will best benefit the participating teachers, based on their input, attitudes, personalities, and knowledge gaps.

(continued on next page)

Table 5.2. *(continued from previous page)*

		For example: Try the **Interview Activity** if teachers have great rapport with each other and seem eager to chat. Try the **Additional Resources and Jigsaw Activity** if the teachers want to read more about issues of teaching, reform, and evaluation.
1–4 weeks later	45–60 minutes	**Build Your Own Evaluation: Part 1** Drawing on Dialogue Focus Group discussion and materials, teachers build a consensus about which features should be included in the evaluation plan for a state or district. The results are compiled in **Build Your Own Evaluation—Group Handout 1** and **Build Your Own Evaluation—Group Handout 2.**
1–4 weeks later	45–60 minutes	**Build Your Own Evaluation: Part 2** The moderator brings printed copies of the **Build Your Own Evaluation—Group Handout 2** and shares them with the whole group. Additional teachers may be invited to this meeting. For further clarification, the group may wish to complete **Build Your Own Evaluation—Group Handout 3.** Depending on the reactions of the group, the moderator makes any necessary modifications before sharing the "ideal" evaluation system with the task force or committee, or with other leaders in the reform.

Sample Plan 3: Core Conversations at the Table

Sometimes schools and districts may not have a long-term plan in place to work with teachers and integrate their views and values, but this shouldn't rule out an opportunity for engaging teachers. Perhaps the individual charged with organizing the engagement process has to report to the task force in a few weeks, or perhaps it is an informal process that a teacher (or group of teachers) is pursuing independently in order to talk things over with fellow teachers in a structured format, maybe even at a coffee shop. Perhaps a school is kicking off or trying out an engagement effort with a "sample preview" at a professional development or in-service day.

In such scenarios, a teacher engagement initiative can be much smaller. In any case, for the effort to be meaningful, it requires significant forethought and planning. This smaller effort can comprise four to six teachers. Table 5.3 shows what the engagement process may look like.

Table 5.3. Sample Plan 3: Core Conversations at the Table

Suggested Timeline	Duration	Activity and Description
Days 1–2	Ongoing	**Teacher Recruitment** During this time period, the teacher engagement team sends some emails to colleagues, employees, and teacher friends; posts the invitation in the staff room; and tries to gather as many RSVPs as possible to have a ballpark figure for how many teachers will show up.
Days 1–2	Ongoing	**Moderator Selection and Training** The engagement team will select a moderator or moderators and provide them with any necessary preparation. (The number of moderators will depend on how many teachers sign up to participate. There should be one moderator per ten to twelve teachers.)
Anytime between day 3 and your deadline	2 hours	**Dialogue Focus Group** (which includes viewing the "Engaging Teachers in Evaluation Reform" video) This focus group protocol presents three different scenarios for teacher evaluation. Each scenario contains different elements in different combinations, none of which are fully right or wrong. This approach offers a starting point for conversations about what an effective evaluation system might look like in your school or district. Teachers will work to build consensus, although it is okay if not everyone agrees and no final consensus is reached.
Anytime between day 4 and your deadline	60 minutes	**Build Your Own Evaluation: Part 1** Drawing on Dialogue Focus Group discussion and materials, teachers build a consensus about which features should be included in the evaluation plan for a state or district. The results are compiled in **Build Your Own Evaluation— Group Handout 1** and **Build Your Own Evaluation— Group Handout 2.** If time allows for subsequent feedback, participants can make modifications before the engagement team shares the "ideal" evaluation system with the task force or committee, or with other leaders in the reform.

For schools or districts that have time for only one meeting or are looking to test the waters during an in-service or professional development day, we suggest one three-hour meeting, combining the **Dialogue Focus Group** with Part 1 of the **Build Your Own Evaluation** activity, as outlined in Table 5.4. A teacher engagement team of four to six teachers should still be assembled. For a more detailed description of this particular scenario, see the "Dialogue Focus Group" section of Chapter Six.

Table 5.4. Sample Plan 3: One Core Conversation at the Table

Suggested Timeline	Duration	Activity and Description
Days 1–2	Ongoing	**Teacher Recruitment and Moderator Preparation** (if applicable) During this time period, the teacher engagement team sends emails to colleagues, employees, and teacher friends; posts the invitation in the staff room; and tries to gather as many RSVPs as possible to have a ballpark figure for how many teachers will show up. The engagement team should also still plan to recruit and prepare enough moderators (one for each group of ten to fourteen teachers). *Note:* If you are using this approach during an in-service or professional day, it may be the case that all the teachers who are present participate, and recruitment will be unnecessary. Moderator selection and preparation will still be a necessary step.
Anytime between Day 3 and your deadline	3 hours	**Dialogue Focus Group** (which includes viewing the "Engaging Teachers in Evaluation Reform" video) This focus group protocol presents three different scenarios for teacher evaluation. Each scenario contains different elements in different combinations, none of which are fully right or wrong. This approach offers a starting point for conversations about what an effective evaluation system might look like in your school or district. Teachers will work to build consensus, although it is okay if not everyone agrees and no final consensus is reached. **Build Your Own Evaluation: Part 1** Drawing on Dialogue Focus Group discussion and materials, teachers build a consensus about which features should be included in the evaluation plan for a state or district. The results are compiled in **Build Your Own Evaluation—Group Handout 1** and **Build Your Own Evaluation—Group Handout 2.** If time allows for subsequent feedback, participants can make modifications before the engagement team shares the "ideal" evaluation system with the task force or committee, or with other leaders in the reform

Of course, there are variations on each of the scenarios we've outlined here. Perhaps you, like Teach Plus Los Angeles, would like to convene a number of teachers—one hundred or more—from across the district for one event that includes the three-hour Dialogue Focus Group. Although it is only one event, there are a lot of logistical considerations, and you will need a number of trained moderators, so a large teacher engagement team is still advisable. Regardless of the approach you choose to take for a teacher engagement initiative, the sample plans here, along with the activities that follow, should help inform your vision and planning.

DRIVING THE INITIATIVE

The teacher engagement initiative can be teacher driven or leader driven. Although the latter scenario will, in all likelihood, lead more directly to a teacher evaluation policy that includes teacher input, teacher-driven engagement can still yield significant outcomes at the policy level. In addition, in an environment where leaders do not initially embrace the inclusion of teachers in decision making, positive outcomes from teacher-driven engagement may help leaders come to recognize the value of this approach and contribute to a broader culture of engagement, as discussed in the previous chapter. In this section, we outline suggestions and options for both teacher-driven and leader-driven engagement.

Strategies for Teacher-Driven Engagement

A teacher-initiated approach to teacher engagement could include a number of scenarios. The initiative could consist of informal brainstorming meetings with teachers on their recommendations for a teacher evaluation system for their school or district. The inclusion of teacher voice in policy decision making is optimal, but even if the outcomes do not directly influence policy, those involved in the engagement process will emerge with a more structured way of communicating teachers' ideas about evaluation with whoever is in charge of leading such reforms.

A teacher-driven initiative could also consist of a much larger, formal engagement process, similar to Sample Plans 1 or 2 described earlier, that directly informs policy. In this case, it is helpful to have the blessing and support of leadership in the school or district. To get leaders on board, teachers initiating a teacher engagement effort can and should present the methodology to a principal or other member of leadership who they feel will be supportive of the effort.

In a worst-case scenario, teachers who would like to initiate teacher engagement may be in a school or district where leadership does not support such an effort. Although this situation is certainly frustrating, teachers need not simply give up. Engaging peers and colleagues in these conversations is still a richly rewarding effort that helps teachers sort through the issues, wrestle with the trade-offs, and decide on what they really value and want to see in an evaluation system. Going through the exercise will prepare teachers to inform decision making if and when the current leadership becomes more supportive of teacher engagement. Furthermore, as we explored in Chapter Four, engagement and dialogue activities can themselves contribute to a collaborative culture and a supportive environment for teacher engagement.

Regardless of the scale of the teacher-driven engagement scenario, it is important that both teachers and relevant decision makers know and understand how teacher input will be shared; and open, honest, early, and repeated communication is key. Teachers want to know that their voices will be heard, and they will appreciate the incentive of knowing that someone—preferably someone in charge of designing evaluation reform—will hear what they are saying and take their input into account. We offer suggestions for how to do this in the "Guide to Next Steps" section of Chapter Six.

Strategies for Leader-Driven Engagement

Education leaders at the school, district, and state level can drive a teacher engagement initiative in a number of ways. Although the initiative itself should be owned and managed by teachers, education leaders can recruit teachers to lead the effort. They can also facilitate and support the communication between engagement teams and decision makers following activities.

Although it goes without saying, there may be strong personalities among the key decision makers in your school or district who will play a part in determining the scope of influence that teachers possess. Thoughtful and empowering leaders would welcome input from teachers when making such important decisions. It should be noted that we have created a *Leaders Involvement Guide* (http://www.everyoneatthetable.org/leadersGuide.php). This includes the "Involving Other School Leaders" video (http://www.everyoneatthetable.org/leadersVideo.php), which is aimed at helping districts, task forces, and other local education leaders understand the importance of engaging teachers in the evaluation reform process.

Education leaders can also facilitate the inclusion of teachers in any decision-making body that may exist. As described in Chapter Two, in a district or state that is confronting the need for evaluation reform, school or district leaders often approach the redesign with an established committee or task force. This task force represents voices from each critical group that will be affected by the reform— administrators, teachers from multiple grade levels and content areas, union or association leadership, principals, parents, the community, and others.

Teachers need to be a central component of this task force. Members of the teacher engagement team can and should sit on the task force, but we encourage a broader representation of teachers as well. Leaders in a school, union, or district can encourage teachers' active involvement—both as representatives on these task forces and as speakers at meetings. They may also be in a position to encourage the task force to involve teachers in this way.

After each team has gone through an engagement process with a broader community of teachers in a state or district (or at selected points during the process), the engagement teams will bring the takeaways and points of consensus and division to the task force for it to consider as it develops the evaluation plan.

The following suggestions—based on interviews and focus groups with teachers and administrators who served as part of a task force—should be considered when assembling a task force:

- This group will be the first set of experts convened to "pitch" the idea of policy and program reform, so the composition of the group must be carefully thought through. The teachers included on the task force should represent the diversity of schools, grade levels, and subjects, as well as the range of genders, cultures, and teacher age or experience levels that exist in a school or district.
- As noted in the discussion of teacher engagement teams, the teachers selected to participate on the task force should not be only the usual suspects.
- In cases where teacher representation is limited, the task force or committee can still invite additional teachers to present their views at meetings on specific topics.
- To ensure that teachers' voices are heard, critical decisions should be made by vote, and teacher representatives' votes should carry significant weight in the final decision.

Task force representatives can also consider engaging task force members using the activities in Chapters Six and Seven during meetings as a way to expand the dialogue beyond teachers.

TEACHERS TOLD US . . .

The following are other recommendations from teachers who have participated on district- or state-level teacher evaluation task forces:

- Devote a separate committee specifically to the task of teacher evaluation and make sure the issue gets focused attention.
- Only start when committee participation is determined and confirmed and all planning is done.
- Have meetings in the daytime, during teachers' regular hours.
- Throughout the process, make sure there are clear channels of communication and collaboration among administration, union, and teachers, and communicate early and often.
- Make sure that clear communication lines exist between the task force and teachers not on the task force.
- Don't back away from discussing sensitive issues.
- Give the task enough time. Give teachers and the task force the opportunity to really examine the details of the plan and make sure that it adequately describes what good teaching looks like.
- Clarify outcomes and be action oriented; avoid tangents during meetings.

ACTIVITY 2
Reflecting on Our Task Force

On your own or during your next task force meeting, take the following self-assessment to determine whether your task force represents teachers as well as you would hope:

1. Does our task force allow teachers to vote?
2. If yes, do teachers' votes carry significant weight?
3. Does our task force schedule meetings at a convenient time for teachers?
4. Does our task force include teachers who are not normally involved?
5. Does our task force include a representative sample of teachers of different subject areas, grades, experience levels, genders, and ethnicities?
6. Does our task force bring in the voice of teachers who are not members of the task force?

If you answered no to any questions, consider whether you wish to continue on the same path or make changes in the operations of your task force.

Bonus activity: Ask the teachers and non-teachers on your task force if their answers are in line with one another.

Once the group has been selected, a kickoff meeting will set the tone for the reform process. The conversation should not address nitty-gritty details but rather be high level and process oriented, addressing big-picture questions about how design and implementation of a new evaluation plan will unfold. For example, if the reform is state driven, what are the elements that districts and schools can control? What elements will require collective bargaining with the union? What are the decision points that teachers can weigh in on? Will there be a pilot process? What is the overall timeline for reform?

To initiate the broader conversation about evaluation planning needs in a school or district, other early task force meetings may include the following topics:

- Defining highly effective teaching
- Conducting a gap analysis of the current evaluation system in relation to the required or ideal system
- Mining the "bright spots" to identify the positive aspects of the existing system that can be retained
- Determining the overall structure of the new system, or understanding the new structure if a mandated state framework has been introduced

This meeting provides an opportunity for the leader or leaders guiding the engagement process to vet their vision of the process and for teachers on the planning teams to understand and weigh in on appropriate decision points for teacher engagement. Task force members can also make recommendations regarding who should lend expertise to the planning and design of the evaluation system, goals for the system, and meeting norms to be established. The initial meeting serves to inspire those involved to recognize both the need for reform and the potential that it brings. One option for task force representatives from the teacher engagement teams is to bring the takeaways from the kickoff meeting to the teams to explore points of existing consensus on evaluation goals and the broader vision of the plan.

Advance Illinois teacher leader Jake Gourley demonstrates one way for district leadership and teachers to work together and drive an engagement process that leads to an effective and well-received teacher evaluation system:

Getting the Right People at the Table

One Leader's Quest to Build Trust and Transform a School District Through Collaboration

Ask Jake Gourley for advice on how to ensure the success of new teacher evaluations, and he will tell you that it's all about getting the right people to the table. Gourley, an award-winning government teacher at an underperforming suburban high school in Illinois, played a central role in doing just that. The result is a new system that not only has been well received by teachers but also has contributed to unprecedented levels of collaboration and cooperation among administrators, the local school board, and the teachers' union.

According to Gourley, although the district was not yet required by the state of Illinois to implement a new process, both the administration and union felt that "it would be to our advantage to be ahead of the curve instead of waiting to see what might come down the pipeline." By starting early, Gourley's district was also able to take the time to pilot new evaluations instead of implementing the "real thing" in the first year.

The district established a joint committee of administrators and teachers, and spent an entire year collaboratively planning, designing, and then piloting the new evaluation system. Teachers—together with administrators—helped design preconference conversations that were much more like interviews than the old "Let's take a look at your grade book" format, structured what informal and formal observations would look like, held tough conversations on potential measurements of student growth, and set up post-evaluation meetings where the whole team walked through each evaluation looking for red flags.

"Knowing that the first year was a pilot allowed us to build teacher understanding of the evaluation's purpose, as well as the flexibility to identify strengths and weaknesses of the new instrument—both of which helped boost trust in outcomes."

Gourley, who also serves as his local union president, worked aggressively to get teachers involved. "In recent years, I found that administrators were far too willing to go it alone." He felt that this contributed to a feeling of distrust—not only in the building and at board meetings but also in his school's existing teacher evaluation procedures. "Teachers were not active partners in the process, they didn't feel good about what they gained from their evaluations, and frankly felt the whole process was more of an obstacle course than a means to improve instruction."

"I knew if we were going to be successful in developing and building a new evaluation system that would both meet the state's requirements and deliver meaningful information to teachers about how to better serve our students, we had to have open discussions, frequent communication, and, of course, have everyone at the table."

In recruiting teachers to serve on the district's joint committee (whose role would be to design and agree on the district's new measures of teacher effectiveness), Gourley looked for individuals who were strongly invested in the school's curriculum work. "In selecting teachers, we took note of who regularly attended the school board's curriculum meetings. To me, there's such a strong relationship between the strength of the curriculum and the whole evaluation process. By looking at various aspects of the evaluation, including measures of where students are (and are not) mastering the curriculum and meeting standards, teachers will be able to see gaps in instruction and address them through alterations in instruction, learning new strategies from other teachers, or focused professional development."

Gourley also looked for those who had demonstrated collaboration skills. "We were focusing on those who were passionate but who were also willing to hear other vantage points. We also tried to get new people involved. This helped us keep the conversation open and away from prior issues that might have bogged us down."

The joint committee also worked to address the time barrier. "For many teacher leaders, competing priorities can derail committee work. To combat this, we appointed an alternate and second alternate for each teacher representative. Alternates were provided immediate updates after each meeting—whether they attended or not—through both materials and face-to-face conversations. If a teacher representative had a conflict, the alternate was already 'in the loop' and could step in to keep the work moving forward. This approach lessened the burden for teacher representatives and also promoted regular, ongoing communication."

Gourley also credits changes at the building level with creating a culture of openness and collaboration that supported a successful evaluation reform process. Specifically, at one of the district's high schools, the administrators restructured the master schedule to provide teachers with shared professional development time.

"When all the teachers in a particular content area share a common professional development period, three days a week, teachers start to see what their peers are doing, share what has or hasn't worked, and become willing to try new things. We saw a kind of renaissance of teacher engagement and enthusiasm. And, even though the common planning time only lasted one year, the trust and camaraderie extended into the evaluation pilot period. People no longer thought twice about sharing their experiences."

Gourley is also a member of the Educator Advisory Council (EAC) at Advance Illinois, an education advocacy organization. The EAC was established by Advance Illinois to ensure teacher voice in state-level education policy, and is made up of approximately twenty recognized teacher leaders. The EAC engages in multiple roles, ranging from developing a set of policy recommendations aimed at elevating the teaching profession to serving on Illinois State Board of Education (ISBE) committees and task forces to offer teachers' professional knowledge and perspectives.

Being a member of the EAC provided Gourley with additional resources and support as he worked on teacher evaluation reform in his district. "It was great to have the inside track. As laws and rules would come out, Advance Illinois would have those things in our hands the next day. To be able to go into the joint committee meeting and say, 'Right now the State Board [ISBE] is talking about this topic' gave me more credibility with the local administration and empowered me as one of the participants. At the same time, Advance Illinois legitimately seeks input from teachers and passes on our perspectives to legislators and state policymakers."

Although the shift to a more positive climate has brought a dramatic change, challenges still exist. For teachers who were assertive and tried to demonstrate leadership in the past, only to be reprimanded and written up, "Old wounds take a long time to heal. . . . It's hard to build trust when you still have personalities involved who were mistreated in the past." Gourley has found that clear, honest communication does the most to counter the harms of the past.

It is worth noting that in fall 2012, just after the pilot year completed, the district's school board ratified a three-year teachers' contract a full year ahead of schedule. Gourley believes that it is safe to attribute the successful, early completion of negotiations to the collaborative climate built while working on curriculum and evaluation issues.

Sources: Interview with Jake Gourley, June 27, 2012, and Elizabeth Dierksheide, May 9, 2012.

ENGAGING TEACHERS WHEN PROGRESS IS ALREADY UNDER WAY

Although we strongly advocate for teacher engagement from the earliest stages of the decision- and policymaking processes, most states have already begun a process of evaluation redesign, often with an inauthentic or suboptimal teacher engagement initiative or with no teacher input at all. In these situations, education leaders can find themselves going back to the drawing board on a number of elements—which they thought had been settled—because those elements end up being unrealistic or difficult to implement.

In these instances, it is particularly helpful to gather teacher input on what is realistic and implementable, and this can be done using the strategies and materials outlined in this book. Although the key Everyone at the Table Choicework discussion guides and materials are designed for schools and districts in the beginning phases of redesign, the documents (available online at www.every oneatthetable.org) are fully customizable and can be tweaked to align with a school or district's unique circumstances. When developing customized Choicework materials, it is important to heed principles that will invoke thoughtful deliberation of a variety of strategies. These include the following, derived from *You Can't Do It Alone* (Johnson, 2012):

- The choices should be realistic and plentiful enough to get people out of yes-no thinking but not too many to overwhelm them. Three or four choices generally work best.
- Employ language and concepts that teachers use and are familiar with, and avoid jargon.
- Offer a variety of choices across a spectrum of viewpoints, and describe the choices in neutral, nonpolitical language.
- Each choice should be presented both with its most positive attributes and with its trade-offs clearly spelled out.
- Focus on the ethics and values inherent in each choice. Whom does it affect and how? Does it match our vision for a supportive school environment that yields the best outcome for kids? Why may some be opposed to this choice?
- The choices should get people thinking about a general direction and not impel them to or suggest that they choose one of the three or four.

You may also wish to revisit the explanation of Choicework in Chapter Four.

One example of teacher engagement in a district that is already knee deep in the reform conversation is the Hazelwood School District in Missouri. In Hazelwood, the district task force solicited some teacher input in the earliest stages of redesigning the evaluation system and later determined that further input from teachers across the district would help guide the decisions that were yet unresolved. The engagement conversations focused on decision points that were of particular interest to the task force at this later stage in the reform process, such as,

- Should observations by master teachers who are external to the district be for informal purposes only, or should they count toward teachers' final evaluations?
- What is the ideal length of time that observers should spend in the classroom?
- If the task force decides to incorporate student surveys into evaluations, what weight should they constitute?
- How should the student learning objectives (SLO) measure adopted by the task force be set—by teachers individually, through professional learning communities, by evaluators, or by district administrators?

By engaging teachers in dialogue about the new system, even after some preliminary decisions had already been made, the district's evaluation task force was able to make more informed decisions while at the same time giving staff across the district an opportunity to reflect on and lead conversations about their practice and how it should be assessed. The new frameworks, observation instruments, SLO guidance, artifact reviews, and goal-setting and professional development plans are being piloted in the 2013–2014 school year, a process that will benefit from the foundation set for two-way teacher communication and engagement during the planning stage.

TEACHER ENGAGEMENT IN ACTION: DETROIT, WASHINGTON, AND COLORADO

In addition to the example of Hazelwood, here we review three real-life examples of teacher engagement on teacher evaluation redesign: at the school level in Detroit, Michigan; at the district and state level in Washington; and at the state level in Colorado. These examples demonstrate how schools, districts, and states across the country have tackled the task of including teachers in decision making.

Engagement at the School Level: Detroit

At the Nataki Talibah Schoolhouse charter school in Detroit, Michigan, several curriculum leaders in the school intended to talk to teachers about evaluation during an upcoming in-service meeting. After hearing about Everyone at the Table during a statewide educator effectiveness meeting in February 2012, the school's principal decided to use the methodology in this book to structure the discussion. She selected a handful of teachers to moderate several dialogue groups during the in-service day. The moderators and the principal had an informal training session via phone with the Everyone at the Table team. On the scheduled day, all the teachers in the school broke into small discussion groups, each led by a moderator.

Calling this meeting "one of the most meaningful conversations" they had had in a long time, teachers were able to work through various elements of teacher evaluation and find common ground on what they wanted—and did not want—included in their evaluation. Most of the teachers who participated in the dialogue shared similar views and values in regard to how a teacher should be evaluated. None were in favor, for example, of the outside observer option that is present in some teacher evaluation conversations across the nation. The teachers also agreed that even if a new evaluation policy did not directly reflect their considerations, the act of having talked through the issues was itself a beneficial one. As one teacher explained, "It's nice if everyone is heard, even if you aren't able to get what you want. And then when decisions are made, you know everybody talked about it and agreed on it, not just one person making the decision."

Engagement at the District and State Level: Washington

When the Washington State legislature passed Engrossed State Senate Bill 6696 in 2010, stakeholder engagement was a top priority of the leaders at the Office of Superintendent of Public Instruction (OSPI). In the interests of serving the dual purposes of communicating about the new policy changes and hearing from educators and community members about their ideas and concerns, the OSPI leaders convened ten regional forums.

These regional forums were supported by the state's network of Education Service Districts (ESDs) that exist to support the districts in their region. The ESDs provided meeting space, coordinated recruitment efforts, and handled logistics related to refreshments, room setup, and communication with participants. Meanwhile, OSPI staff traveled across the state to present in person at each of the ten regional forums. Their presentation was followed by one-hour focus group discussions, in which participants were divided into four groups: teachers, principals, district administrators, and community members. Each group had a moderator to lead, record, and later summarize the discussion, which was framed around questions such as these:

Current Evaluation

1. Tell me about your current evaluation process. What does it entail?
   Probe: How often are you evaluated? By whom?
   Probe: How helpful is the feedback you get?
   Probe: Is your pay or professional development or career progression affected by your evaluation results?
2. What do you like best about the current evaluation process?
3. What is not working well with the current evaluation process?
4. How are principals evaluated?
5. What components would you like to see in principal evaluation?

Future Evaluation

1. If you were to design your own teacher evaluation system, what would it look like?
2. What role do you think the state should play in teacher evaluation?

Examples

- Develop a model teacher evaluation rubric that school districts can consider adopting
- Monitor the evaluation systems in districts or the evaluation scores of individual teachers
- Create laws that require certain rewards or sanctions for teachers who receive strong or poor evaluations

Understanding of New Legislation

1. How familiar are you with the contents of Senate Bill 6696?
   a. Never heard of it before today's forum
   b. Somewhat familiar
   c. Very familiar
2. What do you like about Senate Bill 6696?
3. What most concerns you about Senate Bill 6696?

More recently, OSPI charged districts that participated in the state's evaluation pilot project to conduct district-level facilitated discussions using the Everyone at the Table materials as a basis. Each district was assigned one topic area: rater agreement, student learning growth, or human resource decisions. Using discussion protocols and a discussion summary template designed by the state, districts were required to hold at least two conversations with teachers and principals and to provide summaries of key priorities, ideas, and concerns to OSPI to guide its decisions. Moreover, each district was required to present these findings at a state-sponsored convening to which legislators and statewide education organizations were invited to listen and engage in dialogue alongside OSPI staff.

Engagement at the State Level: Colorado

In Colorado, legislation was passed in 2010 mandating evaluation reform that included little initial involvement or support from the teaching force. Recognizing the benefits of an all-hands-on-deck approach, the state included myriad opportunities for teacher participation at a later point in the process and therefore serves as an example of engaging teachers in the middle of the redesign process.

In designing the state's evaluation law (Senate Bill 10-191), the legislature mandated the creation of a State Council on Educator Effectiveness (SCEE), which would report to the State Board of Education (SBE) on recommendations and guidelines for definitions and standards of teacher and principal effectiveness; guidelines for a fair, rigorous, and transparent system; and recommendations for state policy changes regarding evaluation.

The SCEE included fifteen members, appointed by the governor, with union-member teachers holding more positions than any other group. In addition, teachers were heavily represented on eleven technical advisory groups (TAGs). Each TAG collaborated on recommendations for specific assigned topics, including teacher and principal standards, student growth, and parent and guardian involvement. These recommendations were then integrated into the appendix of the SCEE's *State Council for Educator Effectiveness Report and Recommendations,* which serves as the basis of the state's law.

Teachers were also critical members of the state's Content Collaboratives, along with external content experts, assessment professionals, and a team from the Colorado Department of Education. These collaboratives focused on creating high-quality and accurate student assessments, aligned with state academic standards, for the purpose of informing teacher evaluation system improvements. In future years, the collaboratives will focus on professional development to support teachers' instructional practice.

The following activity will help you envision a clear and lucid engagement strategy for your unique situation, as well as plan for potential challenges.

ACTIVITY 3
What's Your Plan?

Take a moment to reflect on the following questions:

1. What are our goals and intended outcomes?
2. What is our time frame?
3. Given this time frame, which sample plan best fits our district? [Refer back to Activity 1 to choose the best sample plan for your circumstances, if you haven't done so already.]
4. How many teacher engagement teams are appropriate for our school or district?
5. Will our engagement approach be teacher driven or leader driven? Is a task force strategy or a grassroots strategy more appropriate for our situation?
6. What concerns do we have about this plan?
7. How can we address these concerns?
8. Whom else do we need to speak with before taking our next steps?
9. How will we regularly revisit our progress, address challenges that may arise, and maintain momentum for the long term?
10. How will we determine success? How will we measure real outcomes against our intended outcomes?

We hope that the timelines, strategies, and activities in this chapter, combined with the examples of teacher engagement in practice, have adequately prepared you to spark an engagement initiative in your school or district. The following two chapters provide explicit instructions on specific, field-tested activities that generate authentic engagement of teachers.

CHAPTER
SIX

Strategies for Ensuring Authentic Engagement in Evaluation Reform

At this point in the process, the individual or individuals who have taken ownership of initiating the teacher engagement effort in a school, district, or state should

- Understand the difference between dialogue and debate or negotiation, and know how to encourage the former over the latter
- Be familiar with the principles of authentic engagement, return continuously to evaluate how the effort is aligning with those principles during each step of the process, and be prepared to share and explain these principles with and to others
- Know how the engagement process will unfold: either as a small-scale, informal, teacher-led effort or as a formal feedback channel for a school- or district-level task force
- Have a timeline in mind for the process
- Have established teacher engagement teams

Once these elements are in place, it is time to move to the engagement process itself. This chapter and Chapter Seven describe a specific group of exercises for facilitating effective and productive conversations with teachers that foster sustainable policy. The chapters provide thoughtfully designed yet modifiable activities with lesson plans and handouts, offer best practices for moderating effective and authentic teacher engagement activities, and outline strategies to overcome obstacles.

The process outlined in this chapter not only engenders sound engagement but also accelerates participants' Learning Curve on teacher evaluation in the following way (see Chapter Four to review the Learning Curve framework):

1. **Consciousness-raising.** The introductory activities establish the starting-point knowledge and views of teachers. They also build awareness of the facts and issues at hand.

2. **Working through.** The main dialogue focus group activity (and subsequent optional activities) help teachers work through the potential trade-offs inherent in different evaluation plans.

3. **Resolution.** The **Build Your Own Evaluation** activity helps track points of consensus, confusion, and disagreement and provides you with a concrete tool to bring back to decision makers so that they may incorporate the views of teachers.

THE ROLE OF TEACHER ENGAGEMENT TEAMS

At this point, the teacher engagement teams can, and should, take ownership of organizing and facilitating the engagement process, although other leaders in the effort should be familiar with the activities and should regularly check in with the teams.

The teacher engagement teams are the planning teams in this process, and they will organize the nuts and bolts, recruit participants, manage moderators and recorders, and coordinate follow-up and liaise with school and district leadership. You may wish to review the initial discussion of teacher engagement teams in Chapter Five and refer to the box "Teacher Engagement Teams" in this chapter.

Strategies for Recruiting Teachers to the Conversation

One key task of teacher engagement teams is to recruit teachers to participate in the engagement activities. Optimally, teacher participation should represent the diversity of the school or district. As we have previously emphasized, these conversations should include more than just the "usual suspects." If the dialogue includes only those teachers who tend to be vocal or who are already involved, the vital voices of other teachers will be left out. As a result, the overall message

TEACHER ENGAGEMENT TEAMS

Teacher engagement teams are groups of teachers who help organize the engagement process within a school or district and liaise with school and district leadership.

Teacher engagement teams work in concert with the school's or district's task force to implement engagement. Ideally, some members of the teacher engagement team would also be on the task force.

Some engagement team members can also serve as moderators, but not all moderators need to be on the team. Teacher engagement teams should convene on a regular basis.

Here are some additional recommendations for convening teacher engagement teams:

- The size of teacher engagement teams will depend on the scale of the initiative. Of course, no teachers should be turned away, and larger teams or multiple teams should be accommodated.
- It may be appropriate in your context to divide engagement teams among elementary, middle, and secondary levels. Alternatively, depending on the geographical size of your district, it may be appropriate to convene engagement teams based on location.
- A district can have as many teacher engagement teams as it desires, depending on the number of teachers and their interests. It makes sense to convene one engagement team per school.
- For additional recommendations on establishing and defining teacher engagement teams, please refer to the "Engagement Teams" section of Chapter Five.

brought to the table by teachers may become less credible to teachers and administrators alike. The following strategies will help engagement teams reach out to and include all teachers.

- Using emails, flyers, and word of mouth to spread the word about the discussions and their purpose is helpful in encouraging a diversity of teacher voices. We have included a downloadable and customizable **Sample Teacher Recruitment Invitation** in the next section.
- Personal outreach will also help boost participation. We recommend following up an email invitation with a phone call or in-person conversation about the invitation and the initiative.
- In schools and districts with a union presence, union representatives should be recruited and included in these discussions. A formalized partnership with the teachers' union may also be advisable, depending on the situation. Union

leaders and representatives can also take a guiding role in the process (and may even be the ones driving the engagement).

- The time and location of meetings should be designed to accommodate as many teachers' schedules as possible and to be as convenient as possible. It might make sense to vary the time and location of these meetings so that all teachers can participate. It is also possible (although not ideal) to hold these conversations during all-staff in-service or professional development days when nearly all teachers are present.
- There should be enough time to allow for discussion and brainstorming. Typically, one class period would not be enough, and most of the recommended activities require at least one-and-a-half hours.
- Providing snacks, coffee, and other refreshments can create a more relaxed atmosphere. It can also convince teachers who are uncertain about participating to come along for the discussion.
- The sooner teachers can be engaged, the better. It is never too late to involve teachers, but earlier is definitely better.

Sample Teacher Recruitment Invitation

A downloadable and customizable Word version of this **Sample Teacher Recruitment Invitation** is available on the Everyone at the Table website under "Getting Started: Recruitment Strategies" at www.everyoneatthetable.org/gs_recruiting.php.

Understanding the Role of Moderators and Recorders

As discussed in Chapter Four, a skilled moderator is a key element of authentic engagement; and, as we explain later, note-takers—what we call recorders—are important as well. This section describes qualities teacher engagement teams should look for and cultivate as they choose and train moderators and recorders, as well as specific tasks and duties for each. The principles and strategies here are drawn from extensive work in the field of public engagement and compiled in Public Agenda's *Community Conversations Planning Guide* (2012a) and *Facilitator's Handbook* (2012b).

Qualities of the Effective Moderator

Individuals who are selected by the teacher engagement teams to moderate these conversations should be familiar with the materials in this book, though they

Join the Conversation on Evaluating Teacher Effectiveness!

Please join your colleagues for a lively and important focus group discussion about approaches to evaluating teacher effectiveness.

Who: All teachers at [insert school or district name]

What: This [insert name of activity, such as a focus group discussion or other activity] is intended to provide teachers with an opportunity to engage in thoughtful, constructive dialogue on the important topic of measuring teacher effectiveness. The key ideas raised in this dialogue will be brought back to [insert who key decision makers are (for example, the task force or the school board)] by way of [insert how you will share teacher input]. Input from this [insert activity] will inform the conversation as key decisions are made about the design of a new evaluation system for [insert name of district or school].

When: [insert date and time]

Where: [insert place]

Why: So that your voice can be heard!

Light refreshments will be served. Please RSVP by [insert date] to [insert name] at [insert email or phone number].

For more information, please visit the Everyone at the Table website at http://www.everyoneatthetable.org.

---

need not be experts. Generally, effective moderators demonstrate the following skills, knowledge, and background:

- Group facilitation skills and experience, especially in working with diverse groups and with the general public (as opposed to working only with professionals).
- An ability to create an environment in which participants feel safe and comfortable expressing their views.
- An ability to help people articulate the reasoning, experiences, and values behind their positions.
- An ability to challenge participants (in a friendly, civil way) to consider alternate viewpoints.
- Comfort with, and an ability to manage, group conflict.

- An ability to take a nonpartisan moderating stance.
- Nonpartisan credibility. Some people may be able to moderate in a nonpartisan manner but will not be viewed as nonpartisan by members of the group because of past associations.
- Some general familiarity with the issue at hand, although expertise is not required. This attribute is less important than the others.
- Some diversity. Ideally, a moderator team will roughly reflect the demographics of the community being engaged, so it is often a plus to have some diversity of race, ethnicity, gender, and the like among the moderators.

Responsibilities and Objectives of the Effective Moderator

At the most basic level, the task of the moderator is to make sure that the participants in the small group discussions understand what they are supposed to be talking about at any given time so that the discussions stay focused and on schedule. Throughout the conversation, the moderator should make sure that points are well understood by everyone in the group. To this end, it is often helpful to occasionally summarize the discussion to both clarify positions and refocus the conversation when necessary. If there are important points or arguments that are not being covered during the dialogue, the moderator should introduce them. Beyond this, the moderator's job is to make the conversations as participatory and productive as possible. To achieve this, a moderator

- **Creates an environment where people are comfortable expressing ideas.** The materials in this book are carefully designed to foster an environment in which people can honestly explore their thinking and that of others, and engage in constructive and stimulating dialogue about an important public concern. The moderator can contribute to this by establishing a relaxed but focused tone for the session and modeling honest and straightforward, yet civil and respectful, communication.
- **Remains impartial about the subject.** Moderators must avoid expressing their own opinion and must be aware of other, less obvious or purposeful ways in which they may ascribe value to participants' comments—for example, they need to be careful to avoid saying things like "Interesting point!"
- **Does not take on an "expert" role with the subject matter.** A moderator's role is not to teach the participants about the issue—even if it is a subject he or she knows very well.

- **Models cooperative attitudes and skills.** By exhibiting strong listening skills and asking good questions, moderators can model the behaviors that participants will (one hopes) adopt.
- **Manages the group well.** A moderator helps find the right balance between having too much and too little structure to the conversation.
- **Keeps the deliberation focused and on track.** When comments deviate from the topic at hand, a moderator brings participants back to the goals of the session. Moderators should make sure that the goals are clear, even if the conversation is wide ranging.
- **Encourages everyone to join in the conversation.** A major goal of moderators (particularly early on in the discussion) should be to involve as many people as possible. This does not mean making everyone participate equally; rather, it involves creating a situation where everyone has an opportunity to speak, and occasionally checking with people who have not spoken to see if they have anything they would like to add to the discussion. A moderator must be careful in this task. Comments like "That's a good idea" may make the speaker feel welcome in the conversation, but participants who disagree may think the moderator is being biased.
- **Does not allow individuals or subgroups to dominate the discussion.** Encouraging everyone to participate carries with it two key challenges: (1) managing the contributions of the dominant personality, who will talk at such length or with such force that less aggressive members of the group fade into the background; and (2) managing the contributions of those with greater experience and expertise (such as the educators in the room) who simply have more fully formed views and can talk at greater length.

Moderators should not feel the need to police these issues too tightly. A common mistake of novice moderators is to jump in too quickly if someone appears to be "getting out of line." In our experience, it is best to initially let things play out and to allow the group to react and deal with the individual or situation without interference. This is usually all that is needed.

From time to time, however, moderators may need to intervene to keep the conversation open, constructive, and accessible to everyone. The ground rules you set for the discussion (more on this later) will help you do this. A good moderator

- **Intervenes as necessary.** If the conversation begins to focus on personalities rather than issues, a moderator gently reminds the group of the guidelines or refocuses the dialogue back on the issue. An effective moderator creates an atmosphere of acceptance for all ideas and persons and helps give an equal hearing to all perspectives.

- **Asks clarifying questions when necessary.** If the moderator is not sure what a participant means, there is a good chance that others are unsure as well. Moderators may ask participants to clarify what they are trying to say and may paraphrase what a participant has said to ensure that their meaning is understood correctly.
- **Helps people examine their own views, understand the views of others, and communicate effectively about the issues with diverse members of the group.** Moderators should help participants explain why they feel the way they do—for instance, have they had particular experiences that have led them to their current views? In post-meeting surveys, most participants in dialogues facilitated by an effective moderator state that they heard opposing views that had merit and that they reconsidered one of their own positions at least once. Moderators can facilitate these outcomes by looking for ways to encourage people to examine their views, articulate and explain them more clearly, and hear the views of others and perhaps respond to them.
- **Asks thoughtful and probing questions to surface trade-offs and consequences.** A moderator makes sure that participants have considered the potential outcomes of their comments and ideas.
- **Helps participants find common ground and identify and work through key tensions.** Participants will not always agree and may sometimes be in direct conflict with one another. Helping them identify common ground and key tensions will help move the conversation forward in important ways.
- **Encourages deeper reflection.** A moderator will ask participants to share what is important to them about the issue or why they feel a particular approach or strategy is valuable.
- **Helps people prioritize their ideas for action.** Helping people move from exploratory dialogue to concrete action planning is an important role of an effective moderator.

A Note on Group Conflict
Beginning moderators are often anxious about encountering conflict, but what we have found is that groups often wish to avoid confrontation and therefore strive to minimize their conflicts and reframe them as areas of common ground.

This can artificially conceal assumptions that should be exposed and real tensions that need to be explored. It is important, therefore, that moderators take an accepting attitude toward group conflict and disagreement—an attitude that communicates, "This is normal and useful to our understanding."

Moderators should look neither to agitate disagreements nor to shy away from them, but rather should help the group identify and clarify areas of conflict and disagreement, as well as determine which conflicts are trivial and which are more substantive. If the group wants to focus on a particular conflict, moderators should help participants make as much headway as is realistically possible in a short discussion. Later in this chapter, we offer strategies for addressing conflict in a diplomatic and productive manner (see the section "Strategies for Overcoming Obstacles and Troubleshooting").

The Recorder's Role

It is a good idea to have someone other than the moderator taking notes of the discussion so that subsequent teacher meetings can build on the ideas that have previously been raised. The notes also can be used at meetings with the task force or other key decision makers to accurately capture and communicate teachers' ideas and concerns.

Throughout the small group session, recorders will make notes of the discussion on flip charts, and this will allow moderators to concentrate on managing the flow of conversation.

The recorder's job—noting the major points during small group discussions—is a crucial one. Although the recorder is not expected to write down word for word everything that is said, he or she should try to capture the essence of the main points being made by each participant.

It is especially important to record not only each person's position ("I'm for such-and-such"), but also each person's thinking ("I'm for such-and-such because . . ."). It is equally important that recorders do their best to keep their own views out of the way and to record the proceedings as faithfully as possible.

Some practical tips include:

- Recorders should use a flip chart so that the group can see the document being created. On the first sheet, recorders should be sure to identify which group is being recorded and to number the pages as they go.
- Recorders shouldn't worry about noting people's names; they should rather record their perspectives and ideas.

- Recorders should write as large and as legibly as possible without slowing down.
- Recorders can occasionally ask the group or moderator to clarify a point if it is unclear or if things have moved too quickly.
- Ideally, recorders will be able to remove each finished page and tape it onto a wall so that participants can see the pages when they are ready to summarize their conversation. Some rooms don't have walls that work for this, and it is important not to miss anything, so if it's not possible to get the sheets up on a wall, the recorder should simply flip them over as they fill up and keep writing.

Understanding Common Ground

These conversations will help teachers who may come to the conversation with divergent viewpoints to move toward common ground, or a working consensus. The goal of the conversations is *not* to achieve a perfect consensus among all participants; rather, it is to facilitate a positive and stimulating conversation among equals that allows views to be articulated and examined. In this way, we hope the dialogue will clarify

- Areas of common ground
- Important disagreements that will require continued dialogue
- Questions and concerns that deserve further attention
- Ways in which the community can act together on behalf of students and schools

Requiring everyone to completely agree before a conversation is over could actually stymie the honest sharing of opinions—no one wants to be the hanging juror. Figure 6.1 gives some clarifications on building common ground as opposed to achieving consensus.

READY? SET? GO! ABOUT THE ACTIVITIES IN THIS CHAPTER

The remainder of this chapter will walk you through the key activities of *Everyone at the Table,* and it includes moderator "lesson plans" and sample teacher handouts, all of which may be downloaded and modified from the Everyone at the Table website.

We recommend three separate meetings for the three activities, but we understand that this is not possible in all circumstances. Even if there is time for only

Figure 6.1. Clarifications on Building Common Ground

Building common ground means . . .	Building common ground does not mean . . .
All group members contribute.	All group members agree.
Everyone's opinion is heard and encouraged.	The result is everyone's first choice.
Differences are viewed as helpful.	There are no differences in opinion.
Everyone can paraphrase the pros and cons.	Everyone possesses a complete understanding.
Those who disagree agree to give the group's choice a try, at least for a certain period of time.	Conflict and resistance will be overcome immediately.
All members share in the crafting of a decision and understand the trade-offs inherent in that decision.	All members lend their full-fledged support to a decision.
All members agree to take responsibility for implementing the final decision.	All members must advocate for the decision.

Source: Adapted from Arbukle and Murray, 1989, as cited in Regional Educational Laboratory Network Program, 1995, pp. 15–24.

one meeting, it may be sufficient, provided that the meeting is a productive one. If you have time for only one meeting or if you are looking to test the waters with a pilot meeting before including a broader audience, it is possible to incorporate the three activities into a three-hour meeting (although this is not encouraged). If only two hours are available, we recommend the two-hour **Dialogue Focus Group** option. This activity is the most crucial, and insightful, step.

To help you envision the strategy that you will pursue, here are some options for using the materials in this chapter:

3 meetings

> Taking the Temperature: 30 to 60 minutes
> Dialogue Focus Group: 2 hours
> Build Your Own Evaluation: 1 to 2 hours

2 meetings

> Dialogue Focus Group, with a condensed Taking the Temperature activity: 2 hours
> Build Your Own Evaluation: 1 to 2 hours

1 meeting

> Dialogue Focus Group, with condensed Taking the Temperature and Build Your Own Evaluation activities: 3 hours

While reading through these activities, you may find it helpful to refer back to the sample plan you selected from the previous chapter to help you choose the activities that best fit your unique situation and to envision where they fit into the process.

Before the Conversations

Designing a meeting where teachers are able to sit down together and talk honestly about something close to their hearts can be a demanding and sensitive process. It is important to keep certain logistical considerations in mind so that the process does not break down simply because, for example, the video is not working. Here are some obvious but critical (and easily overlooked) things to consider prior to the meetings:

1. **Room setup.** Set the room up in a way that is conducive to discussion and sharing. Arranging the seats in a large circle, and around a table if possible, allows everybody to see one another as they interact. Having the option of moving chairs or using breakout rooms for smaller group brainstorming sessions is also recommended. Any distracting background noises should be minimized.
2. **Audiovisual equipment.** Several of the activities in this chapter will require audiovisual equipment. Always test all the equipment in advance and check for quality sound projection.
3. **Goals and processes.** Be clear, frank, and specific about the goals of these sessions—both for the initiative broadly and the activities individually—and about the processes for sharing input from these sessions with school or district decision makers. These goals and processes should be established *before* the meeting begins. We have explained the intended goals for each activity in this chapter. To avoid any misunderstandings, these goals should be communicated when recruiting participants and at the start of each meeting. You may also have some of your own goals to add.

Opening Up the Conversation

At the kickoff meeting for the engagement initiative, we suggest beginning the discussion with the following opening steps and introductory talking points. It may also be useful to reiterate them at subsequent meetings, especially if new teachers have joined the conversations.

- Provide the agenda and any handouts for the meeting.
- Welcome the teachers and thank them for participating.

- Indicate the purpose of the discussion.
- If you do not intend to include Taking the Temperature Part 2: The "Foundations of Evaluation" slide show, you should still provide information on the national, state, and district backdrop.
- Emphasize the importance of teachers being involved in teacher evaluation reform.
- Explain to participants how their input will be shared with decision makers—with the superintendent, the principal, the evaluation task force, or the teacher representative on the task force. (Again, we strongly recommend that you carefully think through how teachers' ideas and concerns will be shared, prior to launching this process.)
- Typically, leaders will take teachers' input into consideration, but ultimately make their own decisions about the evaluation design. To avoid misunderstanding, we recommend that you state up front that teachers are not making a policy decision but rather are informing those who are making the decisions.
- Emphasize the following rules for constructive dialogue. We also recommend posting these ground rules on the wall in large writing:
  - Be honest and respectful.
  - Listen to understand.
  - It is okay to disagree, but do so with curiosity, not hostility.
  - Build on each other's ideas, but do not speak over one another.
  - Be brief so that everyone has an opportunity to speak.
  - Put your phones on vibrate or turn them off and resist the temptation to check email or multitask.

STRATEGIES FOR STRUCTURING PRELIMINARY ACTIVITIES: TAKING THE TEMPERATURE ON TEACHERS' CURRENT KNOWLEDGE OF EVALUATION CONCEPTS

The goal of the preliminary Taking the Temperature activities is as their name suggests: they are intended to gauge teachers' starting knowledge on the various concepts around teacher evaluation and to ensure their familiarity with those concepts. Collecting this information means that you can avoid alienating participants by talking about concepts that they are not familiar with, and you can avoid boring them with explanations of concepts that they already know about. This activity helps you assess teachers' current knowledge and then provide an initial overview of the topic to help develop a shared understanding of the options and a common language for discussion.

There are two exercises included in this part of the process:

Taking the Temperature Part 1: Consensogram activity. This activity helps you assess teachers' current knowledge and build a common vocabulary through an interactive rating process.

Taking the Temperature Part 2: Viewing the "Foundations of Evaluation" slide show. Through this PowerPoint presentation, you will familiarize teachers with the key teacher evaluation concepts that are being considered in your district. (We provide a modifiable template for the Power Point at www.everyoneatthetable.com.)

Timeline. If you do have time to include this step, it should take place prior to the **Dialogue Focus Group** activity or any other activity.

Together, these two Taking the Temperature activities can make up the first engagement team meeting (one hour). It is also possible to condense these activities into thirty minutes and include them at the start of your **Dialogue Focus Group** activity.

TAKING THE TEMPERATURE PART 1: ALTERNATIVE ACTIVITIES

Although the Consensogram activity is an innovative, interactive, and strongly visual way to measure current knowledge, teachers sometimes don't have the time to dedicate half an hour to the process.

It is easy to measure current knowledge in other ways that would take only five minutes at the beginning of an engagement meeting—this task can then be folded into the beginning of the main Dialogue Focus Group activity.

Current knowledge can be shown through a simple show of hands. If organizers would like to approach the activity in an innovative or visual way, they can use flags or signs, or they can incorporate a clicker activity, provided they have the technology.

For a discussion of clicker activities, including best practices and suggestions, please refer to "Click to Engage: How Keypads Can Enhance Learning and Deliberation," available on the Public Agenda website at http://www.publicagenda.org/pages/click-to-engage.

If time is limited, it is easy to incorporate a more succinct version of this activity. (See the box "Taking the Temperature Part 1: Alternative Activities," for suggestions.) This five-minute version can be included in either the two-hour or three-hour version of the **Dialogue Focus Group** activity.

Taking the Temperature Part 1: Consensogram Activity

A consensogram is a chart that indicates a group's perception of various topics. Members of the group place stickers on the chart to show their responses. By observing the stickers, one can tell at a glance where the group stands.

Moderator's Lesson Plan: Consensogram Activity

Time
About 30 minutes

Overview
Teachers will explore common teacher evaluation topics to determine the group's starting point knowledge of teacher evaluation.

Purposes
The specific purposes of this activity are as follows:

- Assess teachers' knowledge
- Build a common vocabulary

Room Setup
You will need an easel and one sheet of chart paper in a central place in the room.

Materials
- One sheet of chart paper
- Easel
- Large marking pens
- Several sheets of circle-dot stickers (red, yellow, green, and blue)
- Copies of the teacher handout **Consensogram Group Process**

Instructions
 Before the Activity

1. Position the moderator area front and center so that it is easily visible to all participants.

2. Using the large markers, write the following teacher evaluation topics on chart paper before the session (these topics are suggested as starters). Leave plenty of space between items.
   - Peer assistance and review
   - Value added
   - Observation rubrics
   - Multiple measures
   - Multiple performance levels
   - Sole evaluator
   - Measure weights
3. Familiarize yourself with the topics so that you are fully able to make any needed clarifications.

During the Activity

1. Point out the teacher evaluation topics written on the chart paper.
2. Demonstrate your own knowledge of each topic by putting a circle-dot sticker next to it:
   Red: Help! What is this?
   Yellow: I vaguely know what this means.
   Green: All is well; this makes sense to me.
   Blue: I could stand up and explain this in my sleep!
3. Ask participants to take their stickers and place the appropriate color sticker next to each topic.
4. Let participants know that there are no right or wrong answers. The purpose is simply to indicate how familiar they are with different concepts so that you can speak more about the areas in which there is not a lot of current understanding.
5. Lead the discussion to determine which concepts are more or less understood.
6. Focus additional time on less understood topics.

Teacher Handout: Consensogram Group Process

A downloadable and customizable Word version of the **Consensogram Group Process** is available on the Everyone at the Table website under "Getting Teachers Talking: Teacher Handouts" at www.everyoneatthetable.org/gtt_hand outs.php.

Consensogram Group Process

Step 1: Next to each term on the chart, place the appropriate circle-dot sticker to indicate your level of understanding of the concept as it relates to teacher evaluation.

> *Red:* Help! What is this?
> *Yellow:* I vaguely know what this means.
> *Green:* All is well; this makes sense to me.
> *Blue:* I could stand up and explain this in my sleep!

Step 2: After all participants have posted their stickers, the group will analyze and synthesize the information through the following questions:

- Which concepts are well understood?
- Which concepts are not well understood? Who can explain them?
- What other terms have you heard that you do not fully understand?

Taking the Temperature Part 2: Viewing the "Foundations of Evaluation" Slide Show

The "Foundations of Evaluation" slide show (available as a modifiable template on the Everyone at the Table website at www.everyoneatthetable.org/gtt_powerpoint.php) should be used early on. In addition to providing teachers with a basic overview of key teacher evaluation concepts that are being considered in your district, it also helps develop a common language about the elements of an evaluation system.

Note: It is perhaps most appropriate to present the slide show after teachers have completed the Consensogram activity, when you have a sense of teachers' current knowledge base. We recommend presenting the slide show prior to conducting the **Dialogue Focus Group** activity.

Moderator's Lesson Plan: "Foundations of Evaluation" Slide Show

Time
About 30 minutes

Overview
Teachers will view the "Foundations of Evaluation" slide show and be able to ask questions as needed.

Purposes
The specific purposes of this activity are as follows:

- Increase teachers' knowledge of evaluation
- Build a common vocabulary

Room Setup
You will need to set up chairs so that participants can easily view the slide show.

Materials
- Laptop, projector, and screen for slide presentation
- Copy of the "Foundations of Evaluation" slide show

Instructions

Before the Activity

1. Test-run the slide show and make sure that the projector works.
2. Make sure that you are familiar with the content (notes are provided in the slide show).
3. Modify the slides in advance to include district background and other state- and district-specific information.

During the Activity

1. Briefly introduce the slide show.
2. When presenting, spend more time on the slides that address less well understood concepts.
3. Allow time for additional questions and discussion.

STRATEGIES FOR STRUCTURING ESSENTIAL ACTIVITIES FOR PROMOTING TEACHER CONVERSATIONS

Dialogue Focus Group Activity

Ideally, the engagement process will allow time to complete the preliminary activities to ensure that teachers share a common understanding of key concepts and terminology. However, we understand that this is sometimes impossible—the process may be on a fast track, or initiators of the process may not have discovered these materials until late in the game.

If time is limited and only one activity is possible, **this is the one to do!**

Overview of the Activity
This activity consists of five parts:

- Making introductions.
- Watching the video "Engaging Teachers in Evaluation Reform" (available on the Everyone at the Table website at www.everyoneatthetable.org/gtt_video.php).
- Reading and discussing **Three Scenarios for Teacher Evaluation**.
- Discussing next steps.
- Filling out the **Discussion Summary**. This task is completed by the moderator and recorder.

About the Three Scenarios for Teacher Evaluation
The **Three Scenarios for Teacher Evaluation** activity, appearing later in this chapter, is the Choicework component of this process, and it helps structure this intense and important conversation in a productive way. (See the section "The Power of Choicework: Framing for Deliberation" in Chapter Four to review the concept of Choicework.) Each scenario describes a hypothetical school with a specific evaluation approach (each of which has different elements) and includes a series of questions to prompt dialogue.

These three approaches are provided to give some context and to initiate your discussion. The purpose of these scenarios is not to choose which approach is best but rather to establish a platform for discussing the pros and cons of various options in a more concrete—rather than theoretical—manner. Although the conversation will undoubtedly transcend the three-scenario basis, we still recommend that you incorporate discussion of the individual scenarios, as this will tease out teachers' reactions to ideas and policies that are often unfamiliar to them.

TIPS FOR MODERATORS

Moderators for the Dialogue Focus Group activity should be sure to review qualities and objectives of effective moderators. (See the earlier section "Understanding the Role of Moderators and Recorders" in this chapter.) Here are some additional tips:

- Foster critical, reflective thinking through such probes as the following:
  - Can you elaborate on that?
  - Why do you think that was the case?
  - Tell us more.
- Steer the conversation to focus on solutions and problem solving rather than on airing grievances, using probes such as these: How would you suggest getting around that? What would you suggest instead?
- If participants grow negative or disgruntled, use a similar tactic for questioning.
- If participants are quiet, walk through each prompt question instead of just letting the conversation flow. Use prompts for participants to build on one another's points.
- Continually ask the group to compare and contrast aspects of the scenarios to keep all the options at the forefront of their minds.
- Play devil's advocate if the discussion seems to veer toward one specific idea.
- Encourage participants to ask questions.
- Practice using "wait time," three to five seconds of silence after asking a question or starting a discussion.
- Acknowledge all responses either passively or actively and with a neutral demeanor.

Moderator's Lesson Plan: Dialogue Focus Group Activity

Time
Two hours (with the Build Your Own Evaluation component: three hours)

> *Two-hour meeting variation:*
> Group orientation, introductions, and ground rules (15 minutes)
> Introduce and discuss Choicework (50 minutes)
> Discussion summary: common ground, concerns or disagreements, outstanding questions (10–20 minutes)
> Next steps (30 minutes)

Three-hour meeting variation:
> Group orientation, introductions, and ground rules (10 minutes)
> Introduce and discuss Choicework (50 minutes)
> Discussion summary: common ground, concerns or disagreements, outstanding questions (10–20 minutes)
> Build Your Own Evaluation (50 minutes)

Overview
This is the key activity for engaging teachers. If you do nothing else, this is the activity to do! After the participants introduce themselves and watch the "Engaging Teachers in Evaluation Reform" video, you will provide the handout **Three Scenarios for Teacher Evaluation**. The scenarios and the accompanying moderator prompts have been created to serve as a guide for your discussion, but you may wish to slightly modify the content to reflect the realities of your district at this point in time. All of the materials used for this activity are available as customizable Word documents on the Everyone at the Table website.

If you have time for a three-hour meeting, we strongly recommend that you begin the **Build Your Own Evaluation** activity immediately after discussing the three scenarios. This activity involves using a tool from which teachers choose, "à la carte," the various components of an ideal teacher evaluation system for their district. Alternatively, you can include this component of the discussion in a follow-up meeting. This meeting should take place fairly soon after the dialogue session so that the insights gained remain fresh in people's minds (optimally within a week).

Purposes
The specific purposes of this activity are to help teachers engage evaluation issues in ways that enable teachers to

- Master some basic concepts and facts and build a common vocabulary
- Reflect on their values and think critically and creatively about solutions
- Work through trade-offs and values conflicts
- Build common ground on how to improve teacher evaluations

Room Setup
You will need a large meeting table with chairs around it.

Materials
- Laptop, projector, and screen for the video "Engaging Teachers in Evaluation Reform"
- Flip chart and marker for note-taking

- Copies of the **Three Scenarios for Teacher Evaluation** for all participants
- Copies of **Build Your Own Evaluation—Group Handout 1** for all participants if you are using the three-hour variation
- Moderator copies of the prompt questions to promote discussion

Instructions

Before the Activity

1. Make sure that the video works (including lighting and sound quality). It is recommended that you familiarize yourself with the video prior to showing it to the group.
2. Review the three scenarios and the question prompts in detail.
3. If a recorder has not been chosen in advance, designate a participant before the discussion begins and review his or her duties with him or her (see the section "The Recorder's Role" in this chapter for more information). You and the recorder will later work together to fill out the **Discussion Summary**.

During the Activity

A. Group Orientation, Introductions, and Ground Rules (15 Minutes for Two-Hour Variation; 10 Minutes for Three-Hour Variation)
   1. Introduce yourself and explain your role.
   2. Explain the purpose and rationale of the meeting and explain what will happen.
   3. Let the teachers know that you will be summarizing the results of the discussion and filling out a Discussion Summary that will be shared with administrators or other stakeholders. However you decide to share the information, it is critical that you share this fact up front with the teachers in your meetings.
   4. Conduct a brief round of introductions, especially if the teachers present are not already well acquainted. One way to begin is to have each participant state his or her name, the subject(s) and grade(s) taught, years in the classroom, and school (if participants are from more than one school). We recommend making a seating chart for yourself, indicating names, grades, and subjects. This will help you manage the conversation, especially early on when you are trying to get everyone involved.
   5. If there is time remaining in the ten to fifteen minutes allotted for introductions, you may wish to use the following questions to prime participants for the discussion, open up the conversation, and get teachers thinking about teacher effectiveness. You can modify the questions for your context.

- What made you decide to come to this meeting today?
- Do you consider yourself an effective teacher? Why or why not?
- Do you think that most teachers in the profession are effective? What makes you think that?
- What initially influenced you to become a teacher? What do you like best about this profession? Least?

6. Establish ground rules. Cover any simple ground rules you might want to apply to the discussion. We recommended a number of ground rules in the earlier section "Opening Up the Conversation." You should also consider writing down these rules and posting them in a highly visible location. Here are some example talking points you could use:
   - "Let's all work together to keep the conversation on track and to make sure everyone has an equal chance to speak."
   - "We want this to be a session where people feel free to express their views and where they can consider the views of others. It is okay to agree with others, and it is okay to disagree as well. We just ask that you disagree with ideas, not with people. In other words, let's keep this constructive and avoid getting personal."

B. Introduce Choicework and Discuss (50 Minutes)

Introducing the Choicework Materials

1. Let the teachers know that the next part of the activity involves viewing the video "Engaging Teachers in Evaluation Reform." This nine-minute video is intended to get teachers thinking about the different ideas that are presented and to get them excited about the conversation.

2. Before showing the video, provide a short introduction for the group. It helps to introduce the video along these lines:

   "To help us get the conversation started, we're going to watch a short video about including teacher voices in the discussion of evaluation reform. It was filmed with teachers and administrators from around the country who had conversations very similar to the one that your group will be having after the video.

   "The video presents three different approaches to teacher evaluation. After we watch the video, I'm going to ask you which view is closest to your own, and we can start talking about it. You may also have other ideas that aren't on the video, and we can talk about those as well. I hope that you will feel stimulated and inspired after the video and that we can have a very engaging and thoughtful discussion."

3. Show the video.

Reading and Discussing the Scenarios

1. After the video, begin by explaining to the teachers that they've just heard three different ways of looking at teacher evaluation and that you are now going to look at those approaches more in depth. Let participants know that the next activity is to use the scenarios presented in the video as a way to discuss the kind of teacher evaluation approach that would be most helpful to teaching and learning. Distribute copies of the **Three Scenarios for Teacher Evaluation** and give the group a few minutes to review the approaches by saying something like, "The handouts will help you review the choices you just heard about in the video and give you a little more detail about each one. Let's take just a few minutes to review them quickly now individually and then we'll start our discussion."

2. Explain that you want to get things started by asking the teachers which scenario is closest to their own thinking. Tell them that they do not need to stay with their first choice or agree with every aspect of the scenario they choose—they may admire something in another choice or want to put something on the table that is not in the choices at all—but explain that finding out which choice is closest to their view will help get the conversation going. Ask for a show of hands: "How many lean more toward Scenario A? How many lean more toward B? How many lean toward C?" Then begin to ask people *why* they leaned one way or the other, and your discussion has begun.

3. As people talk about their "first choices," use the questions related to each scenario to prompt discussion around the individual elements of that scenario, tease out the pros and cons, and generally deepen people's thinking about the many important issues embedded in teacher evaluation reform.

If people are talking to you (the moderator) rather than to each other, it can be helpful to connect their points so that they can react to one another. If you were discussing the video, for example, you might invite a proponent of Scenario A to respond to a comment made by a champion of Scenario C to help the group realize that it is okay to react to one another's statements.

C. Discussion Summary: Common Ground, Concerns or Disagreements, Outstanding Questions (10–20 Minutes)

1. After the Choicework phase of your discussion, take ten minutes or so to work with the group on the following three summary questions for this first phase of the conversation:

- In our conversation about teacher evaluation, have we discovered any common ground? What do we agree on or have in common?
- What were our important areas of disagreement—the things we would have to keep talking about to work out our differences and move ahead?
- What are the questions and concerns that need more attention? Are there issues about which we need more information?

    Recorder: If you have not done so already, put three flip-chart pages labeled Common Ground, Disagreements, and Questions/Concerns up on the wall. (We recommend putting them up from the beginning, both to save time and because they can be helpful along the way.)

    Explain to the group that you will be covering all three summary topics in a limited amount of time, and encourage everyone to focus. Begin with Common Ground (although you might start jumping around to the different pages as the discussion unfolds). Following are tips for helping manage the discussion summary portion of the activity (Public Agenda, 2012a).

- You should briefly "process" each suggestion by a group member to make sure that most people are comfortable with having it go up on one of the charts. Ask, "Does everyone agree that that was an area of common ground?" before putting it up on the chart. If the issue can't be resolved quickly, it can become a question for further discussion on the Questions/Concerns chart.
- It is important to discourage people from introducing new material here—the task is to sum up the previous conversation, not begin a new one.
- This is one instance where you can introduce your own observations, as can the recorder. If, for example, the group is missing a point of disagreement that you recall clearly, you might say, "I seem to recall some disagreement about _____. Is that accurate?"
- You do not need 100 percent agreement to list something as "common ground." If most people agree (about three-quarters or more), list the item as common ground. Minority views can usually be noted under Questions/Concerns.

D. Next Steps (30 Minutes, Two-Hour Variation Only)
For the two-hour meeting variation, the following questions are options to help the group discuss next steps and sort through the common ground,

disagreements, and outstanding questions that you've arrived at through your dialogue. Choose the option that would be most helpful, depending on your context:

1. Based on today's dialogue, what are our best recommendations to the administration about how a new evaluation reform should be designed and how teachers can continue to have a voice as the design and implementation process unfolds? (Here, the process can include brainstorming followed by prioritizing recommendations.)
2. What are our next steps? Should we
   a. Invite more teachers to engage in the kind of conversation we had today?
   b. Have a follow-up meeting to further explore the issues that were raised today?
   c. Make recommendations to the administration about our thinking?
   d. Something else?
   (In a sense, this is another Choicework conversation, and you will need to figure out how to help them drive it toward a conclusion.)

You may also choose another closing activity that makes sense to you given the situation in your school or district.

If time allows for the three-hour meeting variation, Part 1 of the **Build Your Own Evaluation** activity can be included following the discussion summary. This activity is discussed in the following section.

After the Activity

1. After the teachers have finished discussing teacher evaluation, thank them for their input.
2. As moderator, you then have the task of completing the **Discussion Summary**. We suggest that you fill out this form within twenty-four hours of the Dialogue Focus Group meeting, in collaboration with the recorder.
3. You may wish to send the completed **Discussion Summary** to all the teachers to confirm that it accurately represents their viewpoints. Ultimately, this summary should be shared (verbally or in writing) with key decision makers in the school or district.

Teacher Handout: Three Scenarios for Teacher Evaluation

A downloadable and customizable Word version of **Three Scenarios for Teacher Evaluation** is available on the Everyone at the Table website under "Getting Teachers Talking: Teacher Handouts" at www.everyoneatthetable.org/gtt_handouts.php.

Three Scenarios for Teacher Evaluation

Scenario A: Principal-Centered Approach

What if . . . your principal implements a new system of teacher evaluation that he or she says gauges the quality of the faculty in a rigorous but equitable way? The principal is the sole evaluator, and he or she tries to match up the teachers' evaluation scores with fair and equitable rewards (and, if necessary, sanctions). He or she uses the following measures to create robust evaluations for every teacher:

Frequency

- The principal formally observes all the teachers on staff at least once per year and up to four times a year for nontenured teachers.
- The principal also conducts informal "walk-throughs" of teachers' classrooms, often visiting without warning.

Measures

The principal uses a four-point rating system (*Distinguished, Proficient, Needs Improvement, Unsatisfactory*) that incorporates the following:

- Formal observations (completed by the principal)
- Teacher-submitted portfolios, chronicling growth over the year and any formal professional development
- A student survey conducted at the end of the year

Consequences

- The principal is not shy about giving more than a few teachers unsatisfactory ratings on their year-end evaluations and giving critical—but in most cases effective—feedback. On the flip side, he or she regularly praises teachers openly during faculty meetings if they are doing well, and his or her feedback always comes very soon after an observation.
- He or she is well known for denying tenure to a high proportion of new teachers, but is willing to coach them toward tenure for the future.

Scenario B: Teacher-Centered Approach

What if . . . your district takes a teacher-centered approach to developing evaluations? This system was created with teacher input; in fact, several faculty members sit on the Evaluation Task Force, a committee that oversaw the design and implementation of the system as well as any subsequent modifications. The faculty members on the Evaluation Task Force serve as liaisons with their colleagues in their schools. The evaluation system includes an appeals process through which teachers may work with the Evaluation Task Force and administrative team to produce actionable strategies following a poor review.

The robust evaluations have the following characteristics:

Frequency

- All teachers are formally observed three times a year—once by the principal and twice by their peers.
- Every teacher writes and submits a professional growth plan for each nine-week period, as well as a final professional growth plan at the end of the year. These documents include a teacher's goals for that nine-week period plus a reflection on the feedback given during observations.

Measures

- **Principal observations.** The data collected during principal-led observations translate directly into targeted professional development sessions.
- **Peer observations**
  - Consulting teachers (experienced teachers in different grades or subjects in your school who have performed well on past evaluations) conduct peer reviews several times each year; these reviews are accompanied by meetings in which the reviewed teachers have the opportunity to respond to feedback and ask questions.
  - Several of the consulting teachers serve on the Evaluation Task Force, so these peer-review meetings also offer an opportunity for teachers to provide critical feedback on the program itself.
  - Teachers may "customize" their evaluation plan each year, choosing (with input from their consulting teachers and within certain guidelines) to weight some measures more heavily depending on their subject area and other factors.

Consequences

- Struggling teachers are assigned to an in-house mentor.
- If a struggling teacher continues to receive low marks on peer reviews for three years in a row, he or she is counseled out of the profession (that is, fired, but gently).

Scenario C: External-Centered Approach

What if . . . teacher effectiveness is determined on the basis of student test scores and observations by a core group of external evaluators? The evaluation system does not allow for teacher input, but it does come with hefty financial rewards. Teachers who receive high evaluation scores and have good test results are given a significant bonus.

The robust evaluations have the following characteristics:

Frequency

Teachers are formally evaluated at the end of each year based on both their students' test score growth and the ratings they receive from external evaluators, who conduct four observations throughout the year.

Measures

- **Formal observations.** Formal observations are conducted solely by a team of external evaluators—former teachers who have been extensively trained and have experience with the content and the grade level. They have little or no background knowledge of a school's context. At least one of these observations is conducted remotely via video. The evaluators rate each teacher on a four-point scale (Distinguished, Proficient, Needs Improvement, Unsatisfactory) four times per year and provide extensive written feedback about the lesson, highlighting areas of strength as well as where teachers could improve. Teachers can also review the video to get a better understanding of what the evaluators are seeing.
- **Informal observations.** The principal conducts informal walk-through evaluations. These walk-throughs are not taken into account during evaluations or bonus-pay decisions.
- **Growth-based testing.** Teacher effectiveness is also measured according to students' gains in test scores. Tests are given to students at the beginning of the year and toward the end of the year, and the growth of a student is measured by the difference in the two scores.

Consequences

- For teachers who score low on the rating scale multiple times in one year, the principal will conduct formal observations, provide his or her own feedback to those teachers, and suggest any individual professional development that is needed.
- The external evaluators will help shape the overall schoolwide professional development planning and implementation based on all teacher evaluations.

Questions for the Moderator to Ask About Scenario A

The following questions are recommended to prompt discussion (and keep it going):

- What do you think about Scenario A? What do you like about it? What do you dislike about it?
- Some say that principals are the ones who ought to do all the formal observations that count as your evaluation. After all, they are the leader of the school, and it is their responsibility. Others worry that principals just do not have the time to evaluate the entire staff and still handle their other responsibilities. What do you think?
  - Who else should be responsible for observations?
  - If more than one person is conducting observations, how can you make sure that each person is using the same criteria for evaluation?
- Some say that experienced teachers who have done well on past evaluations do not need to be observed every year and that continuing to evaluate them takes time away from the principal's observing teachers who really need it. Others say that all teachers could benefit from being observed at least once a year (if not more) regardless of their experience. What do you think?
  - How often should new teachers be observed? How often should tenured teachers who have received good evaluations be observed?
- Some say that teacher-created portfolios give teachers a chance to highlight the work and professional development they have done outside the classroom and should be part of the evaluation; others say that portfolios are very subjective, do not really illustrate what a teacher has done, and show only how much time the teacher has spent making a portfolio. What do you think?
- Some say that it makes a lot of sense to include student surveys as part of the evaluation—as long as the questions are written in a way that is fair and non-biased—because students are the ones who really know how the teacher is teaching. Others say that students can never really be unbiased; they will favor the teachers they like, regardless of whether teachers are good at teaching or not. What do you think?
- Some people like the idea that the principal often gives unsatisfactory evaluations and blunt feedback, because it gives teachers the tools and the desire to be more effective. Others say that this type of scoring and feedback is not helpful, that the negativity is actually a barrier to improvement. What do you think?

- Do you like the idea of having a four-point rating scale (Distinguished, Proficient, Needs Improvement, Unsatisfactory)? How would that make the evaluation different from what you have now?
- Now that we have discussed Scenario A, what do you think about the features described in this approach? Does anyone have a different opinion? Please share.

Questions for the Moderator to Ask About Scenario B

The following questions are recommended to prompt discussion (and keep it going):

- What do you think about Scenario B? What do you like about it? What do you dislike about it?
- Some say that it is important for teachers to be extremely involved in the evaluation process, from defining their own goals and documenting performance to doing observations themselves and being involved in defining the review goals. Others point out that because teachers already work such long hours (often with low compensation and little prep time), it is wrong to ask them to do so much more. What do you think?
- Some say that writing and revising a professional growth plan is an important way for teachers to understand, incorporate, and reach their goals. Others say that sharing professional growth plans and using them as part of the evaluation are time consuming for the teacher and really offer no value. What do you think?
- Some say that having your peers evaluate you is a good idea because your fellow teachers know more about teaching in your school than anyone else. Others say that having teachers evaluate other teachers can lead to competition and less collaboration among peers. What do you think?
- Some say that counseling teachers out of the profession, even after three years of poor evaluations and professional development, is too harsh. Some teachers need more time to succeed. Others say that this makes sense; even teachers with tenure who do poorly on evaluations three years in row should leave. What do you think?
- Now that we have discussed Scenario B, what do you think about the features described in this approach? Does anyone have a different opinion? Please share.

Questions for the Moderator to Ask About Scenario C

The following questions are recommended to prompt discussion (and keep it going):

- What do you think about Scenario C? What do you like about it? What do you dislike about it?
- Some people say that having external observers is the only fair way to perform teacher evaluations. External evaluators will have knowledge in a particular subject and grade level. Others say that unless the observers really know a particular school and its students well, they cannot conduct a good observation. What do you think?
- Does having a video of your teaching, that you can review as well, make a difference in your consideration?
- Some people think that using student test scores as part (but not all) of the teacher's evaluation is important; they believe that such scores measure student growth and aptitude and are essential for determining if students are really learning or not. Others think that student testing, in any form, should never be part of a teacher's evaluation. What do you think?
- Are there other ways to tell if teachers are really helping students grow? What are they?
- Some people say that having a bonus based on individual evaluations allows teachers who do well, regardless of seniority, to get more money than they would otherwise. Others say that having bonuses takes away from the collaborative nature of teaching and will hurt the profession overall. What do you think?
- What if the bonus is very large, but to fund the bonus, teacher raises are then smaller?
- Now that we've discussed Scenario C, what do you think about the features described in this approach? Does anyone have a different opinion? Please share.

Teacher Handout: Discussion Summary

A downloadable and customizable Word version of the **Discussion Summary** is available on the Everyone at the Table website under "Getting Teachers Talking: Teacher Handouts" at http://www.everyoneatthetable.org/gtt_handouts.php.

Discussion Summary

Instructions: The moderator should fill out this form within twenty-four hours of the dialogue focus group meeting in collaboration with one other participant who was designated as a recorder prior to the meeting. Note that it may not be possible at this point to answer all questions in Part 2.

Part 1: Three Scenarios for Teacher Evaluation

On _____, 20____, a group of _____ [#] _____ [grade level] teachers from _____ School District convened for a focus group discussion on measuring teacher effectiveness. In the discussion, we reviewed three scenarios for teacher evaluation: a principal-centered approach, a teacher-centered approach, and an external-centered approach.

On most topics, the teachers

❑ 1   ❑ 2   ❑ 3   ❑ 4   ❑ 5
(agreed)   (disagreed)

- The key themes that emerged in the conversation were:

- Of the three approaches reviewed, teachers were *most* in favor of Scenario ____.
- The reasons they like this approach were:

- However, their concerns about this approach included:

- Participants had a high level of agreement for the following:

- Participants disagreed over the following:

- Participants were most excited and enthusiastic about:

- Participants were least excited and enthusiastic about:

- Other aspects of evaluation that they supported or had concerns over—and the reasons why—were as follows:

- We [can/cannot envision] creating a system that would overall satisfy the group because:

Part 2: An Ideal Evaluation System for Our District

On _____, 20____, a group of _____ [#] teachers from _____ School District convened for a focus group discussion on measuring teacher effectiveness. In the discussion, we talked about the merits of different components of an ideal teacher evaluation system.

On most topics, the teachers:

❏ 1	❏ 2	❏ 3	❏ 4	❏ 5
(agreed)				(disagreed)

It was generally agreed that an ideal evaluation system for _____ School District would include the following:

- The individuals who should conduct observations are [for example, principal, peers, and so on]:

- The frequency of observations for tenured teachers should be _____ announced per year, _____ unannounced per year.
- The frequency of observations for nontenured teachers should be _____ announced per year, _____ unannounced per year.
- Aside from teacher observations, the evaluation system would include the following measures of teacher effectiveness [for example, surveys, teacher portfolios, and student test score growth]:

- The weighting of these measures would be approximately as follows:

- The evaluation results would be tied to professional growth and development in the following ways:

- The evaluation results also would be tied more tightly to the following [for example, career ladder, dismissal, tenure, and compensation or nonmonetary rewards]:

- Other aspects of the evaluation system would include the following:

Build Your Own Evaluation

After teachers have examined evaluation from different angles, reflected, and conversed with each other, this activity helps teachers move from dialogue to action by encouraging them to build their ideal evaluation scenario for their own particular context. We suggest that this activity be completed immediately after the discussion of the **Three Scenarios for Teacher Evaluation** or after further engaging teachers with the additional optional activities (see Chapter Seven). We strongly suggest that you do *not* do this activity without first completing the **Dialogue Focus Group** activity. The reflective and in-depth discussion that teachers will have in the Dialogue Focus Group activity will help teachers better understand the nuances, benefits, and consequences of their preferences when it comes to teacher evaluation, will likely affect their responses in the **Build Your Own Evaluation** activity, and will result in much more meaningful information for decision makers.

The evaluation that the teachers build is another tool that you can take to the key decision makers in your school or district (for example, the task force, the committee, the superintendent, or the school board).

Ideally, this activity would take place over two final teacher engagement meetings, and for this reason we have broken the activity down into Parts 1 and 2. In the first meeting, we suggest that teachers use the **Build Your Own Evaluation— Group Handout 1** to build common ground on which features should be included in a teacher evaluation system. Using Scenarios A, B, and C from **Three Scenarios for Teacher Evaluation** as a template, the group should then collaboratively take the findings from this activity (informed by the Dialogue Focus Group around the three scenarios and any other additional activities) and begin to outline a one-page scenario for teacher evaluation in your school system using the **Build Your Own Evaluation—Group Handout 2**.

If there is time and interest in delving into greater detail about the different components of the evaluation system and how teachers can be involved in the process of making these more detailed decisions, use **Build Your Own Evaluation—Group Handout 3**. This handout will help work through additional teacher evaluation details that will need to be addressed by those implementing the new policy.

Prior to the final meeting (Part 2 of the activity), you should type up, polish, and print out the teacher-created scenario (**Build Your Own Evaluation— Group Handout 2**) and share it with the group. At this stage, additional teachers can be invited to share their reactions to this created scenario. Based on their reactions, further modifications can be made (if appropriate) before the "ideal" evaluation system is shared with the task force or other leaders of the reform.

Having participated in ongoing facilitated discussions about teacher evaluation in the context of your school or district, the teachers should be in a strong position to defend their choices and communicate their rationale to other teachers, district leaders, the community, and beyond.

Moderator's Lesson Plan: Build Your Own Evaluation

Time

If you are including this activity in the three-hour **Dialogue Focus Group** meeting variation, we suggest allocating a maximum of fifty minutes for this discussion so that participants don't grow weary. If you are having a separate meeting (or two meetings) for the **Build Your Own Evaluation** activity, a longer time frame provides room for extra examination and exploration. We recommend allocating ninety minutes for Part 1 and thirty minutes for Part 2.

Overview

Part 1. This final activity brings together the previous discussion(s) by facilitating teachers in building their own scenario for evaluation in their school or district using a menu of "à la carte" components of teacher evaluation. First, using **Build Your Own Evaluation—Group Handout 1**, teachers rank the importance of each aspect that could be included in the system, revisiting the pros, cons, and rationales that were brought up in prior discussion(s). After selecting the ideal components, the group should collaboratively outline a one-page scenario for teacher evaluation, using **Build Your Own Evaluation—Group Handout 2**. This scenario will look similar in format to Scenarios A, B, and C in the key **Dialogue Focus Group** activity. An optional additional component to this activity is to flesh out the different elements of the evaluation system in greater detail, and how teachers can be involved in deciding them, using **Build Your Own Evaluation—Group Handout 3**.

Part 2. If possible, you should type up and polish this new, locally developed, teacher-created scenario (and the additional details from **Build Your Own Evaluation—Group Handout 3** if appropriate) and share it with the group to confirm that they agree with what is written. These documents can be shared with additional teachers at a subsequent meeting. Ultimately, these materials should be brought to the key decision makers in the school or district.

Purposes

The specific purposes of this final activity are as follows:

- Build common ground
- Determine the approach and components of the teacher evaluation system that would best meet the needs of your school or district

Room Setup

You will need a large meeting table with chairs around it.

Materials

For Part 1: All three group handouts, flip chart.

For Part 2: Polished copy of **Build Your Own Evaluation—Group Handout 2** (and **Build Your Own Evaluation—Group Handout 3** if appropriate).

Instructions

Before the Activity

1. Review previous notes from group discussions around the evaluation approaches and other activities.
2. For Part 1: Have the recorder note the components from **Build Your Own Evaluation—Group Handout 1** on the flip chart.
3. For Part 2: Type up and polish the scenario created by the group (and additional details, if relevant) so that it can be clearly read by participants.

During the Activity (Part 1)

1. Although we don't encourage inviting additional teachers to join the activity if they have not participated in a **Dialogue Focus Group**, if any new teachers are present, introductory talking points should be revisited to bring these newcomers up to speed on the background and purpose of this initiative.
2. Distribute **Build Your Own Evaluation—Group Handout 1** and ask participants to spend five minutes reading through the evaluation components and rating the importance of each. Tell the group that you would also like each person to choose the three components that he or she thinks are the most essential to valuable feedback.
3. Go quickly around the table, asking each participant to name his or her three top components. (The recorder should make a star on the flip chart beside each component as it gets a vote.)

4. After each person has announced his or her top three, step back and look at the board. Pick the five with the most stars as the group's initial consensus.

5. Give the group a minute to individually weight each of the top five components on the back of their handout. Go around the table again, asking the participants, by a show of hands, which component they weighted first, second, third, and so on. (The recorder should make note of this ranking.) The recorder should rank each of the five components from first to last based on the group's feedback.

6. Distribute copies of **Build Your Own Evaluation—Group Handout 2** to all participants. As a group (and using the **Three Scenarios for Teacher Evaluation** as a template), create a one-page description of the ideal evaluation in your school or context.

7. If time permits, the group may also discuss the questions from **Build Your Own Evaluation–Group Handout 3**.

You should share these points of consensus with the district's evaluation task force (if applicable), as well as with the school's leadership and the broader school community.

During the Activity (Part 2)

1. At this stage, you may wish to include, if possible, a broader audience of teachers in this meeting or a subsequent similar meeting.

2. Distribute a typed, polished copy of Build Your Own Evaluation—Group Handout 2 to all participants. As you did in the Dialogue Focus Group activity, prompt participants to explore the pros and cons of this approach and decide if any part of the plan needs to be tweaked.

Ultimately, this input should also be shared with key decision makers in the school or district.

Teacher Handouts: Build Your Own Evaluation

Downloadable and customizable Word versions of **Group Handout 1, Group Handout 2,** and **Group Handout 3** are available on the Everyone at the Table website under "Getting Teachers Talking: Teacher Handouts" at http://www .everyoneatthetable.org/gtt_handouts.php.

Build Your Own Evaluation—Group Handout 1

We have spent a great deal of time exploring teacher evaluation, and particularly looking at three different scenarios for teacher evaluation. Now it is your turn to build the ideal policy from scratch. In the following table, which components would you select as part of the ideal evaluation. Is anything missing?

Component	Essential to Have	Important but Not Essential	Not Important	Bad Idea
Principal observations				
Teacher observations				
External evaluator observations				
Impromptu walk-through observations				
Student surveys				
Teacher portfolios				

Component	Essential to Have	Important but Not Essential	Not Important	Bad Idea
Professional growth plans				
Video recording of classes				
Growth-based testing				
A four-point evaluation scale (*Distinguished, Proficient, Needs Improvement, Unsatisfactory*)				
Performance bonuses				
Targeted professional development				
Useful, critical feedback				
Public praise				
Denial of tenure for new teachers with poor evaluations				

Component	Essential to Have	Important but Not Essential	Not Important	Bad Idea
Counseling out of the profession for teachers with poor evaluations over multiple years				

Now that you have considered what should be included in your evaluations, write down the top five components that the group has selected and indicate the *weight* (by percentage) that the various measures should carry. You may also include additional measures.

Teacher Evaluation Measure	Percentage of the Total Evaluation
1.	
2.	
3.	
4.	
5.	
Other measures:	
Total	100

Build Your Own Evaluation—Group Handout 2

Teachers' Preferred Approach to Evaluation in [Your School District]

What if . . .

[Write a two- to three-sentence overview of the nature of the evaluation system. To what does it give priority?]

Frequency

Teachers are formally evaluated _____ times per year by _____.

Teachers are formally observed _____ times per year by _____.

Teachers are informally observed for formative purposes _____ times per year by _____.

Measures

The measures included in teachers' evaluations include the following:

Measure 1 [write a detailed description of each measure]

Measure 2 [write a detailed description of each measure]

These measures will be weighted as follows:

There will be [2, 3, 4, 5] levels of performance.

Rewards

For teachers who receive a strong rating, what will happen?

Consequences

For teachers who receive a poor rating, what will happen?

For teachers who consistently receive a poor rating over time [defined how], what will happen?

Build Your Own Evaluation—Group Handout 3

Key Decisions	What Teachers Think
How will we define educator effectiveness?	Who should decide this? How should teachers be involved? What are some key considerations that must be included?
What are the primary goals of the teacher evaluation system?	Who should decide this? How should teachers be involved? What are some key considerations that must be included?
How will we communicate about policy changes and incorporate feedback on an ongoing basis?	Who should decide this? How should teachers be involved? What are some key considerations that must be included?
As we implement the new system, what are our data infrastructure needs?	Who should decide this? How should teachers be involved? What are some key considerations that must be included?
What policy/contractual changes are required by the new system?	Who should decide this? How should teachers be involved? What are some key considerations that must be included?
Is the system aligned with state, federal, or professional requirements?	Who should decide this? How should teachers be involved? What are some key considerations that must be included?

STRATEGIES FOR OVERCOMING OBSTACLES AND TROUBLESHOOTING

The materials provided in this book should facilitate thoughtful, reflective, and constructive conversations. Should something go wrong, however, we have included the following troubleshooting pointers.

What if nobody shows up? To avoid this problem, it is best to advertise widely, include RSVPs, and send a reminder one or two days before the meeting. However, depending on where the meeting is taking place, there is no problem bringing in teachers who have not responded to the invitation at the last minute if the turnout is low. Remember that teachers are incredibly busy and have a lot being asked of them already—this is why it is critical to clearly and concisely explain and advertise the benefits of participating in these activities. It is often helpful to include a meal or other incentives for teacher participation. If the turnout is low, the conversation still can take place with as few as two or three teachers.

What if the teachers are quiet and do not speak up or engage? If teachers are not contributing voluntarily, consider a structured round-robin to give each person a chance to speak. An initial probe as an icebreaker can help here. You can also relate the material to teachers' current evaluation systems and their experiences with it by asking, "How does this compare to the way you are currently evaluated?" This approach might help them shape their opinions. The skills of an effective moderator are also important to keep in mind here. It is important to avoid any language—including value-laden comments like "That's a good idea" or "Good point"—that may alienate or dissuade others from joining a conversation. If there are members of the group who are more introverted, it is important to keep an eye on their body language. If it seems as though someone may have something to say but is hesitant, gently invite him or her to speak.

What if the teachers will not stay on track? Given a personal and hot-button topic such as teacher evaluation, it is possible that the participants may get hung up on the more contentious aspects of the issue, such as a bad evaluation they have experienced, performance-related compensation, or student test scores. If the engagement effort is occurring in a school or district where evaluation has been controversial or where conflict has been common, it is important to provide space and time for venting early in the conversation (for example, by asking the question, "What are the biggest challenges you face in your instruction right now?"). Once teachers have been able to vent their frustrations, they will generally move on to a more productive phase of dialogue. If teachers keep returning to specific issues, let them know that these topics will be covered after the scenario discussions when determining the ideal evaluation for the district (see Part 2 of the **Discussion Summary**). Other ways to move the conversation forward are to remind them that everyone needs a chance to speak, or to ask, "What would you propose as a solution?" and then change the topic after they have had an opportunity to briefly make their points.

What if the teachers are hostile toward one another or toward you? When discussing a sensitive issue such as teacher evaluation, it is not unrealistic to expect some tension among teachers—and addressing these tensions in a productive way is actually a critical part of the problem-solving process. Let participants know that it is okay to disagree, but that they should do so with curiosity, not hostility. This may help them approach the discussion more thoughtfully and diffuse any anger. Nonetheless, conflict and hostility can and do occur. Sometimes it may be best to acknowledge the tension with a statement such as, "It's good that everyone is here so we can talk through these issues together, since it is a topic that involves such strong emotion and opinions." The subject can then be changed to something more neutral, such as student surveys, what type of feedback should emerge from evaluations, or what can be done to bring more teachers into the dialogue and the decision-making process.

There are times when giving the conflict space can be productive to the dialogue. Depending on the type of conflict, the moderator's response will differ. The following suggestions about responding to conflict are adapted from Public Agenda's *Facilitator's Handbook* (2012b):

> *Conflict based on different facts.* If participants with opposing views are working on the basis of fundamentally different facts and if there is no way to resolve those differences with the time, space, or materials at hand, sometimes the best a moderator can do is bracket the discussion and have participants agree to disagree.
>
> *Conflict based on misunderstandings.* The moderator can help by giving opposing sides a clear opportunity to explain themselves and listen. Conflicts based on misunderstandings often dissipate when opposing sides truly understand each other.
>
> *Conflict based on value differences.* Many conflicts are not personal; they are rooted in value differences. A conflict may arise, for example, between two teachers who have widely different stances on the role of testing in teacher evaluation. It may be that one teacher is ranking the value of rigorous expectations highly while another is more concerned with fairness; ultimately, testing may not be the central issue. Clarifying those value differences and having participants engage with them (rather than with false, perceived differences) is key. To facilitate this, isolate the inherent values (for example, convenience versus comprehensiveness) and help participants work through the differences. It may be useful to

ask a probing question like "Would anyone want to try to characterize the differences between these two perspectives?"

Conflict based on outside issues. Sometimes a conflict arises that is based on personality, past history, or other irrelevant factors. If this happens, it is best for the moderator to steer the conversation back to the issue at hand by directing attention away from the participants in the argument and changing the subject.

GUIDE TO NEXT STEPS

These discussions should be the beginning—not the end—of teachers' engagement in evaluation reform. Teacher voice should not exist in a bubble; it is critical that participants' voices are heard and that teachers are able to genuinely influence the decisions that are made. The outcomes of these conversations should be incorporated into the decision-making process, and leaders in the engagement process should determine how this will be achieved *prior to meeting with teachers.* In addition, they should inform teachers of these steps *from the start,* so that the teachers do not begin to wonder if they are meeting and talking for no real purpose. A lot of mistrust can arise if the discussion is shared in ways that the teachers are not prepared for.

The following are some helpful ideas for presenting teacher input to a task force or group of decision makers:

- Tally quantitative data from **Build Your Own Evaluation—Group Handout 1**.
- Summarize the five most common responses from teachers, supported with quotes from the dialogue focus groups.
- Have each engagement team moderator give a presentation to the task force, school board, or other group of decision makers.

We suggest that at the very least you share the outcomes of the **Dialogue Focus Group** activity with key decision makers. You can share the discussion and its outcomes with the superintendent, the evaluation reform committee or task force, or other leaders via an in-person meeting, email, or other format. *These individuals should be informed from the start that teachers are discussing the topic and providing input.* The **Discussion Summary** is intended to assist you in clearly and concisely articulating the outcomes of the discussion.

STRATEGIES FOR SYSTEMATICALLY MAKING TEACHERS' VOICES HEARD AT THE POLICY TABLE

The movement for teacher voice in education policy is not a new or solitary one; there are groups, both formal and informal, around the country that are unified in this effort, including the groups profiled in this book. Nationwide, grassroots and organized efforts are being made to engage teachers—and other diverse stakeholders—in meaningful conversations on many education reform topics. In the Kansas City region, for example, Public Agenda is engaging parents and education leaders on parent involvement in education. It is important that these efforts are not made in isolation from one another.

Leaders at the school, district, and state level can work to unify these efforts through targeted communication—getting the word out about the teacher engagement effort in a school or district and letting others know what is going on. You could coordinate with the teachers' union, for example, or reach out to parent groups to see if they would like to be included. You could connect with other leaders in teacher engagement on social networks like Twitter and keep an eye out for other schools and districts in your area that are involved in teacher engagement efforts.

Teachers (or other leaders) in a teacher engagement process often doubt that decision makers and policymakers will pay attention to their input, and they worry that their efforts will be all for naught. Despite the inherent benefits of an engagement process, this is a legitimate concern, and any effort to engage teachers in education policy needs to be aggressively publicized. Involving more people in the effort makes their collective voice louder and increases the likelihood that policymakers will pay attention and that teachers (and other often-ignored stakeholders) will become decision makers in the education policy process.

Optional Activities for Teacher Engagement in Evaluation Reform

The pair of activities in this chapter are optional, but they help teachers explore the issue of teacher evaluation and its nuances in more depth and in innovative and interactive ways. These activities are intended to help you examine multiple perspectives, reflect on experiences, start discussions, and build consensus and momentum. If you want to complement your teacher engagement process with one or both of these activities, we suggest that you review them and choose which will best suit your context and be most useful to your engagement team, task force, or specific strategy you are using.

The following optional activities, adapted from the North Central Regional Educational Laboratory's *Blueprints: A Practical Toolkit for Designing and Facilitating Professional Development* (2000), are included:

- Interview activity
- Additional Resources and Jigsaw activity

There are additional optional activities available online at the Everyone at the Table website—www.everyoneatthetable.org.

Interview Activity

During the Interview activity, each participant interviews at least four other participants in a multistep process. The interviewers are then grouped with others who asked questions on the same topic, for the purpose of analyzing the multiple responses in depth. In the final step, each group shares its response with the whole group in a debriefing session.

This activity is used for **generating information** on many questions or issues at once. It balances participation and requires active involvement and critical thinking skills. It works well with a group of twelve or more people.

Moderator's Lesson Plan: Interview

Time
75–90 minutes

Overview
In this activity, each participant begins by collecting information (ideas, opinions, or experiences related to the topic) about teacher evaluation by interviewing at least four other participants using a generic interview question provided by the moderator. Some interviewers focus their question on the logistics of the evaluation system, some on the use of the evaluation results, and some on strategies for working with other teachers and administrators to ensure that reforms are implemented in a positive manner. The interviewers are then grouped with others who asked a question on the same topic for the purpose of analyzing the responses in depth. In the final step, each group shares its response with the whole group in a debriefing session.

Purposes
The specific purposes of this activity are as follows:

- Assess knowledge, needs, interests, and attitudes
- Explore multiple perspectives
- Start conversations
- Sustain thinking
- Tap prior knowledge and beliefs

Materials
- Copies of the **Interview Group Process** (one for each participant)
- Copies of the **Interview Recording Sheet** (a different version for each participant, depending on his or her assigned question)

- Chimes or a timer, if desired, to let participants know when it is time to move to the next interview
- Chart paper and markers

Room Setup

- The moderator area should be front and center so that it is easily visible to all participants.
- The arrangement of chairs for interviewing varies. When the group will be exploring six questions total, divide the number of participants by twelve and arrange two sets of six chairs facing one another for each group of twelve. An ideal number of participants would be twelve, twenty-four, or thirty-six. When the number of participants is not evenly divisible by twelve, adjustments can be made by either reducing the number of questions used or adding a chair at the end of a row to form an interview triad.

Instructions

Before the Activity

1. Create a set of interview questions. Each interviewer will ask one question of his or her partner. Use your discretion to assign the questions to interviewers so that all topics are covered, if possible. Some suggested questions (already included on the downloadable teacher handout) are as follows:
   - In what ways can the current evaluation system be improved? What kind of improvements would you like to see?
   - Have you or a colleague been evaluated in the past using a different system? If so, what aspects of that evaluation system would you suggest incorporating into the current system?
   - What concerns you most about evaluation reform?
   - What do you think should happen if a teacher is found to be very ineffective in the classroom?
   - What would you need to help you grow as a professional as a result of the evaluation system?
   - Describe how the ideal evaluation system would work. What would the evaluation system include, and how would the evaluation results be used?
2. Copy the **Interview Group Process** and the **Interview Recording Sheet** for the appropriate number of people.
3. Set up the room.

During the Activity

1. Frame the purpose of this group process and introduce the content topic and related questions.
2. Pass out copies of the **Interview Group Process** and the **Interview Recording Sheet.**
3. Ask participants to move to the prearranged chairs.
4. Outline the steps of the process, as follows:

> **Step 1: Interview.** Begin the interview process by asking each person to introduce himself or herself to the person sitting across from him or her. Let participants know that they will have about three minutes per person (that is, about six minutes per pair) to conduct the interviews. During the first round, you may want to give a subtle signal or reminder at the two-minute mark.
>
> After the first set of pairs have interviewed, have the individuals in one row remain seated while those in the other row move one seat to the right to interview a new partner (the individual seated in the last chair walks around to be at the first chair). The new pairs begin the second interview, with the interviewer posing the same question and responding to a new question. Continue this process for three to five rounds.
>
> **Step 2: Analyze and Synthesize.** When the interviews have been completed, the analysis process begins. Ask participants to join with others who have been asking the same question. Groups should begin by sharing the results of their interviews, analyzing and synthesizing the data, and looking for common themes and important ideas. Ask each group to create a summary metaphor or a visual depiction of its findings on chart paper. This task could involve text, a visual, or a metaphor.
>
> **Step 3: Share.** During the last phase of the process, groups take turns reporting their findings. Ask each group to take two to three minutes to share its visuals. After each presentation, ask the whole group to look for common and different ideas among the reports. You may wish to summarize and record important ideas on chart paper.

Teacher Handouts: Interview Group Process and Interview Recording Sheet

Downloadable and customizable Word versions of the **Interview Group Process** and the **Interview Recording Sheet** are available on the Everyone at the Table website under "Getting Teachers Talking: Teacher Handouts" at http://www.everyoneatthetable.org/gtt_handouts.php.

Interview Group Process

Step 1: Interview

Using your **Interview Recording Sheet,** interview your partner and record responses (2–3 minutes).

Respond to your partner's question (2–3 minutes).

Change partners as directed by the moderator, and repeat the interview process.

Step 2: Analyze and Synthesize

Assemble question-alike groups, share data, and identify themes or trends.

Summarize group conclusions and prepare a group presentation.

Step 3: Share

Share your presentation with the whole group.

Look for commonalities and differences across groups.

Interview Recording Sheet

Directions

Using the questions at the bottom of this handout, interview the person sitting across from you. Record the responses in the space under the question and, if necessary, on the back of this page. You will have 2–3 minutes to conduct each interview. Use interviewing skills and questioning techniques, such as active listening, paraphrasing responses, and probing, among others.

After you have had a chance to interview your partner and your partner has interviewed you, one of the rows will rotate to the right so that everybody has a new partner. Repeat the interview process with your new partner to get a second perspective on the question you are asking. There will be three to five rounds of interviews.

Question

[Insert one of the following interview questions (or your own question) here.]

In what ways can the current evaluation system be improved? What kind of improvements would you like to see?

Have you or a colleague been evaluated in the past using a different system? If so, what aspects of that evaluation system would you like to see incorporated into the current system?

What concerns you most about evaluation reform?

What do you think should happen if a teacher is found to be very ineffective in the classroom?

What would you need to help you grow as a professional as a result of the evaluation system?

Describe how the ideal evaluation system would work. What would the evaluation system include, and how would the evaluation results be used?

Additional Resources and Jigsaw Activity

The Jigsaw is a cooperative learning strategy that enables participants to **develop or build on expertise** in a particular aspect of a topic and then asks them to convey that information to others in a group. Jigsaw reading uses a set of additional resources to develop participant expertise.

Moderator's Lesson Plan: Additional Resources and Jigsaw

Time
45–90 minutes

Overview
The **Additional Resources and Jigsaw activity** aims to bring research-based findings to the table as teachers weigh in on the ideal evaluation system. In many ways, policy is currently ahead of research when it comes to teacher evaluation reform. To the extent possible, however, policy reforms should be based on evidence about what works. Several helpful, research-based reports are available to guide your school or district's successful evaluation reform.

This activity is intended to facilitate teachers' reading these reports and then sharing what they have learned. It involves "dividing and conquering" the reports, whereby each teacher is assigned a few reports to read and the key takeaways are then brought back to the larger group. Using a "jigsaw" approach, teachers begin by turning to a partner to share what they have read and determine commonalities and any contradictions. Next, a second round of sharing takes place in small groups where both partners' key findings are shared. This is followed by whole-group sharing, in which common themes across all the reviewed reports are discussed.

Purposes

The specific purposes of this process are as follows:

- Expand knowledge of best practices
- Expand knowledge of the diversity of practices around the country
- Build a common language
- Facilitate critical thinking about the pros and cons of different approaches
- Aid teachers' reflection and dialogue

Room Setup

Small tables are required.

Materials

- Copies of the handout **Additional Resources on Teacher Evaluation**. *Note:* This list is not exhaustive; it is intended to provide a starting point for your research.
- Index cards for logging the names of key publications and their takeaways
- Pens
- Alarm or timer if desired

Instructions

Before the Activity

1. Using the **Additional Resources on Teacher Evaluation**, assign each participant an article to review.
2. It is advisable that as the moderator, you read several reports ahead of time and come prepared to kick off the discussion based on what you have learned.
3. Several days before the session, remind participants to read their assignment(s).

During the Activity

1. Begin by sharing some of the ideas that you learned from the various reports you read (5 minutes).

2. Ask teachers to turn to a partner to share what they read and determine any commonalities and contradictions (10–15 minutes).

3. Ask teachers to conduct a second round of sharing in small groups at their tables, in which both partners' key findings are shared (10–15 minutes).

4. Lead whole-group sharing, during which common themes across all the reviewed reports are discussed (10–15 minutes).

5. In small groups at their tables, ask teachers to brainstorm ways to incorporate what was learned through the research into the district's reform plans (10–15 minutes).

6. Lead whole-group sharing to brainstorm ways to incorporate what was learned through the research into the district's reform plans (10–15 minutes).

7. Continue with the sessions. There can be anywhere from one to four or five sessions aimed at reviewing reports, depending on the number of individuals and their degree of interest.

Teacher Handout: Additional Resources on Teacher Evaluation
A downloadable and customizable Word version of the **Additional Resources on Teacher Evaluation** is available on the Everyone at the Table website under "Getting Teachers Talking: Teacher Handouts" at http://www.everyoneatthetable. org/gtt_handouts.php.

Additional Resources on Teacher Evaluation

Generating Teaching Effectiveness: The Role of Job-Embedded Professional Learning in Teacher Evaluation

http://www.tqsource.org/publications/GeneratingTeachingEffectiveness.pdf

This brief supports the thinking and efforts of state and district leaders who are designing and implementing evaluation systems that not only measure teaching effectiveness but stimulate it. The brief describes federal policy changes that animate this work, highlights the research on how teachers learn best, offers guidance on how to assess teachers' engagement in learning and collaboration, and outlines the essential conditions for evaluation systems that increase teaching effectiveness.

Linking Teacher Evaluation to Professional Development: Focusing on Improving Teaching and Learning

http://www.tqsource.org/publications/LinkingTeacherEval.pdf

The recent increased attention being paid to teacher evaluation has raised questions about the relationship between evaluation and student outcomes. This brief offers an informal framework for using evaluation results to target professional growth opportunities for teachers within an aligned system of evaluation, leading to improved teacher practice and student learning. It discusses the six components that are essential to include in a teacher evaluation system that can be effectively used for professional development.

Measuring Teacher Effectiveness: A Look "Under the Hood" of Teacher Evaluation in 10 Sites

http://conncan.org/sites/conncan.org/files/research/measuring_teacher_effectiveness.pdf

This report profiles and compares ten early implementers of evaluation reforms: Delaware; Rhode Island; Tennessee; Hillsborough County, Florida; Houston, Texas; New Haven, Connecticut; Pittsburgh, Pennsylvania; Washington, DC; Achievement First (a charter management organization); and Relay Graduate School of Education. Drawing on information from public documents and site interviews, the report describes how its featured sites have structured and implemented teacher evaluation systems. The report includes a foreword, an introductory brief, a cross-case analysis that includes a discussion of implementation challenges across sites, and ten site profiles.

Providing Effective Teachers for All Students: Examples from Five Districts

http://www2.ed.gov/rschstat/eval/teaching/providing-effective-teachers/report.pdf

Commissioned by the U.S. Department of Education and written by researchers from American Institutes for Research (AIR), this report describes the actions of districts and the challenges they face when assessing teacher effectiveness. The report draws on insights from documents and interviews with district-level staff, teachers' association or union representatives, and principals from five districts (Columbus City Schools, Ohio; Hamilton County Public Schools, Tennessee; Eagle County Schools, Colorado; Hillsborough County, Florida; and Houston Independent School District, Texas). Specifically, the report focuses on three areas of policy: identifying effective teachers, using teacher effectiveness data to inform human resource decisions, and using information about teachers' effectiveness to ensure equity in teacher distribution.

Designing and Implementing Teacher Performance Management Systems: Pitfalls and Possibilities

http://www.aspeninstitute.org/publications/designing-implementing-teacher-performance-management-systems-pitfalls-possibilities-0

This paper discusses key themes, takeaways, and six core principles on designing and implementing teacher performance management systems and policies. Using examples from the field, the paper expands on the principles and challenges that emerge when policymakers focus on comprehensive systems rather than "fixes" for discrete problems.

Building Teacher Evaluation Systems: Learning from Leading Efforts

http://www.aspeninstitute.org/publications/building-teacher-evaluation-systems-learning-leading-efforts

This report describes efforts under way to reshape teacher evaluation and performance management in the District of Columbia Public Schools and the Achievement First charter school network. The commonalities, distinctions, and early lessons learned in these initiatives represent an important learning laboratory for the field; and on the basis of lessons learned in these settings, this paper draws out five key questions that reformers should ask.

Approaches to Evaluating Teacher Effectiveness: A Research Synthesis

http://www.tqsource.org/publications/EvaluatingTeachEffectiveness.pdf

This research synthesis examines how teacher effectiveness is measured and provides practical guidance for evaluating teacher effectiveness. It analyzes the research on teacher effectiveness and different instruments used to measure it. In addition, it defines components and indicators that characterize effective teachers, extending this definition beyond teachers' contributions to student achievement gains to include how teachers affect classrooms, schools, and colleagues, as well as how teachers contribute to other important outcomes for students.

Challenges in Evaluating Special Education Teachers and English Language Learner Specialists

http://www.tqsource.org/publications/July2010Brief.pdf

This brief provides a summary of current research and practice in teacher evaluation. It offers policy and practice recommendations for regions, states, and school districts to help their efforts in creating valid, reliable, and comprehensive evaluation systems for all teachers.

Retaining Teacher Talent: Convergence and Contradictions in Teachers' Perceptions of Policy Reform Ideas

http://www.learningpt.org/expertise/educatorquality/genY/Convergence_Contradiction.pdf

This report informs policymakers about teachers' views on the policies that greatly affect their daily lives. It highlights the teacher perspective on the pressing policy issues of assessing, rewarding, and improving teacher effectiveness, with the goal of keeping teachers themselves at the heart of debates about the profession.

Improving Instruction Through Effective Teacher Evaluation: Options for States and Districts

http://www.tqsource.org/publications/February2008Brief.pdf

This brief discusses the measures used in teacher evaluation and focuses on their strengths, limitations, and current use. It underscores aspects of evaluation policies that currently align with best practices and illuminates areas in which policymakers can improve evaluation rules, regulations, and implementation, thereby improving teacher instruction and student performance.

Measuring Teachers' Contributions to Student Learning Growth for Nontested Subjects and Grades

http://www.tqsource.org/publications/MeasuringTeachersContributions.pdf

The purpose of this research and policy brief is to help states consider options for assessing student learning growth for the majority of teachers who teach content that is not assessed through standardized tests. It provides information about options for states to explore, as well as factors to consider when identifying and implementing measures. It also focuses specifically on federal priorities to help ensure that evaluation systems meet the high expectations set for teacher evaluation. Finally, the brief emphasizes the importance of fairly measuring all teachers, including them in the evaluation process, and ensuring validity in measurement.

Measuring Teacher and Leader Performance: Cross-Sector Lessons for Excellent Evaluations

http://www.publicimpact.com/images/stories/performance_measurement_2010.pdf

This brief reports on the staff evaluation systems used by government agencies, non-profit organizations, and for-profit companies and how they can inform the development and implementation of teacher evaluation systems.

Methods of Evaluating Teacher Effectiveness

http://www.tqsource.org/publications/RestoPractice_EvaluatingTeacherEffectiveness.pdf

This brief is intended to help readers consider evaluation methods to clarify policy, develop new strategies, identify effective teachers, or guide and support districts in selecting and using appropriate evaluation methods for various purposes. It includes a five-point definition of teacher effectiveness that the authors developed by analyzing research, policy, and standards that address teacher effectiveness and by consulting experts in the field.

The Other 69 Percent: Fairly Rewarding the Performance of Teachers of Nontested Subjects and Grades

http://cecr.ed.gov/guides/other69Percent.pdf

This paper addresses the means by which states, school districts, and individual schools can fairly and effectively include all teachers in a performance-based compensation system. It specifically focuses on those who teach a grade level or subject area for which standardized achievement tests are not administered, as well as those who teach English language learners or students with disabilities.

A Practical Guide to Designing Comprehensive Teacher Evaluation Systems

http://www.tqsource.org/publications/practicalGuideEvalSystems.pdf

This guide outlines eight key steps for developing and implementing comprehensive teacher evaluation systems. These steps consist of specifying evaluation system goals, securing and sustaining stakeholder investment and cultivating a strategic communication plan, selecting measures, determining the structure of the evaluation system, selecting and training evaluators, ensuring data integrity and transparency, using teacher evaluation results, and evaluating the system.

A Practical Guide to Evaluating Teacher Effectiveness

http://www.tqsource.org/publications/practicalGuide.pdf

This guide offers a definition of teacher effectiveness that states and school districts may adapt to meet local requirements, provides an overview of the many reasons for evaluating teacher effectiveness, and indicates which measures are most suitable to use under different circumstances. The guide also includes summaries of the various measures, such as value-added models, classroom observations, analysis of classroom artifacts, and portfolios. The summaries include descriptions of the measures, along with a note about the research base and strengths and cautions to consider for each measure.

The Widget Effect: Our National Failure to Acknowledge and Act on Differences in Teacher Effectiveness

http://widgeteffect.org/downloads/TheWidgetEffect.pdf

This report argues that current teacher evaluation systems systematically rate all or nearly all teachers as satisfactory or excellent and that this failure to differentiate between degrees of teacher effectiveness is harmful to our nation's students.

ACTIVITY 4
Joining the National Dialogue

In recent years, a number of groups have sprung up across the country to put teachers front and center in policymaking circles. Many of these initiatives are highlighted in this book.

We hope to shine a spotlight on your story too, and to assist all teacher leaders who are working to shape teacher evaluation systems in sharing their successes, challenges, and lessons learned.

Please visit www.everyoneatthetable.org/sharestory.php to share your story of meaningfully engaging teachers in teacher quality reform.

Other Stakeholders

Engaging Principals, Parents, and
Community Members

A range of important issues that affect teachers—both individually and as a profession—are embedded in state and district policies promoting new evaluation systems, and teachers should proactively and continually engage in the policy dialogue. But teachers are not the only stakeholders whose voice matters. Principals, parents, and community members also need a place at the table. It is important that the ideas, concerns, and insights of these critical stakeholder groups are part of the policy dialogue, whether through direct engagement strategies or inclusive communication strategies. This chapter consists of three sections: engaging principals in teacher evaluation; engaging principals in principal evaluation; and engaging parents and community members in teacher and principal evaluation.

THE TRANSITION OF PRINCIPALS TO INSTRUCTIONAL LEADERS

The role of principals has transitioned in recent years from school manager to instructional leader. Now, successful principals not only make sure that the buses run on time and parents are happy but also are increasingly expected to provide leadership for the school's approach to curriculum and instruction—coaching teachers on instructional strategies, and modeling the use of data to inform instructional decisions (Clifford, Behrstock-Sherratt, & Fetters, 2012). They are, furthermore, expected to conduct teacher evaluations that are accurate and meaningful and that lead to improved classroom practice, and their own evaluations increasingly focus on their instructional leadership.

Recent federal initiatives have repeatedly emphasized that the quality of teachers *and school principals* is of utmost importance. The $4.35 billion federal Race to the Top (RTT) initiative, for example, was intended to kick-start educational innovation in public education, and it emphasized both teacher and school leader effectiveness as key to reform. States that successfully secured RTT funding were selected based on, among other things, their plans for

- Improving teacher *and principal* effectiveness based on performance
- Ensuring equitable distribution of effective teachers *and principals*
- Providing high-quality pathways for aspiring teachers *and principals*
- Providing effective support to teachers *and principals*
- Improving the effectiveness of teacher *and principal* preparation programs

This increased emphasis on strong principals stems from a growing body of research which confirms that principals are second only to teachers among school-level factors that influence student achievement (Leithwood, Louis, Anderson, & Wahlstrom, 2004). Although principals are central to the educator effectiveness debates that are alive in their schools today, they, like teachers, too often find that their voices are left out of the wider policy discussion on the topic. Indeed, a policy environment has been created in which many principals "feel invisible" in the debate and frustrated that their concerns—from the emphasis on testing to the time-intensiveness of multifaceted evaluation systems—are not being heard. Despite this, and despite the existence of many grassroots teacher voice organizations, there is no comparable movement that seeks to expand principal voice beyond those elected to local principal associations.

PLANNING FOR PRINCIPAL ENGAGEMENT

Preparing for principal engagement in evaluation reform efforts builds on the same foundational activities that underpin teacher engagement. The reform process should be as inclusive as possible from the very beginning, and it should include multiple opportunities for engagement. Questions such as the following can help guide this early planning.

- Which principals will be included in the conversations (for example, all principals in your district, principals from nearby districts)?

- Which other leaders will be included in the conversations (for example, assistant principals, department heads)?
- Which principal is in the best position to moderate the discussion and bring the outcomes to those making final policy decisions?
- Should there be a single group that meets, or should there be one high school, one middle school, and one elementary school principal engagement team?
- What will you address—teacher evaluation, principal evaluation, or both?
- When and where will your meetings take place? Are there ways to create efficiencies, such as by combining principal engagement meetings with other principal meetings?
- How will principals' input be shared with the key decision makers in a meaningful way?

After reflecting on these questions and deciding on the best approach to incorporating principal voice into the design and implementation of a new evaluation system, the next step is to assemble a principal engagement team and identify a moderator or moderators. The principal engagement team operates much like teacher engagement teams (see Chapter Five). The number of principal engagement teams and the number of individuals on the teams will depend on the size of a district; in many cases, a single committee of three or four principals will suffice. Members of the principal engagement team are responsible for logistical concerns, such as coordinating meetings, providing food, securing a location, and so on. They are also responsible for recruiting other principals to the conversation, selecting and preparing moderators, choosing the most relevant discussion topics and formats, liaising with district or state leaders and task forces to share the outcomes of the principal dialogues, and following up with principals about how the ideas they shared were used.

After this core team has been assembled, the next step is to reach out to invite other principals to participate. The following template may be used as a starting point.

Sample Principal Recruitment Invitation

A downloadable and customizable Word version of this **Sample Principal Recruitment Invitation** is available on the Everyone at the Table website under "Getting Principals Talking: Principal Handouts" at http://www.everyoneatthe table.org/principals_handouts.php.

Join the Conversation on Evaluating Principal Effectiveness!

Please join your colleagues for several lively and important discussion meetings about approaches to evaluating principal effectiveness.

Fellow Principals:

I am writing to you to propose an approach for meaningfully incorporating principals' expertise and ideas into the new principal evaluation system that is being developed in our district. As you likely know, [insert update about the current status of reform in your district].

Specifically, I would like to suggest that we district principals convene as a group for several meetings during the next [insert number] months in order to share ideas, develop priorities, and collaboratively decide on several key recommendations to put forth.

I already have spoken to [insert name of task force leader, superintendent, association leader, or other key decision maker], who agrees that this approach is a good idea. [Insert any other information about avenues for principals to be involved in a task force or how the results of the proposed conversations will likely be brought to the policymaking table].

I hope that you can make time in your busy schedule to attend these meetings. Please let me know if you have any questions or concerns.

Respectfully yours,

[insert name]

As is the case for teachers, principal engagement can include multiple conversations over the course of a year, a few conversations over several months, or a single, in-depth conversation. It will ideally take place at the very beginning of the reform process, but also may take place during the implementation or modification phases. You may wish to collaboratively develop this plan with other leaders during your first meeting, using the sample plans in Chapter Five as a guide.

A critical early step is to determine how principals' voices will be included when the final decisions regarding a new policy, program, or initiative are presented. Here are some possibilities:

- Making regular presentations (or a single one) to a task force, committee, or school board
- Creating a formal document that summarizes the recommendations of principals
- Engaging in informal conversations with a superintendent or other key leader about what principals are thinking on the topic of evaluation

Expectations about how the principal engagement conversations will be used to inform decision making should be communicated to principals from day 1.

ENGAGING PRINCIPALS IN TEACHER EVALUATION

As teacher evaluation systems undergo transformation, significant additional responsibility is falling on principals as the lead evaluators. In some districts, the implementation of new teacher evaluation systems has resulted in as much as 60 percent of principals' time being spent on activities related to teacher evaluations. Typically, principals are required to undergo training to become certified to assess teacher performance, and to incorporate pre-observation meetings, post-observation meetings, written feedback, and summative evaluation forms into the successful conduct of a teacher's annual evaluation.

◉

The key activity for principal engagement around teacher evaluation is essentially the same activity that we recommend for teachers. Although principals are used to discussing policy in meetings, engagement activities require a different kind of conversation. Principal engagement team members and moderators should carefully review the principles for dialogue and engagement and the qualities and strategies of an effective moderator in Chapters Four and Six.

This key activity kicks off with an eight-minute discussion-starter video that can be found on the Everyone at the Table website (www.everyoneatthetable.org) and then delves into three teacher evaluation scenarios for a structured discussion using Yankelovich's Choicework methodology (Yankelovich, 1999). Conversations between principals may differ from conversations between teachers in one key way: principals may want to focus more on the practical and logistical aspects of the components of the systems because of their firsthand knowledge of conducting evaluations.

If your district is also convening teacher engagement teams (which we would recommend), you might consider asking for a summary of the teachers' **Dialogue Focus Group** discussion(s) in advance of this exercise. After the principals discuss teacher evaluation, the summary of teachers' views on the topic can be shared, and areas of similarity and difference in opinion can be fleshed out.

As is the case with teachers, the three scenarios provided in Chapter Six are ideal for schools and districts in the early stages of designing a new system, but can be modified to fit any context. (See Chapter Five for more information about engagement in contexts where reforms already are under way.) In situations where principals have more time to discuss teacher evaluation redesign, the **Build Your Own Evaluation** (Chapter Six) and the additional activities (Chapter Seven) can be easily adapted for principal conversations.

ENGAGING PRINCIPALS IN PRINCIPAL EVALUATION

In many cases, principal evaluation reform policies are passed alongside teacher evaluation policies. In their examination of the status of principal evaluation reform in the United States, Jacques, Clifford, and Hornung (2012) map the thirty-five states that have passed principal evaluation policies since 2005. In 2005, North Carolina was first out of the gate with a statewide reform effort that focused on principal evaluation. Other early adopters included Ohio (2008) and Delaware (2009). In 2010, eight additional states passed principal evaluation legislation, and between 2011 and 2012, an additional twenty-four states followed suit. Tools like Clifford, Hansen, and Wraight's *Practical Guide to Designing Comprehensive Principal Evaluation Systems* (2012) (which can be found at: http://www.tqsource.org/publications/DesigningPrincipalEvalSys.pdf) walk through each step of the principal evaluation redesign process. Principals ought to be involved at each stage of this process, particularly the initial design stage. The engagement strategies discussed in this section are intended to facilitate deep and constructive conversations at this stage, although they can be modified when principal engagement takes place during the policy implementation or modification phases.

Before turning to the essential and optional principal engagement strategies, you may wish to complete Activities 5 and 6 here.

ACTIVITY 5
Measure Your Own Starting-Point Values (Principals)

How much do you agree with the following statements? Rate yourself from 1 to 5;
1 = low agreement and 5 = high.

When measuring principal effectiveness, our evaluation plan should . . .

. . . be fair	1	2	3	4	5
. . . be efficient	1	2	3	4	5
. . . be flexible	1	2	3	4	5
. . . be convenient	1	2	3	4	5
. . . be comprehensive	1	2	3	4	5
. . . have high expectations	1	2	3	4	5
. . . have reasonable expectations	1	2	3	4	5
. . . be collaborative and build community	1	2	3	4	5
. . . be consistent	1	2	3	4	5

If your district has a task force, Activity 6 will help you think through whether current principal representation on the task force is adequate and how it might be improved.

ACTIVITY 6
Reflecting on Our Task Force (Principals)

Consider these questions about the representation of principals on your district task force or evaluation reform committee:

1. Does our task force allow principals to vote?
2. If yes, do principals' votes carry significant weight?
3. Does our task force include a representative sample of principals of different types of schools, genders, and backgrounds?
4. Does our task force bring in the voice of principals who are not members of the task force?
5. If no, how can our task force better include input from principals who are not task force members?
6. Are teachers adequately represented in all of the above ways as well?

> 7. If no, how can principals support the improved representation of teachers in the reform process?
>
> Consider how your responses to this self-assessment can be used to change how your task force is run so that it better reflects principals' and teachers' voices.

The Essential Activity for Promoting Principal Conversations on Principal Evaluation

The key activity for principal engagement is a structured **Dialogue Focus Group** based on the principles of Choicework. This approach presents three evaluation scenarios for principals to consider, each of which has trade-offs, pros, and cons. Participants are able to develop consensus about the best policy for their context and learn about people's reasons for putting forward alternative choices.

The following three principal evaluation scenarios and moderator prompts have been created as guides for widespread discussion among principals. Please review the instructions in Chapter Six for successfully moderating this type of **Dialogue Focus Group.**

Also available on the Everyone at the Table website is a **Principal Discussion Summary** (not included in this book). This template is used for summarizing the principal conversations relating to the three scenarios. It also asks principals to begin thinking about an ideal evaluation system.

Principal Handout: Three Scenarios for Principal Evaluation

A downloadable and customizable Word version of **Three Scenarios for Principal Evaluation** is available on the Everyone at the Table website under "Getting Principals Talking: Principal Handouts" at http://www.everyoneatthetable.org/principals_handouts.php.

Three Scenarios for Principal Evaluation

Scenario A: Multirater Principal Evaluation

What if . . . new district leadership comes on board and decides to implement a 360-degree, multirater evaluation system that is designed to assess principals' performance as school leaders? District leadership chooses to design the 360-degree system to include feedback from the superintendent, teachers and other staff, and the principal's assigned mentor (if available); the principal's self-evaluation; and a portfolio developed by the principal. In addition, parents and students are solicited for input about the school as a whole, and their ratings also are included in the principal's evaluation. The purpose of this comprehensive approach is to allow both the principal and his or her evaluator to obtain a complete picture of potential areas for school and personal improvement, as well as evidence of good leadership practices that may not be ascertained through a single type of assessment (for example, an observation or walk-through).

Frequency
- The principal is formally evaluated annually, with one formative and one summative assessment by the superintendent or other trained district personnel.
- Feedback is formally collected annually from the mentor, teachers and other staff, parents, and students, but additional information from these groups also can be included in the principal's evaluation.
- Feedback and evaluation findings are incorporated into the principal's professional development plan.

Measures
Principals are evaluated on a four-point rating system (for example, *Distinguished, Proficient, Needs Improvement, Unsatisfactory*) that is tied to leadership standards, such as the Interstate School Leaders Licensure Consortium (ISLLC) standards.* The summative evaluations rely on the following:

- Review of the principal-submitted portfolio that chronicles the principal's growth and any formal professional development
- Review of data about teachers (for example, retention and attendance)
- Student achievement scores
- Assessments of a variety of leadership areas: communication, use and analysis of student achievement data to inform school policy, working conditions, teacher engagement and support, management of budget, and related areas

The informal or more formative evaluations consist of the following:

- Drop-in observations by the superintendent or other trained district personnel
- Annual surveys and informal interviews of parents, teachers, and students
- Review of key school documents (for example, parent newsletters)

---

*Council of Chief State School Officers. (2008). *Educational leadership policy standards: ISLLC 2008* (as adopted by the National Policy Board for Educational Administration). Washington, DC: Author. Retrieved from http://www.ccsso.org/Documents/2008/Educational_Leadership_Policy_Standards_2008.pdf.

Evaluators also must be careful to take into account the context of the school. If a principal is dealing with high poverty, student mobility, teacher attrition, low parental involvement, or other challenges, these factors need to be taken into consideration.

Consequences

Having captured an accurate and complete picture of the principal's strengths and weaknesses, the evaluation results are given to a coach, who meets with the principal twice monthly, sometimes over the phone.

There are few consequences if a principal is rated poorly on the four-point scale or fails to improve over time; it is hoped that with the intensive support provided by the coach, the enactment of consequences will not be required.

Scenario B: Observable Practices for Principal Evaluations

What if . . . the district decides to revise its principal evaluation protocol and align it to the teacher evaluation protocol? The task force leading the change is intent on assessing the multiple hats that principals wear in the multiple contexts in which they work: serving as instructional leaders inside the school; navigating district systems and resources outside the school; and engaging with a wide range of stakeholders, including teachers, resource and support staff, students, parents, district administrators, business and community members, and sometimes independent contractors providing professional development or other services. At the same time, the superintendent also recognizes the need to give principals the time, space, and autonomy to focus on their jobs without being unduly burdened by responsibilities related to their evaluation.

Frequency

- Observational data from faculty meetings, leadership team meetings, and whole-group professional development meetings are collected throughout the school year. The observations are announced and arranged ahead of time.
- Observational data from scheduled parent-teacher association meetings and other events that engage parents or community members also are collected throughout the school year. These observations are announced and arranged ahead of time.
- Walk-throughs by the superintendent or other district personnel take place approximately twice each year and are announced and arranged ahead of time.
- Formal evaluations are conducted once every three years and involve a meeting between the principal and the superintendent.

Measures

The observations cover the following practices:

- Ability to run an effective meeting

- Ability to communicate with district leaders, school staff, parents, and other community members
- Inclusive decision making
- Ability to access and secure targeted support from the district as needed
- Ability to set goals, plan, use data, and monitor a meeting to support the meeting's objectives (for example, curriculum planning, teacher scheduling, and analysis of student test data)
- Solid instructional coaching and the creation of a positive school culture

Consequences

Principals who receive strong evaluations are publicly praised for their good work. They also are asked to provide minimal coaching to struggling principals in the district.

Principals who receive poor evaluations are placed on a growth plan that involves attending several courses and being evaluated every year instead of once every three years. Principals who receive three consecutive poor ratings do not have their contracts renewed for the next academic year.

Scenario C: The Turnaround Principal Evaluation

What if . . . the district determines that a new principal evaluation system is needed to take into account its vision of the school principal as a leader of drastic, urgent improvement? Helping teachers raise student achievement levels is central to this new system, and "quick wins" for the school earn high marks for principals. Principals are heavily rewarded, or otherwise penalized, based on student test score growth. To create the extensive, lasting change that is needed, the superintendent believes that there must be distributed leadership throughout the school. Principals are evaluated jointly with their leadership teams, in part on their ability to effectively share leadership and responsibilities among staff.

Frequency

- All principals are evaluated three times each year to allow for continuous feedback and opportunities for improvement and tailored support. Two formative evaluations are conducted to provide feedback, and an end-of-year summative evaluation is conducted. The summative evaluation results are entered into the principal's file.
- School walk-throughs and observations by district staff for evaluative purposes occur regularly and are unannounced.

Who Conducts the Evaluation?

The district superintendent (or other district-assigned designee) conducts the evaluation. This person is required to complete intensive training on the evaluation protocol and ensure interrater reliability because of the high-stakes nature of the evaluations.

Evaluators also are required to complete training in providing critical yet tactful and constructive feedback, which is shared during required pre- and post-evaluation debriefing sessions. After each evaluation, the principal is required to refine his or her professional development goals.

Measures

Diverse amounts of school-level data are collected—including student achievement and growth data, teacher and student retention data, attendance data, teacher working conditions survey results, teacher evaluation results, and other information—to capture key leadership practices, such as evidence of the following:

- Student learning gains
- Shared leadership
- Effective interactions with district leadership (for example, providing timely updates and securing targeted resources)
- Instructional leadership, the use of data, ability to work with parents, and creation of a culture of continuous improvement

Consequences

- Principals who receive two poor evaluation ratings (out of three) in a given year lose their jobs.
- Principals whose schools show large test score gains are given a significant financial bonus.
- All principals receive intensive, ongoing feedback through face-to-face meetings with their supervisors to discuss strengths and weaknesses and suggestions for improvement.

Questions for the Moderator to Ask About Scenario A

- What do you think about Scenario A? What do you like about it? What do you dislike about it?
- Some say that it is important that multiple stakeholder groups have an opportunity to provide feedback on the principal because such groups are the primary constituents that the principal serves. However, there are concerns that students, teachers, and parents cannot really be unbiased, and the most vocal (or unhappy) individuals from each group may impact or skew the type

of feedback received. How, if at all, should the school or district go about ensuring that all voices (positive and negative) are heard? Should equal weight be given to all stakeholder groups?

- Some say that the superintendent, as the leader of the district, ought to conduct all aspects of each principal's evaluation. Others worry that the superintendent may not have the time to evaluate each principal or may not be adequately informed about what principals at certain types of schools (for example, high school and elementary school) do to be effective. What do you think?
  - Who else should be responsible for evaluations?
  - If more than one person in a district is conducting evaluations, how can you make sure that each person is using the same criteria for evaluation?
  - What kind of training would ensure that the superintendent or other individual uses the evaluation tools and rubrics appropriately?
- Do you like the idea of having a four-point scale tied to leadership standards?
  - How would that scale make the evaluation different from what you have now?
  - Should the scale be adjusted for newer principals, who would otherwise likely score low on the scale due to their lack of experience?
- Some say that having principals create portfolios gives them an opportunity to highlight their work and professional development; others say that portfolios are very subjective, do not capture the magnitude of all the principal's responsibilities, and take up precious time that would be better spent running the school. What do you think?
- If portfolios are included in the principal evaluation process, what types of data or information should be covered?
- What is the best role for a principal's mentor or coach in addressing issues that come up in the evaluation? Is it realistic for principals to have a mentor or coach as described in this scenario?
- Should principal evaluation data be given to coaches?
- Now that we've discussed Scenario A, what do you think?
- Does anyone have a different opinion? Please share.

Questions for the Moderator to Ask About Scenario B
- What do you think about Scenario B? What do you like about it? What do you dislike about it?

- In what ways is this scenario similar to your current evaluation system? In what ways is it different?
- Is one evaluation every three years enough? If not, how often should principals be evaluated?
- Does this approach adequately measure those principal practices (for example, conducting meetings, communicating with all staff, making inclusive decisions) that contribute most to student achievement?
- What observable practices are the most relevant to principal evaluation? Are they addressed in this scenario? What are some additional observable practices of a principal that should be captured?
- What important principal practices are not captured in this evaluation system?
- How important is it for a principal to be recognized by district leadership for a job well done? What are the best ways to recognize principals for their successes?
- Which would you prefer: a more hands-off approach (such as this one) or a more intensive evaluation process?
- Now that we've discussed Scenario B, what do you think?
- Does anyone have a different opinion? Please share.

Questions for the Moderator to Ask About Scenario C
- What do you think about Scenario C? What do you like about it? What do you dislike about it?
- Some people think that using test scores as part (but not all) of the principal's evaluation is essential for determining if students are really learning or not. Others think that test score data are less relevant. What weight, if any, do you think student test scores should have in a principal's evaluation?
- Should principals be evaluated based on student achievement (for example, raw student test scores), student growth (for example, the change in test scores from the beginning to the end of the year), or both? Should the evaluator use value-added models of student growth (that is, complex statistical models that take into account students' test score growth over the past several years as well as additional demographic factors that typically influence student achievement)?
- Are there other ways to tell if principals are really helping improve student learning? What are those ways?

- What percentage—70 percent, 50 percent, 30 percent, or some other percentage—of a principal's evaluation should be determined by student test scores? Why did you choose the percentage that you did?
- How should the evaluation be modified to take into account that several months or a year may be necessary for improvements to be seen after some of the significant changes that occur within a turnaround school?
- Should a principal be evaluated on the degree to which leadership is shared?
  - If so, what is the best way to evaluate for the presence of shared leadership?
  - If shared leadership should be included, should the principal be the only person evaluated according to ISLLC or other leadership standards in the school?
- Do you think it is important to include personal goal setting by principals as part of the evaluation?
- In this scenario, the principal is constantly provided with a lot of critical but constructive feedback. Is there ever too much feedback?
- Is it right to give significant financial bonuses to principals who receive strong evaluations?
- Now that we've discussed Scenario C, what do you think?
- Does anyone have a different opinion? Please share.

Build Your Own Evaluation

We recommend that after discussing the three scenarios, you close out the exercise with a **Build Your Own Evaluation** survey. This survey can be tweaked to cover the issues that are relevant in your district. It is important that principals complete the survey *after* the **Dialogue Focus Group.** Unlike typical surveys (which are not preceded by a reflective and in-depth discussion), this Build Your Own Evaluation survey is likely to result in much more meaningful information for decision makers.

Principal Handout: Build Your Own Principal Evaluation
A downloadable and customizable Word version of **Build Your Own Principal Evaluation** is available on the Everyone at the Table website under "Getting Principals Talking: Principal Handouts" at http://www.everyoneatthetable.org/principals_handouts.php.

Build Your Own Principal Evaluation

Instructions: After spending time exploring principal evaluation, particularly looking at the three different scenarios for principal evaluation, it's your turn to build the ideal policy from scratch. In the following chart, review the possible components that could be part of the ideal principal evaluation. Rate each component as essential to have, important but not essential, not important, or bad idea. At the end of this chart, indicate the weight percentages for student test-score data or other important considerations for the principal's evaluation. Is anything missing? If so, add components as needed.

Component	Essential to Have	Important but Not Essential	Not Important	Bad Idea
Evaluation Areas of Focus				
Improved school culture and safety				
Improved teacher working conditions				
Use of student data to make decisions				
Graduation rates				
Teacher retention and attrition				
Teacher placement in subject area of training				
Average teacher evaluation scores above baseline				
Student absences				
Number of discipline referrals				
Ability to communicate with teachers, staff, parents, and students				
Involvement of staff in decision making				
Involvement of parents or community in decision making				
Time spent on instructional leadership				
Establishment of a strong school mission and vision				
Ability to set and meet goals to support school objectives and initiatives				

(continued on next page)

(continued from previous page)

Component	Essential to Have	Important but Not Essential	Not Important	Bad Idea
Distribution or sharing of leadership				
Quality of financial management				
Ability to access and secure targeted support from district as needed				
Solid instructional coaching				
Who Conducts the Principal's Evaluation				
Superintendent				
Other district-assigned evaluator				
Assigned mentor or coach				
Outside or consultant evaluator				
Other *(please specify)*:				
Training of Evaluators				
Required				
Evaluation of Evaluators				
Required				
Who Participates in the Principal's Evaluation (e.g., Stakeholder Groups)				
Superintendent				
Other district personnel				
Assistant principals				
Teachers				
Certified nonteaching staff (e.g., counselors and department chairs)				
Noncertified teaching staff (e.g., secretary)				
Parents				
Students				
Community members				
Assigned mentor or coach				
Other *(please specify)*:				
Evaluation Format				
Observations				
School walk-throughs				

Component	Essential to Have	Important but Not Essential	Not Important	Bad Idea
Data presentation and question-and-answer format from principal				
Other (please specify):				
Type of Evaluation				
Formative				
Summative				
Combination of formative and summative				
Evaluation Frequency				
Annual				
Biannual				
Other (please specify):				
Miscellaneous Evaluation Components				
A four-point evaluation scale or rubric (e.g., Distinguished, Proficient, Needs Improvement, Unsatisfactory)				
A binary evaluation scale or rubric (e.g., Satisfactory versus Unsatisfactory)				
Public praise or acknowledgment of successes				
Performance bonuses				
Targeted professional development				
Revisions to professional goals or growth plans				
Termination of contract				
Evaluation Measures				
Inclusion of school context as part of evaluation				
School climate survey				
Student surveys and interviews				
Teacher surveys and interviews				
Parent surveys				
Self-assessment results				
Review of professional development plan				
Principal portfolio				

(continued on next page)

(continued from previous page)

Component	Essential to Have	Important but Not Essential	Not Important	Bad Idea
Review of other artifacts or school documents (e.g., newsletters)				
Review of staffing data				
360-degree evaluation				
Review of student achievement data or growth-based test data				
Meeting notes from faculty, leadership team, or whole-group professional development meetings				
Other *(please specify)*:				

Percentage of Weight in Evaluation	70%	50%	30%	Other %
Student test score data				
Other *(please specify)*:				
Other *(please specify)*:				
Other *(please specify)*:				

OPTIONAL ACTIVITIES FOR ENGAGING PRINCIPALS IN TEACHER AND PRINCIPAL EVALUATION REFORM

In addition to the key **Dialogue Focus Group** activity and the **Build Your Own Evaluation** activity, additional structured dialogues, similar to those recommended for teachers, can be used by principal engagement teams for the redesign of principal evaluation systems.

Additional Resources and Jigsaw Activity

Principals, as leaders in their schools, ought to *know* as much as possible about "what works" in evaluation, and this makes the Jigsaw reading activity especially apt. The instructions for the Jigsaw reading activity can be found in Chapter Seven.

Although there is less literature on principal evaluation than on teacher evaluation, several principal evaluation resources that can be read and brought back for discussion are listed here.

Additional Resources on Principal Evaluation

State Policies on Principal Evaluation

http://www.tqsource.org/publications/StatePoliciesOnPrincipalEval.pdf

The recent wave of education reform initiatives has resulted in new principal evaluation legislation in the past few years. This policy brief describes the trends in recently passed principal evaluation legislation, with a focus on implementation timelines and pilot programs. In addition, it discusses possible implementation challenges and areas of importance.

The Ripple Effect: A Synthesis of Research on Principal Influence to Inform Performance Evaluation Design

http://www.air.org/files/1707_The_Ripple_Effect_d8_Online.pdf

This brief draws on research literature on principal effectiveness and policy documents created by scholars and national organizations concerned with principal professional practice and its effects. The researchers also reviewed and analyzed policy documents produced by national policy entities, which define principal effectiveness and principal professional standards. Effectiveness definitions and standards were reviewed, and a typology emerged.

The Policies and Practices of Principal Evaluation: A Review of the Literature

http://www.wested.org/online_pubs/resource1104.pdf

This brief discusses the findings that emerge from a review of sixty-eight papers published on principal evaluation from the 1980s to the present. The studies cover the following themes: the implementation of principal evaluation policies, systems, protocols, and processes; the development or validation of various principal evaluation instruments; the uses and characteristics of portfolios in principal evaluation; and the analysis of multiple components of principal evaluation. Key findings from each theme are presented as well as key findings from critical descriptions and commentaries in the literature base.

Interview Activity

The Interview activity (more detailed instructions for which are in Chapter Seven) allows principals, who so often do the interviewing in their schools, to also be interviewed. Each principal interviews at least four other principals on a single question about principal evaluation before sharing what has been learned.

The types of questions that might be used for principal evaluation include the following:

- What are the three greatest benefits and three greatest drawbacks of evaluating principals based on how well principals evaluate teachers?
- What types of data are most demonstrative of a principal's effectiveness? Why?
- How should principal evaluation results be used? Rank the following uses from best to worst and explain your thinking: (1) pay bonuses, (2) contract renewal, (3) coaching, and (4) principal assignment to the most challenging schools in a district.

ENGAGING PARENTS AND COMMUNITY MEMBERS ON TEACHER AND PRINCIPAL EVALUATION

More productive inclusion of the community in the decision-making process can be a powerful complement to school-based teacher or principal engagement. Although community members are probably not interested in engaging on the nitty-gritty details of teacher evaluation in the way that we suggest for teachers and principals, effectively communicating with and engaging parents and the community are, at the very least, helpful to this work, and are at times absolutely critical.

In some cases, parent surveys of teacher and principal effectiveness are on the table for inclusion as one of multiple measures in evaluations. More broadly, engaging parents and the community is helpful because teacher and principal evaluation is, at heart, about helping students learn, and parents and community partners can support and complement the educational efforts of schools. Engagement can also be critical because school reform can become politicized and can self-destruct; sound communication and engagement with parents, taxpayers, and important community leaders can help inoculate reform efforts against these maladies. This is not to say, by any means, that policy disagreements should not be aired—we are not concerned here with a persuasion campaign to manufacture unthinking support. Rather, creating an environment in which honest disagreement can lead to honest dialogue in turn produces sound and sustainable policies that help children learn and can help forge outside support for school reforms.

The dialogue protocols, Choicework discussion materials, and activities presented throughout this book can be modified for parent and community conversations. In Washington State, for example, researchers working with the state department of education conducted ten focus group discussions with parents and community members to solicit feedback on their views of recent teacher and principal evaluation legislation. (See Chapter Five for a more detailed description.) In many cases, despite their interest, parents and community members will not make time for the types of sustained engagement activities described earlier in this book. The focus of the next section is therefore on effective and inclusive communication strategies.

TALKING TO THE PUBLIC: COMMUNICATIONS 101

For parents, questions about teacher effectiveness strike a deeply personal chord. This is not a theoretical exploration of what makes a good teacher; teacher quality is about the quality of education their children are receiving, and, ultimately, their children's opportunity for a better life. Suddenly changing the way a school measures teacher or principal performance may cause parents to wonder about the quality of their child's education in the past. An incomplete or inaccurate picture of evaluation—for example, the release of teachers' test scores for their students without a clear explanation of what the data mean and how they fit into the context of teacher quality—can greatly damage the public's trust and confidence in teachers, schools, and district and state leaders.

The release of teachers' value-added student test scores in New York provides a good example of an unsuccessful community engagement strategy. Even supporters of linking teacher evaluation to student test scores worried that the data would be misunderstood or misused, especially as the scores had a wide margin of error. The ensuing controversy—Randi Weingarten, president of the American Federation of Teachers, called the release a "public flogging," and Sandi Jacobs, vice president of the National Council on Teacher Quality (a group that supports student performance as a component in evaluation), called it "a really bad idea"—diverted the public's attention and prevented a more robust and productive conversation about what makes for effective teaching.

Instead of a data dump, we advocate creating a baseline of public understanding over time, with the caveat that school, district, or community leaders will need to stretch themselves to do this in ways that are credible and easy to understand. If there had been a better exchange with the public about the concept of value-added test scores (something that is difficult even for teachers to understand!) within the context of teacher evaluation, as well as what weight these test scores actually bore, New York might have been able to avoid such a controversial situation.

The following are some important principles for engaging and communicating with the public, drawn in part from past Public Agenda research on school quality (Johnson, Rochkind, Remaley, & Hess, 2011) and from our expertise in stakeholder engagement.

Respect the Basics of Good Communication

The basics of good communication are not especially mysterious, although education reform unfortunately seems to be riddled with examples of breathtakingly clumsy communications missteps—sending a note home in a backpack to communicate about school closure, for example, or releasing teacher test scores without clear context, as in New York.

Communications basics include planning, empathy, and taking a moment to think about what listeners will hear and what questions they may have. When you emphasize the ground rules for good communications, parents, students, teachers, and others in the community will at least know that they are being treated with thoughtfulness and are being given an opportunity to understand the issue at hand. Surprising people, delivering potentially troubling news thoughtlessly or in a cavalier manner, ignoring community ideas and concerns, or showing disrespect for people's emotions are communications missteps that could potentially derail even the most earnest reform policy.

Communicate Early and Often

Let people know what is going on and why. Communicate directly with parents, with important community partners, and with the media, and do so from the beginning. It is ineffective to talk to the community only once a decision has already been made, particularly if it involves an issue that the community cares strongly about or if it is one that is prone to politicization. People need time to absorb and adjust to change, and, in the absence of real communication, rumors can (and do) run rampant and threaten to derail reform.

Communicate Through Trusted Sources

It may be the case that a legacy of distrust exists between the community and the school district. Alternatively, the community may have heard about evaluation mishaps in other districts—or even their own—and be suspicious about the merit of spending time and money on revamping an evaluation plan.

It is often advisable for reformers and education leaders to reach out to trusted allies in the community—for example, religious or organizational leaders, local employers, and higher education officials—to develop the best approach for talking to the community and explaining what is happening and why. **This is no PR maneuver**; leaders should not approach trusted community members expecting them to help "sell" their message. Rather, we suggest reaching out to those who know and understand the community best, so that leaders and reformers are able to communicate using understandable language and can avoid concepts or jargon that may be emotionally loaded or off-putting.

In our experience, teachers often have strong credibility, and, in most cases, they have far more one-on-one interactions with parents and students than do state and district leaders. This is yet another reason why teachers need to be included in the evaluation redesign process—if they believe that the change (and its eventual outcomes) will help make them the best possible teachers for the community's children, that is a powerful message for the community to hear.

Of course, these kinds of relationships and connections cannot be established at the last minute. Reformers and leaders need to reach out to potential allies and partners in the community long before the final decisions are made and the final plans are in place.

Provide Focused Information—Not Too Little and Not Too Much

In the research for *Don't Count Us Out,* Public Agenda (Johnson, Rochkind, & DuPont, 2011) found that information alone does not translate to evidence of effectiveness or help build the public's confidence. In fact, *too* much information, without meaningful context or communication, can actually erode the public's trust because people become skeptical of the accuracy and importance of data, suspicious of the way numbers can be manipulated, or confused and overwhelmed by the detailed information flying past them in the name of "disclosure" and "transparency."

Furthermore, as we examined in our discussion of the Learning Curve (see Chapter Four), more information does not in itself advance individual or shared understanding of a complex issue. At the same time, however, the public does need a foundation of basic facts in order to understand trade-offs and benefits and to judge evaluation policy properly and wisely. Finding this balance is a key challenge in communicating with the public in an inclusive and productive way. The information should also be easily digestible and should help the community understand the complexities of the issue.

It is worth remembering one fundamental rule of good communication in just about any situation: presenting information in formats that invite people to ask questions, exchange views, and make suggestions can be far more effective than the world's most polished PowerPoint flashed on a screen at a news conference or public hearing.

Be Responsive to the Community's Concerns

Education leaders, and those charged with communicating and engaging with the public, should of course be in tune with the deeply personal connection that parents have with the question of the quality of their children's teachers. Another related consideration is that parents may not always judge a teacher's effectiveness based on academics alone. Most parents care deeply about their children's academic progress, but they may be equally concerned about whether teachers care about and nurture their children, promote a safe and orderly classroom, and help their children develop good behavior and a strong character. Ratings systems that focus solely on academics may seem incomplete to some parents. Leaders and teachers need to help parents understand that good teachers succeed in all these areas and that all are captured in the evaluation system.

Remember to Tell Stories

Most people learn and retain more from hearing a compelling story than from a litany of statistics. (See, for example, Goodman, 2010, at http://www.agoodmanonline.com/publications/storytelling/index.html.) Stories have memorable characters, specific settings, rich and interesting details, and a narrative structure that brings people into the situation, and they are a highly effective form of communication. They don't replace more comprehensive statistical information, but they can give the statistics life and meaning. Dry data about test scores, or even a category on a scale, mean so much more, and become so much more effective, when placed in a story that provides context. Who is an effective teacher? What happens when a student learns from a gifted, caring, and effective teacher? What happens in a school filled with effective teachers and principals with vision and empathy? What happens in a community filled with such schools?

Consider Creating Community and Parent Task Forces

Community and parent task forces can provide input into the development of policies and practices. Many business and nonprofit professionals have evaluation experience in their own industries, and they may be able to bring fresh eyes and ideas to conversations about the most effective evaluation policies and practices for teaching and learning. Moreover, a parent task force could help schools develop the most effective strategies for sharing evaluation information with parents.

Conclusion

Teacher Voice in Evaluation and Beyond

The teaching profession is at a crossroads. There is unrelenting political pressure at every level of the education system to strengthen teacher effectiveness by implementing more rigorous evaluation systems. Whether these new systems deliver on the promise of improving instruction and increasing student achievement is in large part dependent on the ability of teachers to authentically engage in reform conversations and policymakers' sincere efforts to act on the resulting recommendations. Teacher voice, input, and involvement in evaluation must increase to ensure that new systems incorporate teachers' wisdom and practical experience, enable teachers to embrace new policies, and expand teacher leadership.

This book has presented a new approach to collaboratively developing and implementing teacher evaluation systems, one that we hope facilitates authentic inclusion of teacher voice as a way to create sustainable and legitimate policy that sticks. We have outlined an extensively field-tested method for including teacher voice in evaluation reform, as well as strategies for increasing the engagement of principals, parents, and community members in evaluation as part of a complete approach to advancing how educator effectiveness is assessed for the twenty-first century. Also important, we have shared stories from the field that demonstrate that this vision is possible to achieve.

Individuals and organizations around the country are taking bold steps to change the teaching profession from one that is disconnected from the policies that are imposed on it to one that leads these changes; we have described some of these leaders in this book, including the following:

- Dina Rock from Hope Street Group in Ohio, where state-of-the-art online discussion forums provide teachers the opportunity to move the policy conversation beyond the teachers' lounge and into the statehouse
- Sydney Morris and Evan Stone from Educators4Excellence, who reach more than six thousand teachers nationwide through intensive policy teams that spend months researching, polling, and thinking about a specific pressing reform issue, and present their white papers to districts, unions, and state leaders
- Teach Plus, which, recognizing that policymakers do value teacher voice, facilitates solutions-oriented conversations between teachers and policymakers—helping teachers from Boston to Los Angeles connect their personal story with larger policy issues
- New Millennium Teachers, which brings together groups of early-career teachers in six cities across the country to develop best practices guides on teacher evaluation
- Seattle-based Teachers United, which advocates for teacher-designed policies and has placed teacher leaders in the boardrooms of nonprofit organizations, in union executive committee meetings, and out in the community
- Jake Gourley from Advance Illinois, who demonstrates how teacher voice organizations can inspire everyday teacher leadership and can influence local politics that lead to positive changes for students
- VIVA Teachers, which has engaged teachers, even those with only a few minutes to contribute, through its online "Idea Exchange" platform where professionally moderated conversations have been the basis for actionable recommendations in Minnesota and elsewhere

Opportunities for teacher leadership are clearly on the rise. That is a welcome development for teacher engagement efforts, as teacher leaders can play a decisive role in effective teacher engagement. Promoting teacher leadership in teacher evaluation is one vital approach to grow leadership skills, knowledge, and interest among teachers while simultaneously developing more meaningful and effective policies.

TEACHER ENGAGEMENT AND LEADERSHIP AS A HUMAN CAPITAL MANAGEMENT STRATEGY

Despite all the advances around teacher leadership, authentic and sustained engagement in teacher evaluation reforms is still in the early stages. It is our hope that as evaluation policies continue to be developed, implemented, and modified, the dozen or so leaders highlighted in this book will serve as models for teachers en masse to come to the table to help establish sound mechanisms for evaluating effectiveness in the teaching profession.

Teacher evaluation is itself but one element in a more comprehensive approach to ensuring teacher effectiveness. The teacher leaders cited in this book, as well as the research and policy community, agree that teacher evaluation on its own will not immediately result in a great teacher in every classroom. Other policies, including those related to teacher preparation and compensation, for example, are also important for ensuring that our education system is populated with talented and effective teachers. Accordingly, the education policy conversation is moving toward the comprehensive overhaul of human capital management in education as a more strategic and sustainable approach to recruiting and retaining effective teachers for all students.

As illustrated in Figure 9.1, human capital management approaches treat teacher evaluation as just one component in a web of critical policies that impact who decides to teach, where they teach, how well they teach, and how long they stay.

Figure 9.1. Example of an Aligned Human Capital Management System

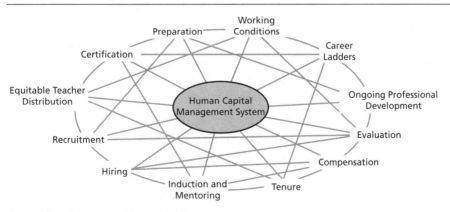

Source: Behrstock-Sherratt and Jacques, 2012.

In our previous book, *Improving Teacher Quality: A Guide for Education Leaders* (Laine, Behrstock-Sherratt, & Lasagna, 2011), we detail the elements of a strategic, comprehensive human capital management system for attracting, retaining, and developing effective teachers. We argue that education leaders at the state and district level must address not only teacher evaluation but also the full spectrum of human capital management strategies—preparation, recruitment, hiring, induction, professional development, compensation, and working conditions—as none of these strategies on their own will result in a profession that attracts and retains the best and the brightest into the teaching force. As they do in teacher evaluation, teachers have the potential to be a powerful and beneficial partner in decision making and problem solving when it comes to human capital management strategies. Teacher voice should guide the restructuring of a human capital management system, and education leaders should strive to support a collaborative system in which leadership and decision making are shared across the policy spectrum.

It is our hope and vision that teachers engage on these issues and strategies and that policymakers include the input of teachers in a systematic, meaningful, and organized way, so that the decisions they make are informed and supported by those most directly impacted by change. For example, teacher leaders may be actively involved in recruiting new talent to their school or district as well as sharing with district leaders the factors that led them to the district, and they may sit on hiring committees. Teacher leaders may serve as mentors and instructional coaches to help their colleagues (particularly those newer to the profession) improve their instructional practice. To create a truly world-class teaching profession, the teacher engagement strategies introduced in this book for the purpose of creating a comprehensive and sustainable evaluation system can and should also be applied to inform the design of new human capital management systems.

We hope we have shown that authentic engagement is not a mysterious and nebulous process, but rather a defined set of principles, practical tools, and methods dedicated to giving stakeholders—in this case teachers—a voice and a means to participate in decisions that affect their lives and profession. Teacher engagement in teacher evaluation can drive continued engagement and teacher leadership opportunities around the full set of issues that attract great teachers to the profession, make them want to stay, and address critical shortages in high-need subject and geographical areas.

Across the country, education leaders are grappling with such challenges as teaching shortages in the STEM fields, high numbers of inexperienced teachers placed in the most high-poverty and high-need schools, and the constant movement of experienced teachers into districts that offer higher pay and less challenging working conditions. Bringing teachers to the table for practical, grounded, solutions-oriented conversations can breathe new life into what traditionally have been top-down reform efforts and increase the likelihood of successful implementation.

As this book repeatedly demonstrates, assessing teacher effectiveness, let alone significantly improving teacher effectiveness, is a complex undertaking. The states and districts that were out of the gate first in terms of redesigning their evaluation systems have seen some success—more than three-quarters (78 percent) of teachers surveyed in 2011 believed that their most recent evaluation was done carefully and taken seriously, and 62 percent received meaningful feedback that improved their instruction (Rosenberg & Silva, 2012).

It is worth noting, however, that the states and districts that are pioneering the design and implementation of new evaluation systems have often tried to keep things simple by avoiding the daunting prospect of developing these policies in collaboration with teachers themselves. As a result, the long-term viability of these newly minted evaluation systems is uncertain, as teacher resistance, misunderstanding, and stress increase. We are confident that this book's alternative approach to reform will lead to policies more likely to stand the test of time. Nevertheless, there is always more to learn about how effectively our research-based tools and strategies engage teachers for the purpose of reimagining teacher evaluation systems and about whether they work at scale—so let us know how your reform efforts go!

Transforming teacher evaluation systems by applying the strategies described in this book requires teachers to take charge of their profession: to step out of the classroom and into the statehouses, district boardrooms, community conversations, and school improvement committees and ensure that their practical wisdom is heard and that it serves as the foundation for a new approach to improving teaching and learning. We sincerely hope that the ideas that are sparked by reading this book, and the collaborations and conversations that emerge, will serve as the beginning of far greater teacher-led improvements, not only to teacher evaluation but also to the profession as a whole. The growing network of teacher leader policy organizations that have been described in this book chart a path for successful teacher engagement in policy reform. It is up to you to chart this path's next course.

USEFUL RESOURCES: SAMPLE POLICY REPORTS FROM TEACHER LEADER ORGANIZATIONS

Advance Illinois

Transforming Teacher Work for a Better Educated Tomorrow
> http://www.advanceillinois.org/filebin/TransformingTeacherWork.pdf

Educators4Excellence

Beyond Satisfactory: A New Teacher Evaluation System for New York
> http://educators4excellence.s3.amazonaws.com/8/b5/5/152/1/E4E_Evaluation_White_Paper_FINAL.pdf

Principals Matter: Principal Evaluations from a Teacher Perspective
> http://educators4excellence.s3.amazonaws.com/8/13/1/349/E4E_Principals_Matter.pdf

Breaking the Stalemate: LA Teachers Take on Teacher Evaluation
> http://educators4excellence.s3.amazonaws.com/8/e7/3/461/E4E-LA.Teacher_Evaluation.final.pdf

Hope Street Group

Policy 2.0: Using Open Innovation to Reform Teacher Evaluation Systems
> http://hopestreetgroup.org/sites/default/files/docs/resources/policy2.0policypaper.pdf

Analysis of Education Reform in the American Recovery and Reinvestment Act of 2009 (ARRA)
> http://hopestreetgroup.org/sites/default/files/docs/resources/ARRA-Analysis-2.11.09.pdf

Teacher Evaluation Playbook
> http://playbook.hopestreetgroup.org

New Millennium Teachers

Making Teacher Evaluation Work for Students: Voices from the Classroom (Denver)
> http://www.teachingquality.org/sites/default/files/denvernm_final.pdf

How Better Teacher and Student Assessment Can Power Up Learning (Washington State)
> http://www.teachingquality.org/sites/default/files/WA_report_FINAL.pdf

Many Ways Up, No Reason to Move Out (Bay Area)

http://www.teachingquality.org/sites/default/files/BAY_AREA_FINAL_Jan2012.pdf

Teach Plus

A Great Evaluator for Every Teacher: 5 Recommendations to Ensure That Teacher Evaluations are Fair, Reliable, and Effective (Boston)
http://www.teachplus.org/uploads/Documents/1336657021_AGreatEvaluatorforEveryTeacher050912.pdf

Peer Assistance and Review (PAR) Implementation Teachers Will Support (Memphis)
http://www.teachplus.org/uploads/Documents/1327432092_PAR%20Implementation%20Teachers%20Will%20Support.pdf

Improving Teacher Evaluation in California (Los Angeles)
http://www.teachplus.org/uploads/1321543495_ETW_TeachPlusLA_Improving%20Teacher%20Evaluation%20in%20CA_web%20booklet.pdf

Guidelines for Observing Teacher Practice in Chicago
http://www.teachplus.org/uploads/Documents/1307025976_GuidelinesForObservingTeacherPracticeInChicago.pdf

VIVA Teachers

Voices from the Classroom: VIVA National Task Force Report
http://vivateachers.org/wp-content/uploads/2011/02/VIVANat.pdf

Opening Doors to Professional Communication and Collaboration (New York)
http://vivateachers.org/wp-content/uploads/2011/02/VIVANy.pdf

REFERENCES

Allensworth, E., Ponisciak, S., & Mazzeo, C. (2009). *The schools teachers leave: Teacher mobility in Chicago Public Schools.* Chicago, IL: Consortium on Chicago School Research. Retrieved from http://ccsr.uchicago.edu/sites/default/files/publications/CCSR_Teacher_Mobility.pdf.

American Institutes for Research. (2012a). *Performance Management Advantage: The implementation path.* Washington, DC: Author.

American Institutes for Research. (2012b). *Teacher performance management: Scorecard for district policymakers.* Washington, DC: Author. Retrieved from http://educator-talent.org/inc/docs/PMA_TeacherPerfMgmt_DistrictScorecard.pdf.

Arbuckle, M. A., & Murray, L. B. (1989). *Building systems for professional growth: An action guide.* Andover, MA: Regional Laboratory for Educational Improvement of the Northeast and Islands.

Banchero, S. (2012, February 25). Teacher ratings aired in New York. *Wall Street Journal.* Retrieved from http://online.wsj.com/article/SB10001424052970203918304577243591163104860.html.

Behrstock-Sherratt, E., & Jacques, C. (2012). *Aligning evaluation results and professional development: Driving systemic human capital management reform.* Washington, DC: U.S. Department of Education.

Berry, B. (2011). *Teaching 2030: What we must do for our students and our public schools— now and in the future.* New York, NY: Teachers College Press.

Bill & Melinda Gates Foundation. (2010). *Working with teachers to develop fair and reliable measures of effective teaching.* Retrieved from http://www.metproject.org/downloads/met-framing-paper.pdf.

225

Bill & Melinda Gates Foundation. (2013). *Ensuring fair and reliable measures of effective teaching: Culminating findings from the MET project's three-year study.* Retrieved from http://www.edweek.org/media/17teach-met1.pdf.

Bittle, S., Haller, C., & Kadlec, A. (2009). *Promising practices in online engagement.* New York, NY: Center for Advances in Public Engagement at Public Agenda.

Brandt, C., Mathers, C., Oliva, M., Brown-Sims, M., & Hess, J. (2007). *Examining district guidance to schools on teacher evaluation policies in the Midwest region.* Naperville, IL: Regional Education Laboratory Midwest. Retrieved from http://ies.ed.gov/ncee/edlabs/regions/midwest/pdf/REL_2007030.pdf.

Bushaw, W., & Lopez, S. (2011). Betting on teachers: The 43rd annual Phi Delta Kappan/Gallup Poll of the public's attitudes toward the public schools. *Kappan 93*(1), 9–26. Retrieved from http://www.pdkintl.org/poll/docs/pdkpoll43_2011.pdf.

Center for Advances in Public Engagement. (2008). *Public engagement: A primer from Public Agenda.* New York, NY: Author.

Clifford, M., Behrstock-Sherratt, E., & Fetters, J. (2012). *The ripple effect: A synthesis of research on principal influence to inform performance evaluation design.* Washington, DC: American Institutes for Research. Retrieved from http://www.air.org/files/1707_The_Ripple_Effect_d8_Online.pdf.

Clifford, M., Hansen, U. & Wraight, S. (2012). *A practical guide to designing comprehensive principal evaluation systems: A tool to assist in the development of principal evaluation systems.* Washington, DC: National Comprehensive Center for Teacher Quality. Retrieved from http://www.tqsource.org/publications/DesigningPrincipalEvalSys.pdf.

Clotfelter, C. T., Ladd, H. F., Vigdor, J. L., & Wheeler, J. (2007, March). *High-poverty schools and the distribution of teachers and principals* (Working Paper 1). Washington, DC: National Center for Analysis of Longitudinal Data in Education Research.

Cody, A. (2012, January 10). Dialogue with the Gates Foundation: How do we build the teaching profession? *Education Week Teacher.* Retrieved from http://blogs.edweek.org/teachers/living-in-dialogue/2012/07/dialogue_with_the_gates_founda.html?cmpENL-TU-VIEWS2.

Coggshall, J. (2007). *Communication framework for measuring teacher quality and effectiveness.* Washington, DC: National Comprehensive Center for Teacher Quality. Retrieved from http://www.tqsource.org/publications/NCCTQCommFramework.pdf.

Coggshall, J., Behrstock-Sherratt, E., & Drill, K. (2011). *Workplaces that support high-performing teaching and learning: Insights from generation Y teachers.* Washington, DC: American Institutes for Research and American Federation of Teachers. Retrieved from http://www.aft.org/pdfs/teachers/genyreport0411.pdf.

Commission on Effective Teachers and Teaching. (2011). *Transforming teaching: Connecting professional responsibility with student learning.* Washington, DC: Author. Retrieved from http://www.nea.org/assets/docs/Transformingteaching2012.pdf.

Condon, C., & Clifford, M. (2012). *Measuring principal performance: How rigorous are commonly used principal performance assessment instruments?* Washington, DC: American Institutes for Research. Retrieved from http://www.learningpt.org/pdfs/QSLBrief2.pdf.

Covey, S. (with Merrill, R). (2006). *The speed of trust: The one thing that changes everything.* New York, NY: Free Press.

Daley, G., & Kim, L. (2010*). A teacher evaluation system that works.* Santa Monica, CA: National Institute for Excellence in Teaching. Retrieved from http://www.tapsystem.org/publications/wp_eval.pdf.

Danielson, C. (1996). *Enhancing professional practice: A framework for teaching.* Alexandria, VA: Association for Supervision and Curriculum Development.

Darling-Hammond, L., LaPointe, M., Meyerson, D., & Orr, M. T. (2007). *Preparing school leaders for a changing world: Executive summary.* Stanford, CA: Stanford University, Stanford Educational Leadership Institute.

Davis, S., Kearney, K., Sanders, N., Thomas, C., & Leon, R. (2011). *The policies and practices of principal evaluation: A review of the literature.* San Francisco, CA: WestEd.

DeAngelis, K., Peddle, M., Trott, C., & Bergeron, L. (2002). *Teacher supply in Illinois: Evidence from the Illinois Teacher Study.* Edwardsville: Illinois Education Research Council.

Delaware Performance Appraisal System II, Del. Code Ann. tit. 14, §§ 1270-75 (2012). Retrieved from http://delcode.delaware.gov/title14/c012/sc07/index.shtml.

Doyle, D., & Han, J. G. (2012). *Measuring teacher effectiveness: A look "under the hood" of teacher evaluation in 10 sites.* New York, NY: 50CAN; New Haven, CT: ConnCAN; and Chapel Hill, NC: Public Impact. Retrieved from http://www.conncan.org/learn/research/teachers/measuring-teacher-effectiveness.

Duffett, A., Farkas, S., Rotherham, A. J., & Silva, E. (2008). *Waiting to be won over: Teachers speak on the profession, unions, and reform.* Washington, DC: Education Sector. Retrieved from http://www.educationsector.org/sites/default/files/publications/WaitingToBeWonOver_0.pdf.

Evaluation of Educators, 603 Mass. Code Regs. 35 (2011). Retrieved from http://www.doe.mass.edu/lawsregs/603cmr35.html.

Farkas, S., Foley, P., & Duffett, A. (with Foleno, T., & Johnson, J.). (2001). *Just waiting to be asked? A fresh look at attitudes on public engagement.* New York, NY: Public Agenda. Retrieved from http://www.publicagenda.org/files/pdf/just_waiting_to_be_asked.pdf.

Farkas, S., Johnson, J., & Duffett, A. (with Moye, L., & Vine, J.). (2003). *Stand by me: What teachers really think about unions, merit pay and other professional matters.* Washington, DC: Public Agenda. Retrieved from http://www.publicagenda.org/files/pdf/stand_by_me.pdf.

Forman, K. K. (2012). An exemption for individually identifiable teacher performance data under state freedom of information laws. *Seton Hall Legislative Journal, 36*, 379–407.

Friedman, W., Kadlec, A., & Birnback, L. (2007). *Transforming public life: A decade of citizen engagement in Bridgeport, CT.* New York, NY: Center for Advances in Public Engagement at Public Agenda.

Gates, B. (2012, February 22). Shame is not the solution. *New York Times.* Retrieved from http://www.nytimes.com/2012/02/23/opinion/for-teachers-shame-is-no-solution. html?_r1.

Glazerman, S., & Max, J. (2011, April). *Do low-income students have equal access to the highest-performing teachers?* Washington, DC: Institute of Education Sciences, National Center for Education Evaluation and Regional Assistance.

Goe, L. (2010). *Evaluating teachers with multiple measures.* Washington, DC: American Federation of Teachers. Retrieved from www.atfunion.org/files/dmfile/ EvaluatingTeachingwithMultipleMeasures.pdf.

Goe, L., Bell, C., & Little, O. (2008). *Approaches to evaluating teacher effectiveness: A review of the literature.* Washington, DC: National Comprehensive Center for Teacher Quality. Retrieved from http://www.tqsource.org/publications/EvaluatingTeachEffectiveness.pdf.

Goodman, A. (2010). *Storytelling as best practice* (5th ed.). Los Angeles: Goodman Center.

Hagelskamp, C., & DiStasi, C. (2013). *Failure is not an option.* New York, NY: Public Agenda.

Hatry, H. P., & Greiner, J. M. (1985). *Issues and case studies in teacher incentive plans.* Washington, DC: Urban Institute Press.

Heitin, L. (2012, April 24). 2012 National Teacher of the Year hopes to "restore dignity" to teachers. *Education Week Teacher.* Retrieved from http://www.edweek.org/tm/ articles/2012/04/24/ntoy_2012.html?tknYVRFQGZ2NSoBe7P%2Fy7gGEs46%2Fod FoFeiEX0X&cmpENL-EU-NEWS2.

Humphrey, D. C., Koppich, J. E., Bland, J. A., & Bosetti, K. R. (2011). *Peer review: Getting serious about teacher evaluation.* Menlo Park, CA: SRI International.

Jacob, B., & Lefgren, L. (2005). *Principals as agents: Subjective performance measurement in education.* Working Paper 11463. Cambridge, MA: National Bureau of Economic Research. Retrieved from http://www.nber.org/papers/w11463.pdf.

Jacques, C., Clifford, M., & Hornung, K. (2012). *State policies on principal evaluation: Trends in a changing landscape.* Washington, DC: National Comprehensive Center for Teacher Quality. Retrieved from http://www.tqsource.org/publications/ StatePoliciesOnPrincipalEval.pdf.

Johnson, J. (2012). *You can't do it alone: A communications and engagement manual for school leaders committed to reform.* Lanham, MD: Rowman & Littlefield Education.

Johnson, J., Rochkind, J., & DuPont, S. (2011). *Don't count us out: How an overreliance on accountability could undermine the public's confidence in schools, business, government, and more.* New York, NY: Public Agenda and the Kettering Foundation.

Johnson, J., Rochkind, J., Remaley, M., & Hess, J. (2011). *What's trust got to do with it?* New York, NY: Public Agenda.

Kadlec, A., & Friedman, W. (2010). *Changing the conversation about productivity: Strategies for engaging faculties and institutional leaders.* New York, NY: Public Agenda. Retrieved from http://www.publicagenda.org/files/pdf/changing-conversation-college-productivity_0.pdf.

Kane, T., & Darling-Hammond, L. (2012, June 24). Should test scores be used to evaluate teachers? *Wall Street Journal.* Retrieved from http://online.wsj.com/article/SB100014 24052702304723304577366023832205042.html.

Kaplan, T. (2012, June 22). Albany to limit the disclosure of teacher evaluations. *New York Times,* p. A21.

Koppich, J. E. (2010). *Meeting the challenges of stakeholder engagement and communication: Lessons from Teacher Incentive Fund grantees.* Washington, DC: Center for Educator Compensation Reform, U.S. Department of Education, Office of Elementary and Secondary Education.

Kowal, J., & Hassel, E. (2010). *Measuring teacher and leader performance: Cross-sector lessons for excellent evaluations.* Chapel Hill, NC: Public Impact. Retrieved from http://www.publicimpact.com/images/performance_measurement-public-impact.pdf.

Lachlan-Haché, L., Cushing, E., & Bivona, L. (2012). *Student learning objectives (SLOs) as a measure of educator effectiveness: The basics.* Washington, DC: American Institutes for Research. Retrieved from http://educatortalent.org/inc/docs/SLOs_Measures_of_Educator_Effectiveness.pdf.

Laine, S., Behrstock-Sherratt, E., & Lasagna, M. (2010). *Improving teacher quality: A guide for education leaders.* San Francisco, CA: Jossey-Bass.

LaRock, J. D., & Rodriguez-Farrar, H. (2005, Winter). Interview: U.S. Secretary of Education Margaret Spellings. *Harvard Educational Review.* Retrieved June 16, 2012, from http://www.hepg.org/her/abstract/2.

Leithwood, K., Louis, K., Anderson, S., & Wahlstrom, K. (2004). *How leadership influences student learning.* New York, NY: Wallace Foundation. Retrieved from http://www.wallacefoundation.org/knowledge-center/school-leadership/key-research/Documents/How-Leadership-Influences-Student-Learning.pdf.

Leo, S. F., & Lachlan-Haché, L. (2012). *Creating summative educator effectiveness score: Approaches to combining measures.* Washington, DC: American Institutes for Research. Retrieved from http://www.educatortalent.org/inc/docs/Creating%20Summative%20EE%20Scores_FINAL.PDF.

Little, O., Bell, C., & Goe, L. (2009). A practical guide to evaluating teacher effectiveness. Washington, DC: National Comprehensive Center for Teacher Quality. Retrieved from http://www.tqsource.org/publications/practicalGuide.pdf.

Markow, D., & Pieters, A. (2012). *The MetLife survey of the American teacher: Teachers, parents, and the economy.* New York, NY: MetLife Foundation. Retrieved from http://www.metlife.com/assets/cao/contributions/foundation/american-teacher/MetLife-Teacher-Survey-2011.pdf.

Mathews, J. (2012, June 22). D.C. keeps ignoring its test erasure scandal. *Washington Post.* Retrieved from http://www.washingtonpost.com/blogs/class-struggle/post/dc-keeps-ignoring-its-test-erasure-scandal/2012/06/22/gJQAEzT2vV_blog.html.

McNeil, M. (2012, January 10). Big Race to the Top problems in Hawaii, Florida, New York, says Ed. Department. *Education Week.* Retrieved from http://blogs.edweek.org/edweek/campaign-K–12/2012/01/race_to_the_top.html?cmpENL-EU-NEWS1.

Mead, S., Rotherham, A., & Brown, R. (2012). *The hangover: Thinking about the unintended consequences of the nation's teacher evaluation binge.* Washington, DC: American Enterprise Institute. Retrieved from http://www.aei.org/files/2012/09/25/-the-hang-over-thinking-about-the-unintended-consequences-of-the-nations-teacher-evalua-tion-binge_144008786960.pdf.

National Council on Teacher Quality. (2011). *State of the states: Trends and early lessons on teacher evaluation and effectiveness policies.* Washington, DC: Author.

National Education Association. (2010). *Teacher assessment and evaluation: The National Education Association's framework for supporting education systems to support effec-tive teaching and improve student learning.* Retrieved from http://www.nea.org/assets/docs/HE/TeachrAssmntWhtPaperTransform10_2.pdf.

New York State Department of Education. (2012). *Summary of revised APPR provisions.* Retrieved from http://engageny.org/wp-content/uploads/2012/03/nys-evaluation-plansguidance-memo.pdf.

Paulson, A. (2012, August 12). Back to school: How to measure a good teacher. *Christian Science Monitor.* Retrieved from http://www.csmonitor.com/USA/Education/2012/0812/Back-to-school-How-to-measure-a-good-teacher.

Performance Evaluation Reform Act, P.A. 96-0861 (2010). Retrieved from http://www.isbe.net/peac/pdf/PA096-0861_SB315.pdf.

Personnel Evaluation Procedures and Criteria, Fla. Stat. § 1012.34 (2012). Retrieved from http://www.leg.state.fl.us/statutes/index.cfm?App_mode=Display_Statute&Search_String=&URL=1000-1099/1012/Sections/1012.34.html.

Public Agenda. (2010). *Retaining Teacher Talent Survey of Teachers: Full survey data.* Retrieved from http://www.learningpt.org/expertise/educatorquality/genY/FullSurveyData.pdf.

Public Agenda. (2012a). *Community conversations planning guide.* New York, NY: Author.

Public Agenda. (2012b). *Facilitator's handbook.* New York, NY: Author.

Public Agenda & Achieving the Dream. (2011). *Engaging adjunct and full-time faculty in student success innovation.* New York, NY: Author. Retrieved from http://www.publicagenda.org/files/pdf/ATD_engaging_faculty_in_student_success.pdf.

Rebora, A. (2012, October 31). Teacher-leadership degrees aim to fill career gaps. *Education Week.* Retrieved from http://www.edweek.org/ew/articles/2012/10/31/

10leaders.h32.html?tknTXCCNHks21FQ3mIuscHz9AEIr1CtjV%2FezsE8&cmp clp-sb-ascd.

Regional Educational Laboratory Network Program. (1995). *Facilitating systemic change in science and mathematics education: A toolkit for professional developers.* Andover, MA: Regional Laboratory for Educational Improvement of the Northeast and Islands.

Rice, J. K. (2010). The impact of teacher experience: Examining the evidence and policy implications. Washington, DC: National Center for the Analysis of Longitudinal Data in Education Research. Retrieved from http://www.urban.org/UploadedPDF/1001455-impact-teacher-experience.pdf.

Rosenberg, S., & Silva, E. (2012). *Trending toward reform: Teachers speak on unions and the future of the profession.* Washington, DC: Education Sector. Retrieved from http://www.educationsector.org/sites/default/files/publications/REPORT-Teacher Survey3f.pdf.

Sarrio, J. (2011, July 13). Atlanta's testing scandal adds fuel to U.S. debate. *Atlanta Journal-Constitution.* Retrieved from http://www.ajc.com/news/atlanta/atlantas-testing-scandal-adds-1007201.html.

Sartain, L., Stoelinga, S., & Brown, E. (2011). *Rethinking teacher evaluation in Chicago: Lessons learned from classroom observations, principal-teacher conferences, and district implementation.* Chicago, IL: CCSR. Retrieved from http://ccsr.uchicago.edu/sites/default/files/publications/Teacher%20Eval%20Report%20FINAL.pdf.

Scholastic & Bill & Melinda Gates Foundation. (2012). *Primary sources 2012: America's teachers on the teaching profession.* Retrieved from http://www.scholastic.com/primarysources/pdfs/Gates2012_full.pdf.

Thomas, S. L., & Bretz, R. D. (1994). Research and practice in performance appraisal: Evaluating employee performance in America's largest companies. *SAM Advanced Management Journal,* 59(2), 28–34.

Weisberg, D., Sexton, S., Mulhern, J., & Keeling, D. (2009). *The widget effect: Our national failure to acknowledge and act on differences in teacher effectiveness.* The New Teacher Project. Retrieved from http://widgeteffect.org/downloads/TheWidgetEffect.pdf.

Yankelovich, D. (1999). *The magic of dialogue.* New York, NY: Simon & Schuster.

Yankelovich, D., & Friedman, W. (Eds.). (2011). *Toward wiser public judgment.* Nashville, TN: Vanderbilt University Press.

Zavis, A., & Barboza, T. (2010, September 28). Teacher's suicide shocks school. *Los Angeles Times,* p. A4.

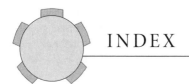

INDEX

Page references followed by *fig* indicate an illustrated figure; followed by *t* indicate a table.

Management Scorecard for Districts on, 72–73; teacher role as, 77–80. *See also* Teacher evaluation

Evans, E., 101–102

Everyone at the Table website: additional optional activities available on, 179; Additional Resources on Teacher Evaluation handout available on, 186; Build Your Own Evaluation available on, 206; Build Your Own Evaluation Group handouts available on, 169; Discussion Summary handout available on, 162–165; "Engaging Teachers in Evaluation Reform" video available on, 149; Interview Group Process handout available on, 182; Interview Recording Sheet handout available on, 182; Principal Discussion Summary available on, 199; Sample Principal Recruitment Invitation available on, 194; Sample Teacher Recruitment Invitation available on, 133, 134, 135; sharing your own story on engaging teachers on the, 191; Three Scenarios for Principal Evaluation available on, 199

Expert speak mistake, 93

F

Facebook, 100

Facilitation: mistake of partisan, 93; as teacher engagement principle, 89–90. *See also* Moderators

Facilitator's Handbook (2012b) [Public Agenda], 134

Failure to communicate mistake, 93

Farkas, S., 5

Feedback: culture of engagement that encourages, 96, 98–99; Gen Y teachers expressing desire for, 65–66; teachers reporting on their evaluation, 221; 360-degree performance assessment, 80

Fennell, M., 13

Fenwick, M., 49–50

Fetters, J., 192

A Few Key Conversations at the Table (sample plan): overview of the, 112–113; suggested timeline for, 113*t*–114*t*

Firing teachers: as cost-cutting measure, 23; due to poor effectiveness ratings, 46*fig*–47

Florida Comprehensive Assessment Test (FCAT), 38

Foley, P., 5

Forman, K. K., 44

"Foundations of Evaluation" slide show: moderator's lesson plan for, 148; purpose and timeline for using, 144, 147; sample plans for using, 111*t*, 113*t*; when you don't include the, 143

Framework for Teaching, 24, 25*fig*

Framing for deliberation: Choicework discussion starters for, 86–89; definition of, 86

Framing for persuasion mistake, 93

Friedman, W., 83, 86, 94

Fung, J., 13

G

Gaget, Gauthier & Cie, 19

Gates, B., 45

Gen Y teachers: positive attitude toward walkthroughs and feedback by, 65–66; views on performance tied to salaries, 42, 43–44*fig*

Glazerman, S., 47

Goal setting for meetings, 142

Goe, L., 24, 30, 35

Goodman, A., 216

Gourley, Jake, 122–124, 218

Greiner, J. M., 43

Group conflict. *See* Conflict

Guide to Evaluation Projects, 68

H

Hagelskamp, C., 99

Haller, C., 99

Han, J. G., 39

Handouts. *See* Teacher handouts

Harrison County teacher evaluations, 39

Hassel, E., 40

Hatry, H. P., 43

Hazelwood School District in Missouri, 126

Heenan, A., 12

Heitin, L., 7

Hess, J., 23, 214

Hess, R., 12

Highly effective teachers (HETs): creating assessments based on outcomes, 22; transitioning from HQTs to, 22

Highly qualified teachers (HQTs): No Child Left Behind requiring reports on, 20–21; percentage over time of, 21*fig*; transitioning toward HETs (highly effective teachers) from, 22

Hillsborough County Public Schools, 37–38

Hope Street Colloquium (2012), 37

Hope Street Group, 36–37, 100, 218, 222

Hornung, K., 197

Human capital management: example of aligned system of, 219*fig*; teacher engagement and leadership as, 219–221

Humphrey, D. C., 77

I

Illinois: evaluation requirements and standards in, 58; Illinois State Board of Education (ISBE) of, 124; Jake Gourley interview on redesigning teacher evaluation in, 122–124, 218

Improving Teacher Quality: A Guide for Education Leaders (Laine, Behrstock-Sherratt, & Lasagna), 220

Inequitable teacher distribution, 47–49

Institute for Educational Leadership, 94

Instruction: effective teacher evaluation for improving, 189; effective teaching domain of, 25*fig*

Instruction artifacts: alignment of purpose of evaluation with analysis of, 33*t*–34*t*; teacher effectiveness measured using, 31

Internet online engagement, 99–100. *See also* Websites

Interstate School Leaders Licensure Consortium (ISLLC) standards, 200

Interview activity (principal), 211–212

Interview activity (teachers): used for generating information, 180; Interview Group Process handout on, 181, 182, 183; Interview Recording Sheet handout on, 181, 182, 183–184; moderator's lesson plan on, 180–182; sample plans for using, 112*t*, 114*t*

Interview Group Process handout, 181, 182, 183

Interview Recording Sheet handout, 181, 182, 183–184

Interviews: Alesha Daughtrey of the Center for Teaching Quality (CTQ), 62–63; Chris Eide of Teachers United, 16–17, 218; Dina Rock of Hope Street Group, 36–37, 218; Elizabeth Evans of VIVA Teachers, 101–102, 218; Jake Gourley on redesigning teacher evaluation, 122–124, 218; Maria Fenwick of Teach Plus Boston, 49–50; Sydney Morris and Evan Stone of Educators4Excellence, 10–11, 2218. *See also* Teacher engagement; Teacher leadership

"Involving Others School Leaders" video, 119

J

Jacob, B., 52

Jacobs, S., 45, 213

Jacques, C., 197

Johnson, J., 5, 125, 214, 215

Join the Conversation on Evaluating Principal Effectiveness!, 195

Join the Conversation on Evaluating Teacher Effectiveness!, 135

Joining the National Dialogue activity, 191

K

Kadlec, A., 86, 94, 99

Kane, T., 52

Kaplan, T., 45

Kearney, K., 15

Keeling, D., 19

Klein, J., 37

KODAK group, 14

Koppich, J. E., 43, 77

Kowal, J., 40

L

Lachlan-Haché, L., 40, 78

Ladd, H. F., 47

Laine, S., 220

LaPointe, M., 15

LaRock, J. D., 47

Lasagna, M., 220

Leaders Involvement Guide, 119

Learning Curve: consciousness-raising phase of, 83, 84*fig*, 132; description of theory, 83; Everyone at the Table activities to accelerate, 85, 132; evolution of public adoption of, 84–85;

resolution phase of, 84*fig*, 132; working through phase of, 83–84*fig*, 132

Lee, John, 81

Lefgren, L., 52

Leithwood, K., 193

Leo, S. F., 40

Leon, R., 15

LinkedIn, 100

Little, O., 24

Lopez, S., 20

Los Angeles (LA) school district, 81–82

Los Angeles Times, 11

Louis, K., 193

M

The Magic of Dialogue (Yankelovich), 91

Making Teacher Evaluation Work for Students: Voices from the Classroom report (CDE), 63

Markow, D., 7

Marshall, L., 13

Massachusetts: Boston Public School teachers, 13–14; evaluation requirements and standards in, 58; Teach Plus Boston in, 49–50; teacher self-evaluation and goal setting practice in, 78–79; VIVA Teachers' presentation on closing the achievement gap in, 102

Master teachers, 38

Mathers, C., 23

Mathews, J., 8

Max, J., 47

Mazzeo, C., 47

McNeil, M., 9

Mead, S., 22

Means to an End report (Aspen Institute), 68, 69

Measure Your Own Starting-Point Values (principal activity), 198

Measures of Effective Teaching initiative (Gates Foundation), 54

Measures of Effective Teaching Project, 32

Meeting the Challenges of Stakeholder Engagement and Communication (Koppich), 43

Meetings. *See* Teacher engagement team meetings

Mentoring: Community Conversations outcome of, 95; mentor teachers engaged in, 38

The MetLife Survey of the American Teacher (Markow & Pieters), 7

Meyerson, D., 15

Minkel, J., 13

Minnesota Department of Education, 101

Moderator questions: on Scenario A: Multirater Principal Evaluation, 203–204; on Scenario A: Teacher Evaluation activity, 160–161; on Scenario B: Observable Practices for Principal Evaluations, 204–205; on Scenario B: Teacher Evaluation activity, 161; on Scenario C: The Turnaround Principal Evaluation, 205–206

Moderators: care in choosing and training, 89–90; Dialogue Focus Group activity tips for, 150; Discussion Summary role of, 156; group conflict management by, 138–139, 176–177; qualities of an effective, 134–136; questions to ask about Scenario C: Teacher Evaluation activity, 162; responsibilities and objectives of the effective, 136–138; teacher engagement team role of, 134–138; three sample plans for selecting and training, 111*t*, 113*t*, 115*t*. *See also* Facilitation

Moderator's lesson plans: Additional Resources and Jigsaw activity, 184–186; Build Your Own Evaluation activity, 167–169; Dialogue Focus Group activity, 150–156; Interview activity, 180–182; Taking the Temperature Part 1: Consensogram activity, 145–146; Taking the Temperature Part 2: "Foundations of Evaluation" slide show, 148

Montclair State University, 14

Morris, S., 10, 11, 218

Mulhern, J., 19

Multiple Conversations at the Table (sample plan): overview of the, 110–111; suggested timeline for, 111*t*–112*t*

Murray, L. B., 141

N

Nataki Talibah Schoolhouse charter school (Detroit), 127

National Board Certified Teachers (NBCTs), 12

National Board for Professional Teaching Standards certification, 47

National Center for the Analysis of Longitudinal Data in Education Research, 21

National Comprehensive Center for Teacher Quality, 23

principals in, 197–210. *See also* Teacher evaluation

Principals: culture of engagement leadership by, 96–98; giving teachers a stake in evaluating, 80; making the teacher evaluation experience meaningful, 75–77; online evaluation design resources for, 68–69; six steps to guide teacher evaluation design for, 59–61*t*; Teacher Evaluation Scenario A: Principal-Centered Approach for, 157, 160–161; 360-degree performance assessments of, 80; transition to instructional leaders, 192–193. *See also* Stakeholders

Professional development: Additional Resources and Jigsaw activity for, 112*t*, 114*t*, 184–186; Additional Resources on Teacher Evaluation handout on, 185, 186–190; The Teacher Performance Management Scorecard for Districts on, 74. *See also* Teacher leadership

Professional responsibilities domain, 25*fig*

Public Agenda: "Click to Engage: How Keypads Can Enhance Learning and Deliberation" by, 144; *Community Conversations Planning Guide* (2012a) by, 134; Community Conversations series project of, 94; *Education: A Citizens' Solutions Guide* by, 87; engagement-supporting leadership qualities identified by, 97; *Facilitator's Handbook* (2012b) by, 134; research on citizen forums on the national debt conducted by, 85; Retaining Teacher Talent project research by, 53; on self-reported reason for becoming a teacher, 48; on teachers interested in schools run by teachers, 15; on teacher opinion on firing ineffective teachers, 46; working toward engaging community in improving schools, 178

Public Engagement: A Primer from Public Agenda (Center for Advances in Public Engagement), 85

Public Impact, 40

Public's Attitudes Toward the Public Schools poll (2011), 20

R

Race to the Top (RTT) initiative, 9, 193

Rebora, A., 14

Recorders: description of, 139; Discussion Summary role of, 152, 155; teacher engagement team role of, 139–140

Reflecting on Our Task Force activity: for principal engagement, 198–199; for teacher engagement, 121

"Reform fatigue," 9

Reliability: decision point on what constitutes, 65; description of teacher evaluation, 32

Remaley, M., 214

Resolution phase of Learning Curve: activities to use during, 132; description of, 84*fig*

RESPECT project (U.S. Department of Education), 6–7

Retaining Teacher Talent project, 53

Rice, J. K., 22

Rigged game mistake, 93

Rochkind, J., 214, 215

Rock, D., 36–37, 218

Rodriguez-Farrar, H., 47

Room setup: for Additional Resources and Jigsaw activity, 185; for Interview activity, 181; for Taking the Temperature Part 1: Consensogram activity, 145; for Taking the Temperature Part 2: "Foundations of Evaluation" slide show, 148; for teacher engagement team meeting and conversation, 142; for Three Scenarios for Teacher Evaluation, 151. *See also* Teacher engagement team meetings

Rosenberg, S., 53

Rotherham, A. J., 5, 22

S

Sample Principal Recruitment Invitation, 194–196

Sample Teacher Recruitment Invitation, 133, 134, 135

Sanders, N., 15

Sarrio, J., 8

Sartain, L., 24

"Scarlet Letter policy," 45

Scholastic & Bill & Melinda Gates Foundation, 15

School district teacher engagement: Colorado's SCEE (State Council on Educator Effectiveness) guidelines for, 129; engaging teachers when progress is already under way, 125–126;

Teacher evaluation task forces: decision points discussion by, 63–66, 69, 108, 122; leader-driven engagement in, 119–122; planning and preparation for, 107–117; recommendations by teachers on, 120; Reflecting on Our Task Force activity, 121; teacher-driven engagement in, 118–119; topics to discuss in early meetings, 121

Teacher evaluators: giving them a stake in evaluating principals, 80; PAR (peer assistance and review) role of, 77; professional dialogue in meetings between observers and, 79; SLOs (student learning objectives) role of, 77–78; teacher self-evaluation and goal setting by, 78–79

Teacher handouts: Additional Resources on Teacher Evaluation, 185, 186–190; Build Your Own Evaluation Group Handout 1, 112*t*, 114*t*, 115*t*, 152, 167, 168, 169, 170–172, 177; Build Your Own Evaluation Group Handout 2, 112*t*, 114*t*, 115*t*, 116*t*, 166, 167, 168, 169, 173; Build Your Own Evaluation Group Handout 3, 112*t*, 114*t*, 166, 167, 168, 169, 174; Consensogram Group Process, 145, 146–147; Discussion Summary, 162–165; Interview Group Process, 181, 182, 183; Interview Recording Sheet, 181, 182, 183–184; Three Scenarios for Teacher Evaluation, 151, 152, 154

Teacher Incentive Fund, 43

Teacher Leader Certificate program (Boston), 13–14

Teacher leader certifications, 14

Teacher leadership: as critical national effort, 15; culture of engagement and role of, 96–98; efforts to expand, 11–12; examining strategies to promote, 14–16; as a human capital management strategy, 219*fig*–221; increasing opportunities for, 218; recent developments in promoting, 13–14; resources on measuring, 189. *See also* Interviews; Professional development

Teacher Leadership Resource Center (Boston), 13

Teacher performance: Danielson's Framework for Teaching levels of, 24–25*fig*, 54; resources on designing and implementing systems of, 187–188; resources on measuring, 189; resources on rewarding, 190; The Teacher Performance Management Scorecard for Districts on, 69–75. *See also* Assessment instruments; Performance evaluation; Teacher evaluation

Teacher Performance Management Scorecard for Districts, 69–75

Teacher portfolios: alignment of purpose of evaluation with, 33*t*–34*t*; teacher effectiveness measured by, 31

Teacher quality: Danielson's Framework for Teaching, 24–25*fig*, 54; federal initiatives on importance of, 193; public concerns with, 3–4; research showing teachers without a voice in, 5–6; seven dimensions of, 26, 27*t*–29*t*

Teacher quality dimensions: teacher capacity, 28*t*; teacher character, 28*t*; teacher effectiveness, 27*t*; teacher expertise, 28*t*; teacher performance, 29*t*; teacher qualifications, 27*t*; teacher success, 29*t*

Teacher recruitment: Sample Teacher Recruitment Invitation for, 133, 134, 135; teacher engagement team strategies for, 132–134; three sample plans for, 111*t*, 113*t*, 115*t*

Teacher salaries: Gen Y versus older teacher views on performance tied to, 42, 43–44*fig*; teacher survey on effectiveness of tying performance to, 42*fig*; tying teacher effectiveness ratings to, 41–44; Washington, DC schools' IMPACT program linking evaluation to, 39

Teacher self-assessment: alignment of purpose of evaluation with, 33*t*–34*t*; teacher effectiveness measured by, 31

Teacher self-evaluations, 78–79

Teacher turnaround teams ("T3s"), 48

Teacher unions: American Federation of Teachers, 213; Education Minnesota involvement in VIVA Idea Exchange, 101; evaluation policies negotiated through, 59

Teachers: assigned based on their effectiveness, 47–49; English language learner specialists, 188; expressing satisfaction with their evaluations, 221; feeling excluded from the quality movement, 5–6; firing for purposes of cost-cutting, 23; firing those who receive poor effectiveness ratings, 46*fig*–47; five

VIVA Idea Exchange, 101, 102, 218
VIVA Teachers, 101–102, 218, 223
"Voices from the Classroom" report (VIVA Teachers), 102

W

Wahlstrom, K., 193
Walkthroughs, 65–66
Wall Street Journal, 52
Washington, DC schools: cheating scandal, 8; IMPACT program linking salary to evaluation, 39
Washington State: Education Service Districts (ESDs), 127–129; Engrossed State Senate Bill 6696 (2010), 127; Office of Superintendent of Public Instruction (OSPI), 127–129
Websites: Additional Resources on Teacher Evaluation for professional development, 186–190; AIR Performance Management Scorecard, 69; Build Your Own Evaluation Group Handouts, 169; Choicework discussion starters, 88; "Click to Engage: How Keypads Can Enhance Learning and Deliberation" (Public Agenda), 144; *Education: A Citizens' Solutions Guide* (Public Agenda), 87; "Engaging Teachers in Evaluation Reform" video, 149; evaluation design resources, 68–69; Everyone at the Table, 134; Guide to Evaluation Products, 68; "Involving Others School Leaders" video, 119; *Leaders Involvement Guide,* 119; *Means to*

an End report (Aspen Institute), 68, 69; posting teacher effectiveness data on New York State, 45; *Practical Guide to Designing Comprehensive Principal Evaluation Systems,* 197; Sample Teacher Recruitment Invitation download, 133, 134, 135; *State of the States* report, 68; state teacher and principal evaluation policy databases, 68; Teacher Evaluation Playbook (Hope Street Group), 37; TEMP tool for redesigning teacher evaluation, 67–68; *The Widget Effect* report (2009), 190. *See also* Internet online engagement
Weingarten, R., 213
Weisberg, D., 19, 23, 30
What's Your Plan? activity, 130
Wheeler, J., 47
Widget, 19
The Widget Effect report (2009), 19–20, 22, 190
William Casper Graustein Memorial Fund, 94
Working consensus, 140, 141*fig*
Working through phase of Learning Curve: activities to use during, 132; description of, 83–84*fig*

Y

Yankelovich, D., 83, 91, 94, 196
You Can't Do It Alone (Johnson), 125

Z

Zavis, A., 45

JB JOSSEY-BASS | Education

Jossey-Bass provides educators with practical knowledge and tools to create a positive and lifelong impact on student learning.

For more information about our resources, authors, and events please visit us at: www.josseybasseducation.com.

You may also find us on Facebook, Twitter, and Pinterest.

f Jossey-Bass K–12 Education

🐦 jbeducation

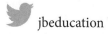 jbeducation